The AI for Good Handbook

Meeting the sustainable development goals with artificial intelligence

First Edition

Minh Trinh, PhD

Rodeo Press

The Artificial Intelligence Handbook Series

The AI Project Handbook: How to manage a successful artificial intelligence project

The AI Model Handbook: A guide to the world of artificial intelligence modeling

The AI Strategy Handbook: Business strategy in the era of artificial intelligence

The AI for Good Handbook:
Meeting the sustainable development goals with artificial intelligence

Library of Congress Cataloging-in-Publication Data

Name: Trinh, Minh, author

Title: The AI for good handbook: meeting the sustainable development goals with artificial intelligence / Minh Trinh.

Description: First Edition. |New York: Rodeo Press, [2022]|Summary: "This book is a guide to use artificial intelligence to meet the sustainable development goals. […]"-- Provided by publisher.| Series: The artificial intelligence handbook series; 4

Identifiers: LCCN 2022916945 |ISBN 9798986928104 (paperback)| 9798986928111 (hardback)

LC record available at https://lccn.loc.gov/2022916945

Rodeo Press

ISBN-13: 979-8-9869281-0-4

In Memory of my Father Trinh Công Trinh

About the Author

Minh Trinh works in finance and technology in New York. He is the Managing Partner of a digital transformation consulting company applying AI to solve complex and challenging problems. He is a graduate of the French Ecole Polytechnique and Harvard University, where he received his Ph.D. in economics.

Table of Contents

Preface │ The Sustainable Development Goals

> "Sustainable development is the pathway to the future we want for all. It offers a framework to generate economic growth, achieve social justice, exercise environmental stewardship and strengthen governance."
>
> Ban Ki-moon

Figure 1. The UN Sustainable Development Goals

Fifty years ago, the United Nations held a Conference on the Human Environment in Stockholm for the first time. It adopted a list of 26 principles:

1. Human rights must be asserted, apartheid and colonialism condemned

2. Natural resources must be safeguarded

3. The Earth's capacity to produce renewable resources must be maintained

4. Wildlife must be safeguarded

5. Non-renewable resources must be shared and not exhausted

6. Pollution must not exceed the environment's capacity to clean itself

7. Damaging oceanic pollution must be prevented

8. Development is needed to improve the environment

9. Developing countries, therefore, need assistance

10. Developing countries need reasonable prices for exports to carry out environmental management

11. Environment policy must not hamper development

12. Developing countries need money to develop environmental safeguards

13. Integrated development planning is needed

14. Rational planning should resolve conflicts between environment and development

15. Human settlements must be planned to eliminate environmental problems

16. Governments should plan their own appropriate population policies

17. National institutions must plan development of states' natural resources

18. Science and technology must be used to improve the environment

19. Environmental education is essential

20. Environmental research must be promoted, particularly in developing countries

21. States may exploit their resources as they wish but must not endanger others

22. Compensation is due to states thus endangered

23. Each nation must establish its own standards

24. There must be cooperation on international issues

25. International organizations should help to improve the environment

26. Weapons of mass destruction must be eliminated

Numerous other meetings and conferences have followed, such as the 1992 Rio Earth Summit, the 2002 Johannesburg Earth Summit, and the 2012 Rio+20 Earth Summit, which have affirmed the close link between economic development and environmental protection.

The Sustainable Development Goals (Figure 1) were defined in 2015 as part of the United Nations 2030 Agenda. They were followed by specific targets in 2017. Many of the Goals are focused on environmental protection, such as Goal 7 (Affordable and clean energy), Goal 11 (Sustainable Cities and Communities), Goal 12 (Responsible Consumption and Production), Goal 13 (Climate action), Goal 14 (Life below water), and Goal 15 (Life on land).

Fifty years after the Stockholm Summit, "only around one-tenth of the hundreds of global environment and sustainable development targets agreed by countries have been achieved or seen significant progress" (SEI CEEW, 2022). As for the Sustainable Development Goals, "the world is no longer making progress on the SDGs. The average SDG Index score slightly declined in 2021, partly due to slow or nonexistent recovery in poor and vulnerable countries. Multiple and overlapping health and security crises have led to a reversal in SDG progress" (Sachs et al., 2022). It is, therefore, clear that there is a severe risk of not meeting these SDGs by 2030.

At the same time, AI has made significant progress since 2011. I previously stated (Trinh, 2021a) that "AI is the new PC" and that it could be compared to the personal computer, in particular, the IBM PC in 1981, and its first killer application, the spreadsheet software Lotus 123.

Today, political leaders and all parties interested in the SDGs must consider adopting AI to help them achieve the Sustainable Development Goals. Like the PC and the spreadsheet, they should expect AI to impact all sectors of human activities profoundly.

The AI for Good Handbook was written to provide a roadmap to reach the SDGs, from eliminating poverty and hunger, and providing health, education, and opportunities for all, to addressing climate change and protecting our seas and lands.

Who Should Read This Book?

This book should interest political leaders, public officials, NGOs, and business leaders, as well as AI experts, engineers, and data scientists who want to help achieve some of the Sustainable Development Goals with the help of AI.

Scope This Book

In this book, we will go over the different SDGs and see how AI can help achieve these goals. It is intentionally not a computer science book. It will not go over the various machine learning models in detail (it is the topic of the AI Model Handbook (Trinh, 2021a)), nor will it go over AI project management (it is the topic of the AI Project Handbook (Trinh, 2021b)).

Outline of This Book

The first part of the book is about People. It covers Poverty reduction (Chapter 1), Hunger (Chapter 2), Health (Chapter 3), Education (Chapter 4), Work, gender equality, and inequalities (Chapter 5), and Cities and communities (Chapter 6). The second part concerns climate and Energy (Chapters 7 and 8). The third part covers Nature, Land ecosystems (Chapter 9), and Water ecosystems (Chapter 10). The book's last part is on Sustainable Growth and goes over Sustainable infrastructure, industrialization, and innovation (Chapter 11), Sustainable economy (Chapter 12), Peace and justice (Chapter 13), and Partnerships for sustainable development (Chapter 14).

Acknowledgments

I learned a lot about development economics during my days at Harvard and benefited from the lectures of Professors Janos Kornai, Jeffrey Sachs, Amartya Sen, and Peter Timmer. I was fortunate to have spent a summer in the India division of the World Bank, thanks to Jamil Baz and Philippe Auffret.

I became familiar with the energy sector and renewable energies when I worked as a chief economist for the power utility sector at the General Directorate for Energy and Raw Materials in the French Ministry of Economy, Finance, and Industry.

I have also been very fortunate to find some time to learn from state-of-the-art AI academic and industrial research. I, like many others, am standing on the shoulders of giants in the field of AI research. Like many practitioners, I learned the basics of AI and machine learning by studying Andrew Ng's online classes, the exceptional Stanford University and UC Berkeley AI-related lectures, and reading the numerous papers on Arxiv.org and elsewhere.

I also learned a lot from the wonderful academics and experts who generously gave presentations to the Artificial Intelligence for Good group in New York: Andrew Ross, Hannah Kerner, Alex Vaughan, Anton Korinek, Graham Taylor, Daniele Silvestro, Sukwoong Choi, and Raphaël Millière. Prafulla Nabar and Christine Dinh-Tan provided insightful comments. Paris Trinh made the illustrations at the beginning of each chapter. Marsha Fulton did the proofreading.

PART I PEOPLE

Chapter 1 | Poverty Reduction

"In this new century, millions of people in the world's poorest countries remain imprisoned, enslaved and in chains. They are trapped in the prison of poverty. It is time to set them free."

Nelson Mandela

1.1 The State of World Poverty

Goal 1 of the SDGs is to "end poverty in all its forms everywhere" ("Goal 1 | Department of Economic and Social Affairs").

Poverty Trend

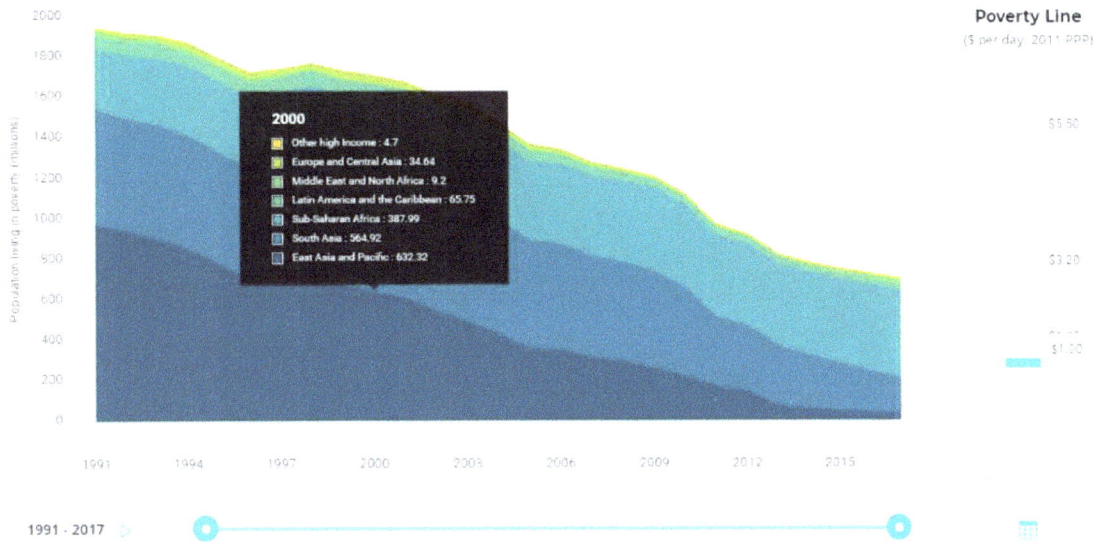

Figure 1.1 Poverty line. Population living in extreme poverty (less than $1.90 per day, 2011 PPP) Source: https://pip.worldbank.org/home

World Poverty, as measured by the population living under some income threshold (the poverty line, usually less than two dollars a day), has been trending down since at least the 1990s (Figure 1.1). China has achieved significant progress, with hundreds of millions of people lifted out of poverty. Poverty and extreme poverty tend to decline with high economic growth. In 1990, 1.9 billion people lived under the poverty line. That population fell to 698 million people in 2017.

The poor are concentrated in Sub-Saharan Africa, where poverty has not improved, and South Asia. In these regions, poverty disproportionately affects children, women, the less educated, and the rural populations (Figure 1.2).

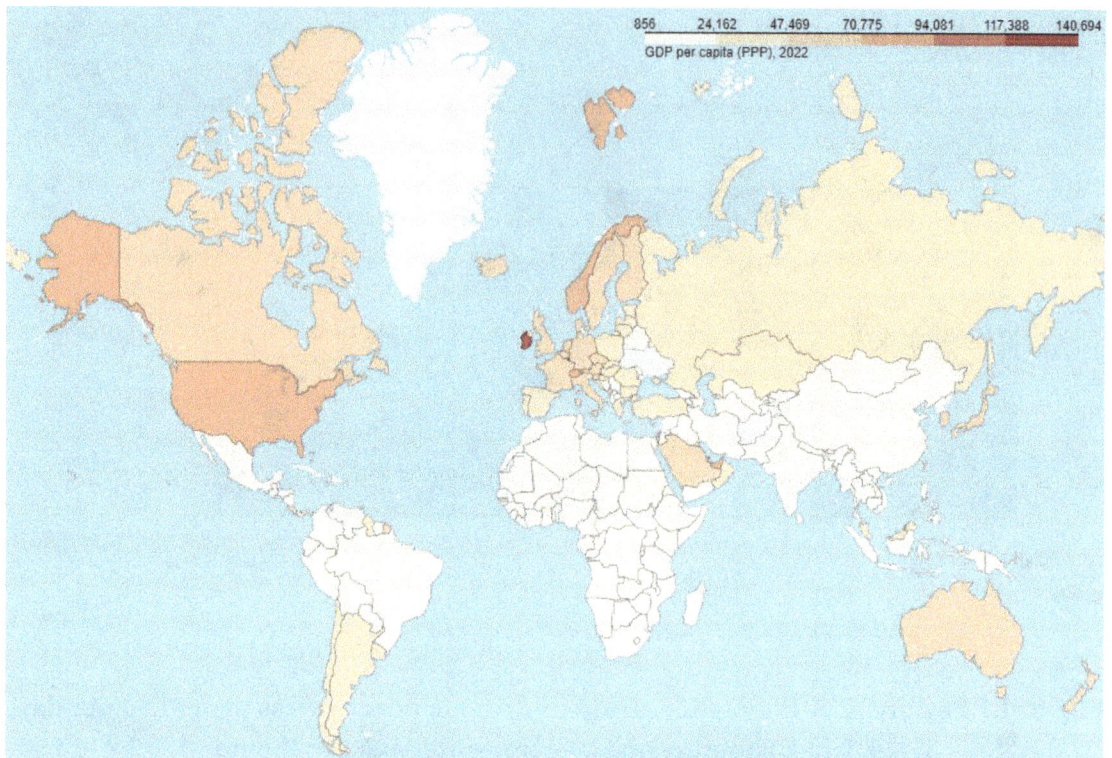

Figure 1.2. GDP (PPP) per capita. Source: Wikipedia, IMF

Besides the poverty line, there are other proxies to measure poverty, such as not having access to proper housing, a sewer system, running water, electricity, and healthcare, and children not having access to education. Typically, populations living in slums are considered poor. An estimated 900 million people live in these conditions ("The World's Largest Slums," 2017).

The PPP (purchasing power parity) adjustment is essential. Real income, as measured by the nominal income divided by the cost of living, is more relevant. With a given income, if prices of food, energy, housing, and essential services increase, people will be poorer.

Multidimensional Poverty

Poverty is not only measured by income level. The economist Amartya Sen defined poverty based not only on GDP or income but on several life quality measures. He was instrumental in creating the Human Development Index ("Human Development Report 2020," 2020), which included life expectancy, education, and per capita income.

Being malnourished, chronically sick, having a low life expectancy, and being unable to read or write are also strong indicators of poverty. Being destitute and not having any assets is also a good proxy for poverty. To have no legal ownership of any assets means that an individual cannot secure a loan and invest in productive assets that could yield some future income, such as getting seeds for planting or baby animals for raising.

The Multidimensional Poverty Index or MPI (Programme (UNDP) and Initiative (OPHI), 2021) attempts to account for the many dimensions of poverty. The indicator aggregates ten measures: nutrition, child mortality, years of schooling, school attendance, cooking fuel, sanitation, drinking water, electricity, housing, and assets. We will focus on income and assets in this Chapter but will cover the other dimensions in other Chapters: hunger (Chapter 2), health (Chapter 3), drinking water (Chapter 10), and energy (Chapter 8).

The Causes of Poverty

There are many causes of poverty. For instance, a person can be poor if she or her household earns a low or no income or owns very little or no assets. If someone (like a child, a student, a retired person, a domestic partner, or a spouse) is not working but lives in a high-earning household, he is not considered poor. The same principle works for owning little or no assets in a home with many assets.

Employment

To alleviate poverty is to raise people's income above the subsistence level. Work opportunities must be present for people to be employed, and people must be available to work. They must be sufficiently nourished and healthy, have access to training and education, and essential services such as transportation and children's care and education.

It is also vital for women, who tend to be responsible for a larger share of the household work and childcare. If they have to spend their days gathering wood to burn, looking for food to feed their family, and staying home to watch their children, they cannot earn a living by themselves.

Wage income will depend on the demand for labor. If many jobs are available from various economic sectors, wage income will be higher. High-productive sectors such as export-oriented industries or high-tech manufacturing might offer higher wages than labor-intensive agriculture. Because of that productivity differential, average wages in lower-income countries tend to be higher in cities than in rural areas. That difference explains the massive migration to the towns observed in Great Britain, Continental Europe, and North America during the industrial revolution. The same phenomenon has been seen more recently in China and other emerging economies.

Suppose the demand for labor is low or shrinks, for instance. In that case, because firms cannot access credit or are faced with broken supply chains or export restrictions, income will fall, and unemployment will increase, as it has during the Covid-19 pandemic.

Income will also depend on the supply of labor. If more workers are available, wages will be lower unless workers acquire skills and become more productive. Education (Chapter 4), therefore, plays an important role. If they compete against automatized labor (machines) or foreign-based labor (through imports), their income might also drop. Automatization, offshoring, outsourcing, and importation from lower-cost countries can be disruptive to the labor market, pressure wages, and increase unemployment. If the workers cannot acquire or do not have the skills to be productively employed, they might end up unemployed.

In general, the balance of power between workers and employers will also affect wages. Automatization or sourcing labor from abroad can be cheaper outside options for employers that put pressure on wages. If only a few employers make the labor market not very competitive, wages will also be lower. If employees are very productive, for instance, because they have the skills to command heavy machinery, their salaries can be higher.

Economic Growth

Alleviating poverty has been achieved successfully at a large scale in many countries with investments in health, education, and infrastructure, market reforms, property rights, and international trade. Many of these topics are covered in other chapters: Health in Chapter 3, Education in Chapter 4, Work in Chapter 5, and Infrastructure in Chapter 11.

The main driver has been economic growth. Without economic growth, such investments are impossible without massive external financial aid. It is evident when we measure poverty as income per capita below a poverty level. Economic growth increases national income, and if population growth is not excessive, it will also increase income per capita. Economic growth also increases inequality as some workers become more productive, but generally, the living standards rise for everyone at different speeds.

Economic stagnation or low economic growth can increase poverty, especially among the youth. Young people graduate from school and even sometimes from college but cannot find employment because firms have no extra demand for their products or services and are not hiring. With the rising cost of living, they cannot escape poverty and stay with their parents for a very long time, unable to find affordable housing. This happens even in rich countries like South Korea and Japan. Youth unemployment is usually high across the world (ILO, 2020).

There has been a global slowdown in productivity (Dieppe, 2021) after the 2008 great financial crisis. Each economic crisis affects productivity growth at a country level, especially among developing countries. Pandemics can also have devastating consequences for economic growth and productivity. Lower capital investments, education attainment level, supply-chain disruptions, and fewer technology spillovers affect productivity negatively.

Poverty Traps

Having no or minimal assets or income can make it impossible to escape poverty. This is the poverty trap (Balboni et al., 2021). A farmer who is unable to buy seeds cannot grow crops. If she cannot purchase chicks or feed them, she cannot raise chickens and sell eggs to the market. If she cannot afford to send her children to the neighboring school, her children will remain uneducated, with minimal job opportunities. Without assets, she cannot get credit and invest to earn more income tomorrow.

Poverty traps can also happen when healthcare, education, and infrastructure are lacking. If someone is too sick or physically too weak to work, she cannot work to earn an income. Then if she cannot make a living, she cannot purchase the right amount and quality of food. If she is not sufficiently educated, e.g., she cannot read or write, many job opportunities will be out of reach, and she will not be able to learn on the job and acquire skills. If she has no access to electricity, she cannot use any electrical or electronic devices and be better informed of opportunities. If running water is not available, she has to spend a lot of time carrying water from a well to her home (even though the well can be a good meeting place and source of information sharing). Long traveling time will limit access and work opportunities for remote villages or towns if roads or bridges are not built or well-maintained.

Natural disasters, armed conflicts, and famines are extreme bad outcomes that can also force people into poverty traps. The poor are very exposed to such risks having minimal resources to self-insure. People might lose their only assets and have to migrate and become refugees if their homes or villages are destroyed or become unlivable because of drought (no water), flood (no place to stay), or risk of being robbed, harmed, or killed (by soldiers, rebels, gangs, or militias), or lack of food (drought, bad harvest).

Public Policies

Public policies can play an essential role in alleviating poverty. Public investments are required to provide the population with healthcare, education, and infrastructure (such as energy, water, communication, transportation, and financial services). Governments can deliver the service directly or use alternatives such as private-public partnerships if they have limited financial resources.

Poor public policies can make things worse. A country with high inflation makes people poorer if their wages do not adjust fast enough. Food and energy become a much larger share of their consumption, and their income might not be sufficient to cover their expenditures. Besides inflation, war is a serious problem. They often go hand in hand. The government of a country that goes through a civil war or a war against its neighbors will favor its military forces and neglect its poor.

There should be a safety net to allocate resources to the poor who cannot sustain themselves. A government needs revenues to redistribute. This can only be done if a country has a working economy and companies, goods, services, and people to tax or direct access to revenues from natural resources. Foreign aid, international organizations such as the United Nations, the World Bank, or the International Monetary Fund can provide some assistance. However, the track record of foreign aid has been controversial (Easterly, 2007).

In many low-income countries, Poor people often live outside the regular economy. They do not have access to public infrastructures and services such as clean water, sanitation, the electricity grid, communication networks, healthcare, or banking. They live in rural areas or shanty towns, unable to escape poverty. Many of these services should be provided by national or local governments but are not because of limited public funding.

Other Factors

In his book The End of Poverty (Sachs, 2006), Professor Jeffrey Sachs lists other factors causing poverty. They include government corruption; legal and social disparities based on gender, ethnicity, or caste; diseases such as AIDS and malaria; lack of infrastructure (including transportation, communications, health, and trade); unstable political landscapes; protectionism; and geographic barriers.

Effect of Covid-19

Covid-19 has reversed the trend of poverty improvement and pushed 90 to 110 million more people into poverty, with the most significant effect in South Asia, followed by sub-Saharan Africa (World Bank, 2020). Many people were from urban populations who used to work in services but became jobless and lost their livelihoods. Covid-19 has highlighted the lack of access of the poor to public health, social protection, insurance, credit, and education and their extreme vulnerability. This is in addition to their lack of housing, basic infrastructure, employment, and economic opportunities, especially when that population is forced to migrate due to conflicts or climate change.

1.2   The SDG Targets

A set of SDG targets have been defined to reach this SDG goal. They include eliminating the most extreme poverty and providing access to public goods:

Target 1.1: By 2030, eradicate extreme poverty for all people everywhere, currently measured as people living on less than $1.25 a day

Target 1.2: By 2030, reduce at least by half the proportion of men, women, and children of all ages living in poverty in all its dimensions according to national definitions

Target 1.3: Implement nationally appropriate social protection systems and measures for all, including floors, and by 2030 achieve substantial coverage of the poor and the vulnerable

Target 1.4: By 2030, ensure that all men and women, in particular the poor and the vulnerable, have equal rights to economic resources, as well as access to basic services, ownership and control over land and other forms of property, inheritance, natural resources, appropriate new technology, and financial services, including microfinance

Target 1.5: By 2030, build the resilience of the poor and those in vulnerable situations and reduce their exposure and vulnerability to climate-related extreme events and other economic, social, and environmental shocks and disasters

Target 1.a: Ensure significant mobilization of resources from a variety of sources, including through enhanced development cooperation, in order to provide adequate and predictable means for developing countries, in particular least developed countries, to implement programmes and policies to end poverty in all its dimensions

Target 1.b: Create sound policy frameworks at the national, regional, and international levels, based on pro-poor and gender-sensitive development strategies, to support accelerated investment in poverty eradication actions

Simply by observing the number of people living in slums in Africa or South Asia, it seems unlikely that some of these targets will be reached in 2030. A horizon of 2050 would be more feasible as they have indeed disappeared in East Asia in the span of a couple of decades, but it would rely on high economic growth.

1.3   How to Alleviate Poverty

Measurement

Alleviating poverty can be done by addressing the causes and consequences of poverty. It has to start with good measurement, data, and statistics. An accurate measure of poverty and its change over time is necessary to monitor progress and evaluate interventions and policies. With no precise measurement, policymakers cannot tell if an intervention is effective or not and cannot scale up successful strategies.

As the Commission on Global Poverty (World Bank, 2017) indicates, monitoring global poverty is not a trivial task and is subject to much uncertainty. Poverty is traditionally measured with household surveys, often using the level of consumption but sometimes income level. The population counting might not be accurate, and the consumption basket of the poor and its value might be measured with errors.

Employment and Economic Growth

Poverty will tend to decrease when there is economic growth and people gain employment (see Chapter 5 on Work). Governments and individuals acquire financial resources that can lift them from dire economic conditions. Economic growth depends on a lot of factors, including functioning institutions and markets, good political, economic, and social governance, macroeconomic, financial, and geopolitical stability, prudent risk management, investments in resilient infrastructure, capital and technology, and human capital to develop and maintain a skilled workforce.

Obviously, not all countries have these factors, and the poorest countries are often lacking in many. The key is to build out of the country's strengths and generate enough economic surplus to invest in the missing factors.

Some countries have precious natural resources (energy, commodities, land) but cannot invest the financial profits that these resources generate and are exposed to economic cycles and market downturns. Their economies end up being dominated by a few companies or individuals that exploit these resources and are unable to prepare any transitions for when these resources run out or become less attractive.

Some countries have cheap labor, often coming from rural areas and moving to the cities. However, they need to invest in upskilling the workers and infrastructure to remain competitive as technological, business requirements, and consumer tastes can evolve. For instance, a reliable power grid is necessary to attract manufacturing facilities, and a dedicated communication network is essential to develop an information technology sector.

Food, Health, and Education

The poor need to have access to food (Chapter 2), health (Chapter 3), education (Chapter 4), and jobs (Chapter 5). This is especially critical if the lack of access leads to a poverty trap, as we have described previously. These are necessary but not always sufficient conditions to escape from poverty.

Institutions, Laws, and Governance

According to Acemoglu and Robinson (2012), institutions can lead to poverty when the government is not making the investments to promote economic growth but only to favor specific social and economic elite groups. They become extractive institutions and block any changes that could threaten the status quo unless the ruling elite could directly benefit. Some non-democratic countries are especially subject to this problem as corrupt rulers are not voted out of power and continue with exploitative policies for a long time. Acemoglu and Robinson give many insightful examples, such as Sierra Leone, ruled by some chiefs inherited from the British colonial times, and Guatemala, ruled by descendants of the Spanish Conquistadors. Chapter 13 on Peace, Justice, and Institutions addresses this topic in more detail.

Investments and Loans, and Foreign Aid

One way to solve the poverty trap at the macro level is to invest massively to boost people's productivity. Because saving is usually scarce in developing countries, investments need to be financed by large capital inflows that take the form of foreign aid, debts, loans, or foreign direct investments. Professor Jeffrey Sachs is a proponent of this approach (Sachs et al., 2022) and suggests borrowing up to more than 30 times of GDP for some low-income countries.

This level of borrowing is probably not realistic. One reason is the country's institutional, organizational, and labor capacities that these investments would require. In particular, a skilled macro policy is needed to manage this level of debt. A second reason is the risk of shock to the economy, similar to oil discovery. A third reason is the risk of fraud and misused funds ("Elite Capture of Foreign Aid : Evidence from Offshore Bank Accounts," n.d.).

Randomized Control Trials

Another popular approach used in the research stage is using Randomized Control Trials (RCTs), as popularized by the 2019 Nobel Prize laureates Professors Abhijit Banerjee, Esther Duflo, and Michael Kremer. Interventions are assessed in experimental settings with test and control populations. RCTs allow better identification of causation. A limitation is the scalability of these results, as one might never be sure if a positive impact documented in a few villages would generalize to a whole country.

1.4   How AI Can Alleviate Poverty

Prediction

As mentioned in the previous section, being able to measure poverty is essential. AI can help measure aggregate poverty using satellite imaging, traffic data, internet data, survey data, mobile and payment data, and search data. AI can also measure poverty from photos, the size of children and adults, health data, education, and cognitive data.

This is especially important when poverty is measured only intermittently or very infrequently. For instance, during the Covid-19 pandemic, no workers were available to conduct surveys. AI can therefore help to do nowcasting and estimating poverty in real-time.

From data on crops, food supply chain data, weather data, population displacement data, calorie intakes, health and education data, inflation data, and financial and economic data, AI can help predict the impact of poverty.

When people need to borrow, for instance, with microfinance, AI can help predict the default risk based on socio-economic features, purpose, and size of the loan. An AI might be more cost-effective for very small loans than a loan officer or a consumer credit report. AI could also use alternative data if the loan applicant lacks financial documentation.

Coordination

With the assessments of poverty and its root causes, it is possible to coordinate the types of intervention. Health, education, nutrition, and economic activity can be estimated or predicted and triggered remediation if their levels are too low. Specialists or community workers in different domains can intervene.

AI can also coordinate supply and demand and complement the role of markets. Data on food or medicine inventory in medical facilities and on the needs of the population can be collected to coordinate the supply chain and reduce waste. Local farmers might want to let the local people know what products it has and at what price and assess the demand before they travel to the market.

Optimization

Optimization will determine the optimal amount of intervention allocated to individuals or groups in the population. Costs and total availability will constrain the allocation. For instance, community healthcare workers can visit only a few villages daily and transport a limited number of vaccines. Food aid can be rationed and should be prioritized for the most vulnerable population. AI can help find where the people with the most children live or where food shortage is more likely to occur.

Control

The control or intervention step involves deploying the assistance to the people in need and ensuring it is done correctly. Community workers can be sent routing or visiting schedules with relevant information, and reports can be collected and analyzed by AI to detect any discrepancies or issues that need to be discussed or reevaluated.

1.5 Case Studies

Satellite Data

Satellite imaging can complement the traditional measures of poverty made from infrequent and expensive national surveys such as the Demographic and Health Surveys (DHS) on household consumption and wealth levels. Government employees or contractors have to be sent across the country to reach out to some representative households to collect the survey data. Researchers Yeh et al. (2020) have used publicly available satellite imagery and deep learning to understand the economic well-being in Africa.

The authors use asset wealth survey data from DHS for geographical clusters in 23 African countries between 2009 and 2016 to train several computer vision models (convolutional neural networks or CNNs) on satellite images collected from nighttime lights and multispectral daytime imagery systems. The models predict the level of asset wealth and the changes. Data on nighttime lights are collected by several satellites. The idea is that the amount of nighttime light visible from space is a good proxy for economic activity and the asset wealth of the local population. Multispectral data (from visible to infrared and thermal spectrums) are produced by the Landsat satellites equipped with special sensors, part of a joint program of NASA and the United States Geological Survey to study global landmasses ("Landsat 8," 2022).

They find that their model can explain out-of-sample (country-year) 70% of the variation of ground-based asset wealth levels. They can predict the different wealth levels across countries but also within countries. Using data from the Livings Standards Measurement Surveys (LSMS) to measure cluster-level wealth changes, they can predict 35% of the variation in time of wealth asset levels.

They apply their model to two downstream tasks. The first is to understand the relationship between wealth and extreme temperature. The second is to target cash transfers to households in poor areas. They find that wealth first increases and then decreases when the maximum temperature rises. A hypothetical cash transfer using satellite imagery effectively targets the poorest households.

Mobile Data

An alternative to using satellite imagery is mobile data. In the writing of Aiken et al. (2021), the authors study an emergency cash transfer program in Togo during the Covid-19 pandemic. The initial program, Novissi, targeted individuals with cell phones who signed up for the program, were registered to vote in some specific regions, and who declared that they worked in an informal occupation. The aim was to reach out to the poorest individuals in the poorest areas. This approach has some limitations as we can expect destitute people not to have a mobile phone or not to be literate and be able to register online.

The researchers propose an enhancement using mobile data. They used two field surveys by the National Institute of Statistics and Economic and Demographic Studies (INSEED): One in-person national representative survey conducted in 2018 and 2019 and one phone survey in rural areas done in 2020 to collect economic, asset, consumption (for the 2018, 2019 survey), demographic, and residence data that are mapped to their daily phone consumption and phone metadata (call detail records or CDR) obtained by the two mobile phone networks in Togo. These data are then used to calculate consumption estimates and then in a supervised machine learning model (gradient boosting regression) to estimate consumption from mobile phone usage and features ("phone targeting approach"). They used around 700 mobile phone features related to phone calls and SMS messages.

To simulate geographical targeting at the prefecture level, they use data from INSEED. At the canton level, they use micro-estimates of relative wealth from the Poverty Map using satellite imagery (Chi et al., 2022a) to construct relative wealth estimates by cantons in Togo. They can then check if the phone targeting is reaching the right population.

They find that the phone targeting approach outperforms the previous implementation of the Novissi program and other counterfactual approaches available to the Togo government, such as geographical or occupation-based targeting, when the targeting is done towards the poorest people in the 100 poorest cantons or at the national level. In particular, they make fewer exclusion errors (exclude individuals who should be included) and inclusion errors (include individuals who should be excluded).

Poverty Map

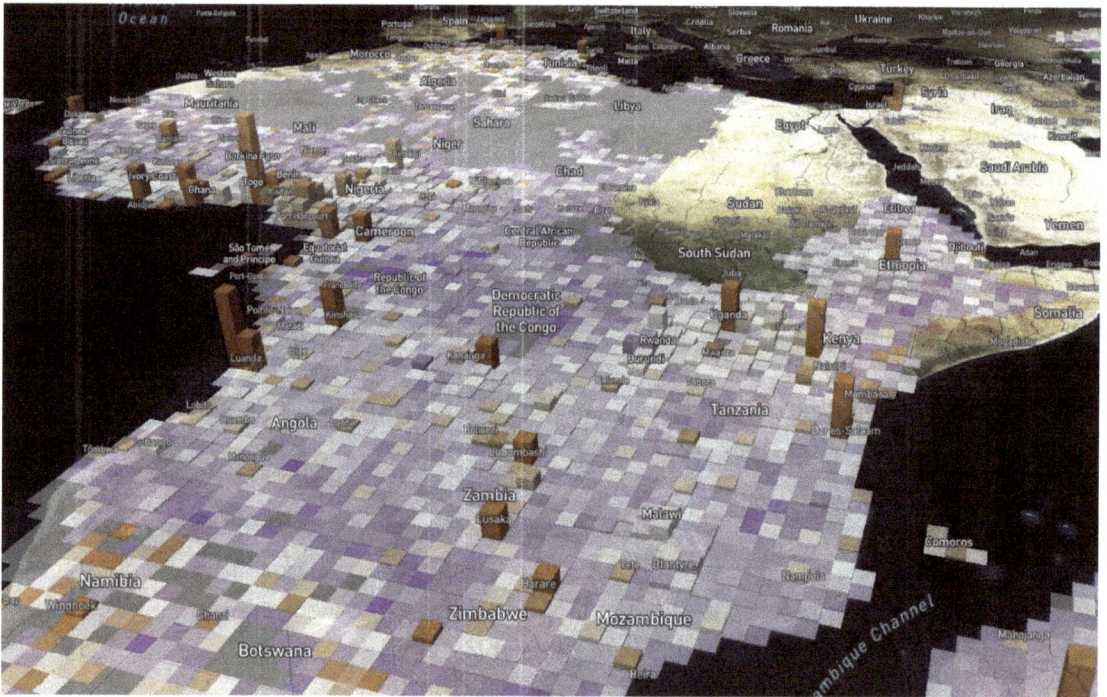

Figure 1.3. Poverty map in Africa. The height of each bar is the absolute wealth in dollars, and the color is the relative wealth estimate

The Poverty Map ("Global Poverty Map," n.d.) is an ambitious project to build micro-estimates of absolute and relative wealth in 2.4 km by 2.4 km micro areas covering 135 low and medium-income countries (LMICs) using geographical, demographic, and alternative digital data such as satellite, mobile, and Facebook (now Meta) social media data. This allows the distribution of wealth and poverty across and within countries. The research is summarized in Chi et al. (2022b).

Their model uses ground truth household survey data from the Demographic and Health Surveys (DHS), sponsored by the U.S. Agency for International Development (USAID). The model features include (Table S2): road density, urban or built-up, elevation, slope, precipitation, population, number of cell towers, WIFI access points, mobile devices, Android devices, IOS devices, nightlights/radiance, and satellite imagery data (principal component data). The machine learning model is a gradient boosting tree model and predicts a relative wealth index at the 2.4 km by 2.4 km grid cell level. The connectivity data, along with radiance, road density, and population, seem to be the most critical feature.

They validate their model using several cross-validation procedures and independent survey data collected by governments in Togo and Nigeria, among others. Their wealth estimates correlate well (high R2) with the wealth and consumption data from the surveys.

Like in the mobile data paper from the previous section, they also simulate anti-poverty programs using national survey data in Togo and Nigeria and compare the welfare distribution with alternative approaches. They find that the machine learning approach performs as well as methods based on DHS, which is vital since the DHS surveys are not performed frequently and do not cover the whole population.

Chapter 2 | Hunger

> "If we can conquer space, we can conquer childhood hunger."
> Buzz Aldrin

2.1 The State of World Hunger

Goal 2 is to "end hunger, achieve food security and improved nutrition and promote sustainable agriculture." ("Goal 2 | Department of Economic and Social Affairs").

Hunger Trend

According to the World Food Programme ("A hunger catastrophe | World Food Programme," n.d.), over 800 million people are hungry, 276 million people face food insecurity, and 44 million people are close to famine. It projects that if the trend persists, the number of hungry people will reach 840 million by 2030 (Figure 2.1), while the SDG was to eliminate hunger by that same date.

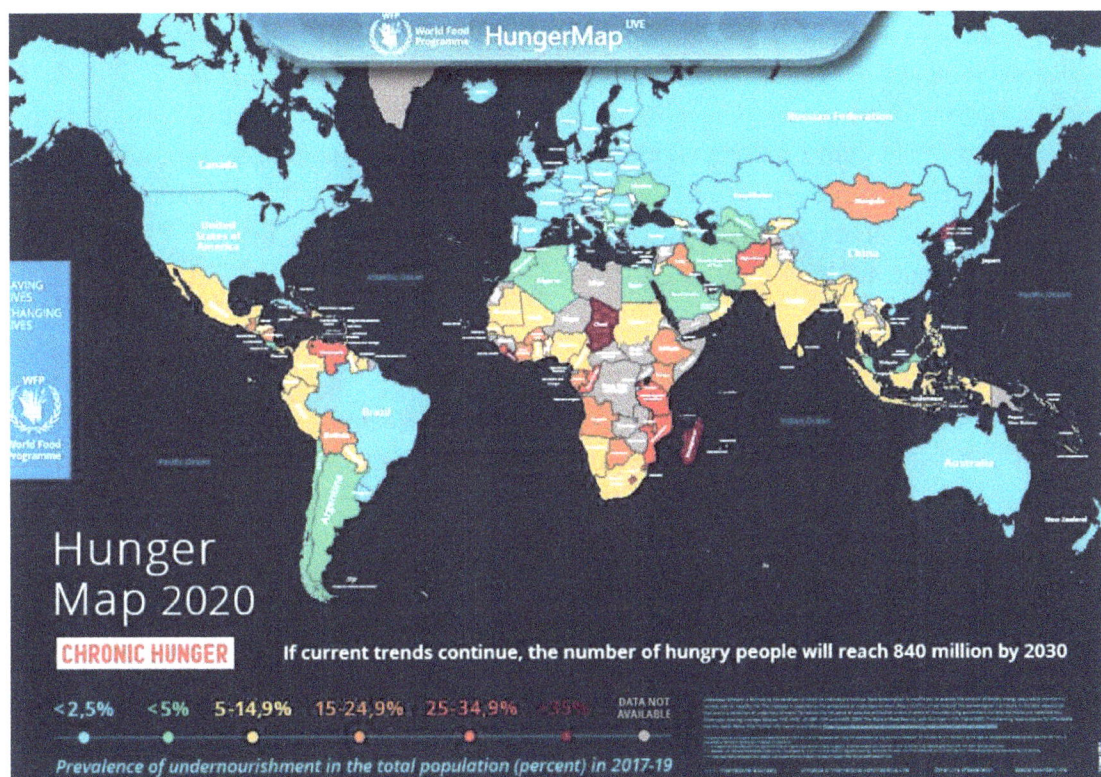

Figure 2.1. Hunger Map 2020. Source: World Food Programme

Hunger is concentrated in sub-Saharan Africa and in some parts of Latin America and Asia. Current food emergencies are in Afghanistan, the Democratic Republic of Congo, Haiti, Northeastern Nigeria, Sahel, Southern Madagascar, South Sudan, Syria, Ukraine, and Yemen.

By 2050, the world population is expected to increase by 50% and therefore put pressure on the food supply. Because of the limited available lands and the impact of climate change, agriculture will have to increase its production without offering the same product variety typical in the diet of developed countries. In particular, it seems infeasible to raise enough livestock to produce enough meat and dairy to feed the world in the same way it provides the western countries. Agriculture needs to be much more sustainable.

Food Insecurity and Malnutrition

To better assess, measure, inform, and communicate about food insecurity and malnutrition, the Integrated Food Security Phase Classification (IPC) Partners, regroup major intergovernmental and nongovernmental organizations and agencies such as the Action Against Hunger and the World Food Program (IPC Global Partners, 2021). They have tools, procedures, and common global classifications for Acute Food Insecurity, Chronic Food Insecurity, and Acute Malnutrition. Each category has its own scale.

The report defines Acute Food Insecurity as "food deprivation that threatens lives or livelihoods, regardless of the causes, context or duration" and uses a scale of 1 to 5 (1: Minimal/None, 2: Stressed, 3: Crisis, 4: Emergency, 5: Catastrophe/Famine); Chronic Food Insecurity as "persistent or seasonal inability to consume adequate diets for a healthy and active life, mainly due to structural causes" with a scale from 1 to 4 (1: Minimal/None, 2: Mild, 3: Moderate, 4: Severe); and Acute Malnutrition as measured by "thinness of individuals or presence of edema" with a scale from 1 to 5 (1: Acceptable, 2: Alert, 3: Serious, 4: Critical, 5: Extremely Critical).

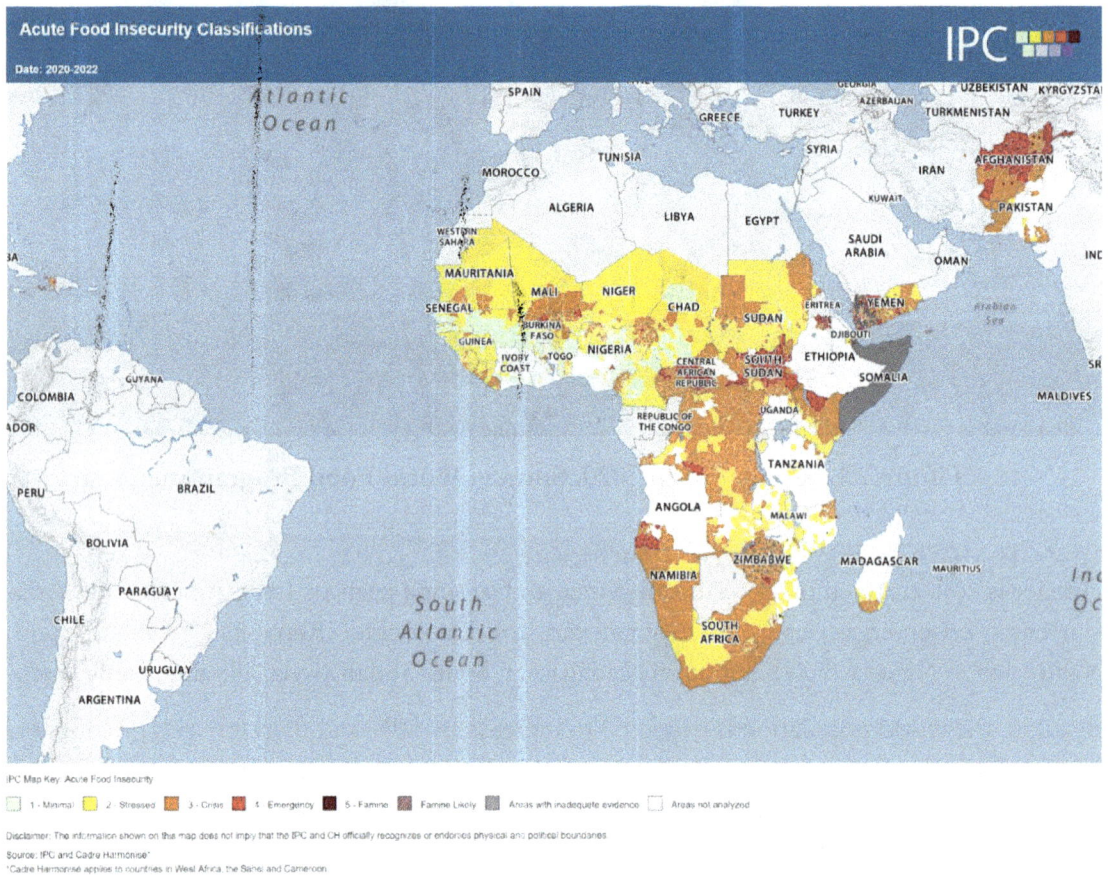

Figure 2.2. Acute Food Insecurity. Source: IPC

Famines are extreme versions of food insecurity. The IPC report also defines a Famine as "The requirement of reliable evidence on the three outcomes – food consumption or livelihood change, global acute malnutrition (GAM), and crude death rate (CDR). All of which are either currently above or projected to be above Famine thresholds (>20% of households with extreme food gaps, >30% of children acutely malnourished, and CDR> 2/10,000/day).”

Malnutrition is usually caused by an unhealthy, undiversified, and irregular diet. An unhealthy diet could lack micronutrients. Malnutrition can also be caused by diseases such as diarrhea, dysentery, malaria/fever, acute respiratory infection (ARI), HIV/AIDS prevalence, cholera or acute watery diarrhea (AWD), or measles (IPC Global Partners, 2021). It causes wasting (during acute undernutrition, children are too thin for their height) and stunting (during chronic undernutrition, children are too short for their age or weight) in children also sometimes makes them overweight and obese (more prevalent in developed countries but becoming more common in middle-income countries such as India or Mexico) as measured by an indicator such as the Body Mass Index (BMI).

The Causes of Hunger

In normal circumstances, hunger is solved by having efficient agriculture, a reliable food supply chain, and affordable prices, so households avoid allocating all their earnings to food. This means having farmers who can reliably produce crops, fruits, and vegetables and raise animals in quantity and distributors who can sell their production up to the retail level to the general population efficiently and cheaply.

Hunger tends to be explained by the four Cs: Conflicts, Climate change, Covid-19, and Costs ("A hunger catastrophe | World Food Programme," n.d.). Because of conflicts, families have to leave their homes and jobs and often move without resources to feed themselves, and they might be stuck in remote areas without access to food aid and food supply. Conflicts also destroy food supply chains and infrastructures such as irrigations, warehouses, and transportation and distribution hubs and disrupt the normal functioning of markets. Armed government forces and militia might deprive civilians and seize the food supply by force. Recent famines that were caused fully or partially by war include Tigray, Ethiopia (2020-present), South Sudan (2017-present), Yemen (2016-present), Darfur (2003-2005), the Democratic Republic of the Congo (1998-2004), Ethiopia (1998-2000) ("List of famines," 2022).

Climate change causes drought, floods, and extreme weather events that can devastate harvests. Climate change combined with intensive agriculture can ruin the environment and food production's sustainability. Most agricultural production depends on rain and not on irrigation. When it relies on irrigation, it might overuse water resources and contaminate the water with excess nutrients. Soils can also be harmed by excessive drought, turning into dust, or being displaced by excessive water overrun during flooding. Recent famines that were caused fully or partially by drought include Madagascar (2021-present), Somalia (2017-present), West Africa and Sahel (2012), Somalia (2011-2012), and Niger (2005-2006).

Covid-19 has disrupted food supply, food production and distribution systems, and the normal functioning of markets. Labor might not be available to complete the harvest on time; transportation might be restricted or considerably slowed down between regions and countries, and the supply chain might be disrupted by closing or financially distressed intermediaries.

Lastly, food price inflation has raised the cost of feeding people, especially the very poor who can least afford higher prices. High energy prices, food export restrictions to importing countries, high international commodity prices, supply disruption such as lack of agricultural labor, and domestic currency devaluation are factors causing food price inflation. Measures such as price control can sometimes lead to supply being diverted to international markets or a reduction in domestic production because domestic food prices do not cover input prices (energy, fertilizer, seeds, labor) and exacerbate the penury of food.

2.2 The SDG Targets

The Sustainable Development Goal is supported by the following Targets:

Target 2.1: By 2030, end hunger and ensure access by all people, in particular the poor and people in vulnerable situations, including infants, to safe, nutritious, and sufficient food all year round

Target 2.2: By 2030, end all forms of malnutrition, including achieving, by 2025, the internationally agreed targets on stunting and wasting in children under 5 years of age, and address the nutritional needs of adolescent girls, pregnant and lactating women, and older persons

Target 2.3: By 2030, double the agricultural productivity and incomes of small-scale food producers, in particular women, indigenous peoples, family farmers, pastoralists, and fishers, including through secure and equal access to land, other productive resources, and inputs, knowledge, financial services, markets and opportunities for value addition and non-farm employment

Target 2.4: By 2030, ensure sustainable food production systems and implement resilient agricultural practices that increase productivity and production, that help maintain ecosystems, that strengthen capacity for adaptation to climate change, extreme weather, drought, flooding, and other disasters, and that progressively improve land and soil quality

Target 2.5: By 2020, maintain the genetic diversity of seeds, cultivated plants, and farmed and domesticated animals and their related wild species, including through soundly managed and diversified seed and plant banks at the national, regional, and international levels, and promote access to and fair and equitable sharing of benefits arising from the utilization of genetic resources and associated traditional knowledge, as internationally agreed

Target 2.a: Increase investment, including through enhanced international cooperation, in rural infrastructure, agricultural research and extension services, technology development, and plant and livestock gene banks in order to enhance agricultural productive capacity in developing countries, in particular, least developed countries

Target 2.b: Correct and prevent trade restrictions and distortions in world agricultural markets, including through the parallel elimination of all forms of agricultural export subsidies and all export measures with equivalent effect, in accordance with the mandate of the Doha Development Round

Target 2.c: Adopt measures to ensure the proper functioning of food commodity markets and their derivatives and facilitate timely access to market information, including on food reserves, in order to help limit extreme food price volatility

2.3 How to Alleviate Hunger

The World Food Programme has mentioned the 4 Cs: Conflicts, Climate change, Covid-19, and Costs. Covid-19 is a recent phenomenon, but it is safe to replace it with pandemics. Any future pandemic at the same scale will disrupt economies if it forces businesses and markets to close and increase unemployment.

Conflicts

Hunger caused by conflicts seems to be hard to prevent. A reason is that the victims of hunger often do not have a voice. They are the poorest of society and not critical assets in armed conflicts. Many end up in refugee camps built or operated by the United Nations and international and non-governmental associations. Economic sanctions against the belligerents would often hurt the poorest more than the armed forces. The best outcome for hunger would be to cease the conflict and find a peaceful resolution (Chapter 13).

Climate Change

Climate change (Chapter 7) has an enormous impact on the food system. Droughts and floods occur more often. In countries that rely on rainfalls and are not using much irrigation, a drought or a flood can have catastrophic consequences on crops and livestock. Plants and crops will fail to grow in either condition and will not produce feed for animals.

Climate change requires more mitigation, such as relying more on irrigation systems and less on rainfalls, better water resource management, and more adaptation, such as using more drought-resistant seeds and introducing agroforestry (combining trees and fields) to build a more robust agricultural system that is more resistant to soil deterioration and high temperature.

Costs

The cost of food is usually determined by the productive capacity of domestic agriculture, the food supply chain, and the availability of food imports and food exports.

Agriculture productivity depends on many factors. At the farm level, factors include the type of crops, the quality of the soil, the use of fertilizers, water availability, technological farming development, economies of scale, and availability of workers (Covid-19 has negatively impacted farming employment). Environmental factors include such as the weather (rains, drought), pests, and diseases, the type of livestock, the land and water available, feed for the livestock, and health and growth rate of the livestock. The farm production then needs to be efficiently transported, transformed, and distributed to the final consumers. If any of these steps in the food value chain is inefficient such as wasting too much food, then the cost can be high, especially for the poorer population.

Food imports can complement local agriculture but expose the population to international prices and export restrictions in times of geopolitical crisis. Food exports can also affect the local population as high global prices could motivate farmers to sell their products abroad instead of domestically.

Without a gain in productivity, the yield of domestic agriculture will decline, especially if the same crop is planted year after year. At the same time, agriculture needs to be sustainable as the overuse of fertilizers, soil erosion, and excessive water consumption can cause irreversible adverse impacts on the environment and the soil quality. Extreme weather conditions can cause damage to the soil and sharply decrease its productivity.

Farming requires investment in mechanization and sustainable agriculture practices, more diversified and resistant crops, potentially less intensive production techniques for livestock, and innovations such as precision agriculture, methane and carbon capture, genetic engineering, and vertical farming.

Warning Systems

In the context of the Horn of Africa (Ethiopia, Kenya, and Somalia), Oxfam (Farr et al., 2022) reviews the timeline of the recent food 2021-2022 crisis with the early warnings from the Famine Early Warning System Network (FEWS NET), the Food Security and Nutrition Working Groups (FSNWG), the Food Security and Nutrition Analysis Unit - Somalia (FSNAU), the Food and Agriculture Organization (FAO), and the World Food Programme (WFP). The signs were available ahead of the crisis but failed to prevent it and concluded that failure is a political failure.

It makes some important recommendations for anticipatory action to prevent food crises instead of reacting when it is too late: 1. Scale up anticipatory action, 2. Have a common risk management strategy between disaster risk reduction, resilience building, climate adaptation, anticipatory action, and early action, 3. Support locally-led early warning and action, 4. Streamline analysis of projections and forecasts, 5. Expand inclusive and shock-responsible social protection systems, and 6. Promote the participation and leadership of women.

Humanitarian Aid

When a severe food crisis strikes, foreign humanitarian aid is often required. Donor countries might not act fast enough and might not supply enough funding. There are serious concerns that aid might not reach the victims of the food crisis, for instance, if the humanitarian aid organizations cannot reach that population or if the aid is diverted by the armed forces or some local militias. There is also a risk of moral hazard if the local government relies on humanitarian aid to assist its population instead of investing in preventative measures.

2.4 What Can AI Do to Alleviate Hunger

Prediction

The first step is to forecast the demand for food based on the population's needs, such as calorie intake and diet requirements, but also the food budget relative to income. Food could be abundant but unaffordable, especially in an inflationary environment or when a country relies heavily on food imports. Very fine-grained accurate forecasts, ideally at the household or individual level, would necessitate more advanced forecasting techniques.

A second step is to forecast the supply of food, the price, and the quantity. Availability of farmland, cropland, grazeland, water, fertilizer, agriculture productivity, mechanization, wholesale market prices, weather conditions, total precipitation, fertilizer prices, the availability and wage of workers, transportation and distribution costs and reliability (supply chain), risk of disease, climate change, and conflicts can all affect the supply side. As for the demand side, very fine-grained forecasts, at a local market or village level, are valuable as they readily address people's needs and can be compared with realized observed values.

The prediction of supply and demand, a projection of food shortage, food insecurity, and famine, can be made for a specific time period and specific location. The prediction could be made to be consistent with the Integrated Food Security Phase Classification (IPC): acute food insecurity, chronic food insecurity, and acute malnutrition.

In parallel, we can measure the state of hunger and food insecurity by collecting health data from the population. Data and wasting of stunting of children, birthweights, and anemia of mothers are very good indicators of current food insecurity and malnourishment conditions (The State of Food Security and Nutrition in the World 2021, 2021). Data on a diet can inform about the lack of categories and micronutrients.

Coordination

This step involves the planning of resources to manage the food gap. Coordination is required on the supply side so that all the required inputs (seeds, fertilizers, soil, water, livestock, fisheries), labor, and technology are available in sufficient quantity and in time. For instance, harvests require temporary manual work for a specific time during the year. The food products must be transported and refrigerated before reaching the end consumers.

If domestically produced food is in short supply, imports and food aid have to compensate for the shortfall. Coordinating with foreign and humanitarian aid must happen ahead of the shortage and requires reliable forecasts to avoid crisis situations. Different scenarios need to be explored to coordinate the efforts under all contingencies. The information necessary for the coordination will need to come from various sources, including household survey data, health records, commodities market data, retail inventories and prices, and earth image data.

Optimization

The coordination effort can be optimized so that resources are used efficiently in all steps, and the food gap is reduced at the lowest cost. This means adopting more precision farming techniques to reduce water, energy, and fertilizer usage in agriculture. Along the supply chain, transportation and distribution must be efficient to reduce food loss. This can require better infrastructure, such as better roads, to shorten the transportation time.

Control

This step involves the control of resources in the food supply chain to manage the food gap. Monitoring systems such as sensors can be used to detect any disturbances and problems in the supply chain. The amount and quality of water, soil quality and nutrients, agricultural inputs, livestock, and plant health conditions, storage capacities, and the number of workers should be closely monitored and managed to produce food sustainably. Food aid must be tracked to assure donors that it reaches the needy population.

2.5 Case Studies

Satellite Imaging

CropHarvest (Tseng et al., 2021) is a comprehensive dataset of geo-referenced agricultural class labels with remote sensing data inputs. It contains longitude, latitude, an agricultural label, and a pixel time series. Labels can be binary or multi-class with extensive agricultural class labels. It facilitates using such data for environmental and agricultural applications such as land use, crop classification and monitoring, water content measurement, and vegetation health.

The satellite input data come from four products: multispectral (MS) image data, synthetic aperture radar (SAR) data, meteorological data, and topographic data. These data come from different satellites and satellite sensors.

Multispectral (MS) image data are collected from the European Space Agency (ESA) satellites Copernicus Sentinel 2 (A and B) thanks to passive sensors covering the visible, near-infrared, and short wave infrared of the spectrum. Different landmasses, plants, and crops reflect these wavelength lights differently depending on their composition, shape, and water content. This allows the identification of different types of crops, such as maize or corn, and the growth stage of these crops. These satellites cover land surfaces, seas, and oceans at least every ten days at a resolution of 10m, 20m, and 60m.

Contrary to Sentinel 2 sensors, radar sensors are active and can see through clouds in the atmosphere and operate days and nights. In a radar, radio signals are emitted and reflected back to the sensors. The Synthetic Aperture Radar (SAR) data are collected from Copernicus Sentinel 1 satellites (A and B). They are used for sea and land ice monitoring, land change use and agriculture, deforestation, and land deformation, as well as for emergency responses.

Other satellites provide meteorological data and topographic data that complement the previous remote sensing data, as the weather (temperature and precipitation) and elevation can affect crops, crop types, and crop growth. It is critical as the planet is going through a period of climate change with severe effects for agriculture.

The authors define some benchmark tasks to compare models. The tasks include identifying pixels containing a particular specific crop or not (crop vs. rest) and containing any crops or not (crop vs. non-crop). They also run several models, three neural networks (Long-Short Term Memory or LSTM) models, and a random forest model on these benchmark tasks.

Crop Yield Predictions

Crop yield prediction is an essential task for AI and machine learning. In Cedric et al. (2022), the authors build several models to predict crop yields in West Africa. They examine the yields of rice, maize, cassava, seed cotton, yams, and bananas in nine countries at the national level: Burkina Faso, Gambia, Ghana, Guinea, Mali, Mauritania, Niger, Senegal, and Togo.

They use data from the Food and Agriculture Organization (FAO) and the World Bank covering 1990 to 2000. The features in their models are average temperature in a year, average precipitation in a year, pesticide per hectare per year, emitted nitrogen dioxide per year, yield in weight per hectare, year, and country/area. They use three models: a multivariate logistic regression, a decision tree, and a k-nearest neighbor. Using the R2 statistics and Mean Absolute Error applied to test data, they find that the k-nearest neighbor model performs the best after hyperparameter tuning and that they are able to forecast crop yields accurately.

Extension of their work should probably include more granular forecasts, ideally at the land plot level or crop area level, and a higher frequency than just yearly and use other alternative data such as satellite imagery to measure crop development, growth, and health such as it is proposed by Crop Harvest.

Robotics

Automation and robotics can help increase agricultural productivity, and AI is critical to guide robots to perform practical and efficient tasks. This can be seen with the development of a model of robotic navigation in vineyards and orchards (Martini et al., 2022) that does not depend on precise GPS positioning or visual odometry (determining a position based on camera images).

The authors simulate the navigation of an Unmanned Ground Vehicle (UGV) in row crops and vineyards. The navigation is done using deep reinforcement learning, a technique that guides the actions of the agent driving the vehicle based on some observed states with the objective of maximizing the cumulative sum of some future rewards. The state includes a depth image, the yaw, and linear and angular velocities of the vehicle. The reward is a combination of angular positioning, distance to the target (end of the crop row), and successful task completion.

They test the agent on different row shapes (straight, hybrid, curved), moving forward or in reverse, and compare the mean absolute errors (MAE) and root mean square errors (RMSE) from the ideal trajectories, the velocities, and the successful completion rates. They also position the agent initially randomly to create more opportunities to explore new states. They find that the agent can successfully guide the vehicle along previously unseen crop and vineyard rows without the need for precise positioning.

Chapter 3 | Human Health

> "He who has health has hope; and he who has hope, has everything."
>
> Thomas Carlyle

3.1 The State of World Health

Goal 3 is to "ensure healthy lives and promote well-being for all at all ages." ("Goal 3 | Department of Economic and Social Affairs").

Health Trend

Health is an important goal to maintain and improve people's welfare. Poor health can significantly affect poverty, morbidity, mortality, employability, and dependency. Being in poor health or having dependents in poor health limits economic opportunities if it prevents working in some jobs or draws down financial resources.

In return, poverty and unemployment also affect health. The health of a population depends on many factors, such as socioeconomic conditions. It is correlated (imperfectly) with average household income and country GDP per capita. It also depends on healthcare public policy, infrastructures and resources, systems and services, the availability of primary care, and the accessibility and availability of qualified healthcare workers. Individual circumstances can lead to very different health outcomes in the same population. It is also impacted by the environment, pollution, and climate change through natural disasters, extreme weather events, and ecosystem, water, and agricultural damages.

The global distribution of health is unequal across the world. It tends to be better in more developed countries and worse in low-income countries, even though that correlation is not perfect. It is common to look at three indicators: infant mortality, maternal mortality, and life expectancy.

Infant Mortality

An important indicator of health is infant mortality. While infant mortality is low in developed countries such as Western Europe, Canada, Japan, or Australia, it is higher in lower-income countries. It tends to be concentrated in Sub-Saharan Africa and Asia (Figure 3.1). The causes are also different across regions.

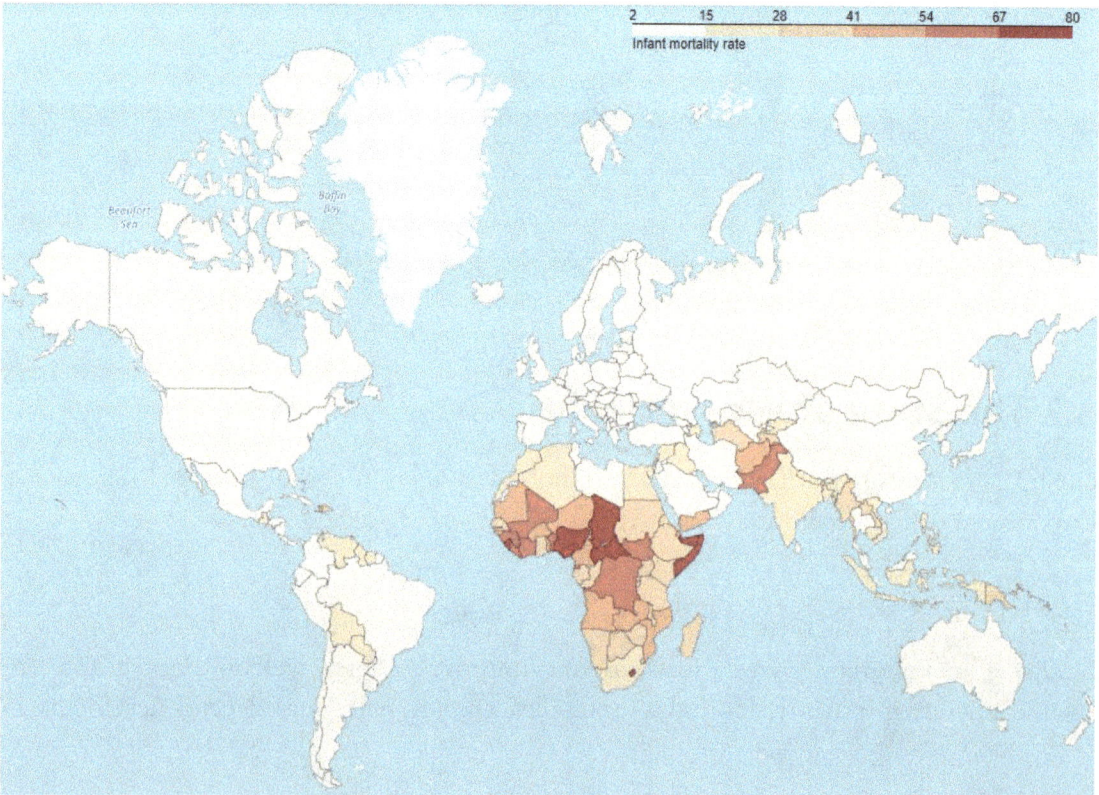

Figure 3.1. Infant mortality rate below one-year-old per 1000 live births. Source: WHO https://www.who.int/data/gho/data/indicators/indicator-details/GHO/infant-mortality-rate-(probability-of-dying-between-birth-and-age-1-per-1000-live-births)

We can compare the causes of infant mortality in Africa and Europe. Some causes are common such as prematurity or birth asphyxia and birth trauma, but some are more prevalent in Africa, such as diarrhoeal diseases, malaria, and HIV/AIDS.

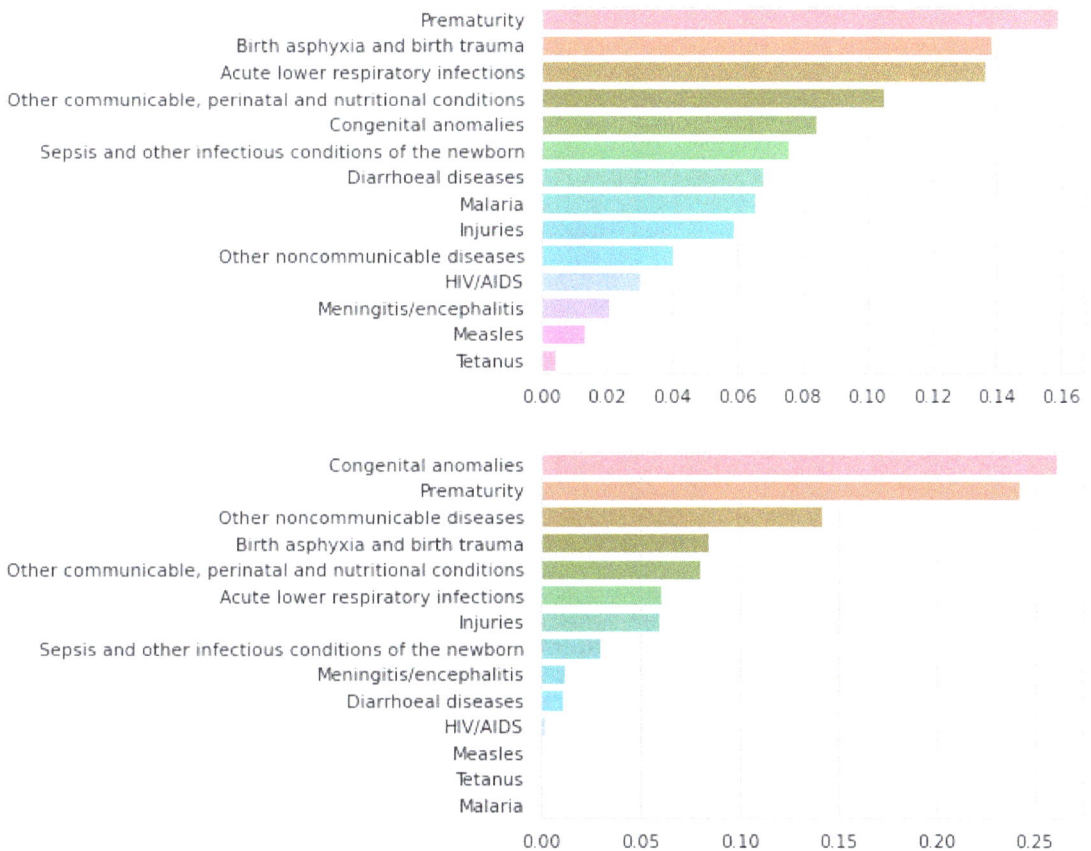

Figure 3.2. Average distribution of causes of infant mortality in Africa (top) and in Europe (bottom)

Maternal Mortality

Maternal mortality can be measured by the number of maternal deaths per 100,000 live births (maternal mortality ratio or MMR) or by the lifetime risk of maternal death (probably of dying from giving birth in her lifetime for a 15-year-old woman) (World Health Organization,

2019). The difference between low and high-income countries is, on average, very large: 462 per 100,000 vs. 11 per 100,000 for MMR and 1 in 5,400 vs.1 in 45 for lifetime maternal death probability.

Maternal mortality differs significantly between countries and reaches very high levels in Africa (Figure 3.2, data from 2016) and some parts of Asia. These are regions where access to quality care is not universal, and poverty and food insecurity are also high.

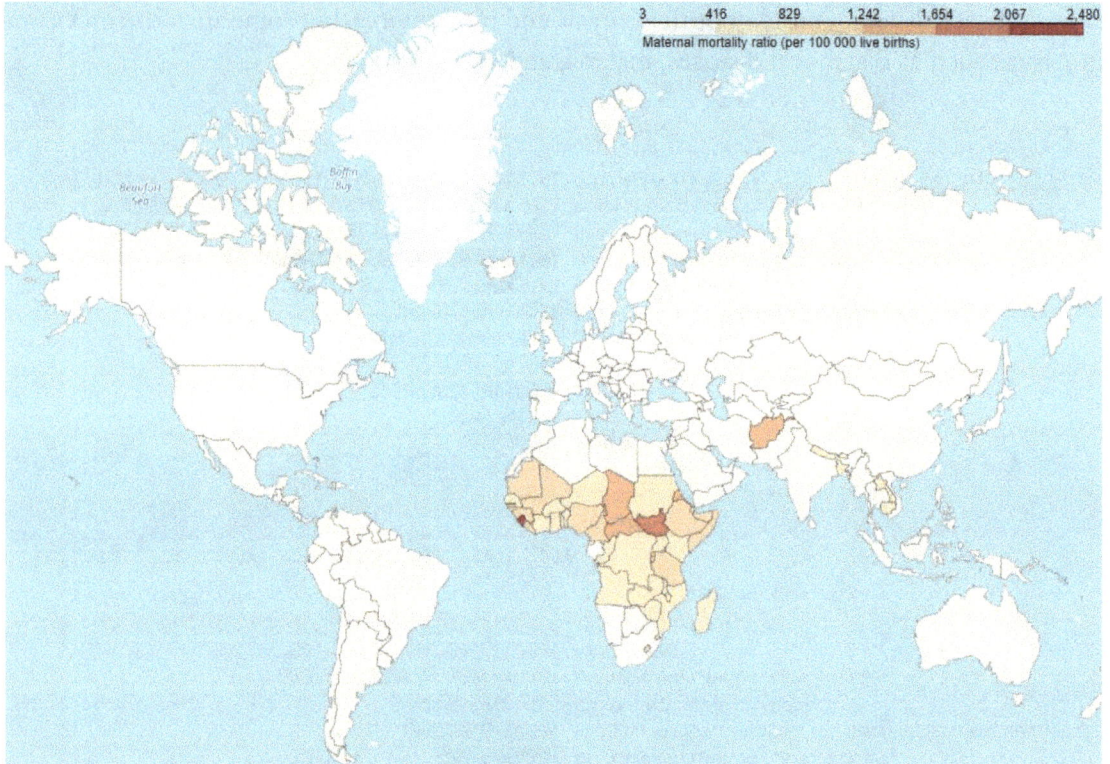

Figure 3.3. Maternal mortality ratio

Life Expectancy

The last indicator is life expectancy. Life expectancy was very low in the 1800s and has improved a lot from the 1950s till now. In Deaton (2013), economist Angus Deaton points out that the early low life expectancy was due to the high infant mortality rate. Families had many children, and not all were expected to survive to adulthood. Once infant mortality decreases to the level of developed countries, progress in life expectancy is harder to achieve, especially if it involves noncommunicable diseases with no cure or the environment.

Life expectancy differs greatly across countries and does not always follow the income level. Some low and middle-income countries, such as Vietnam, have a life expectancy of 76 years vs. 79 years for the United States, which is one of the wealthiest countries in the world. Within a country, there are also differences between socio-economic groups and regions.

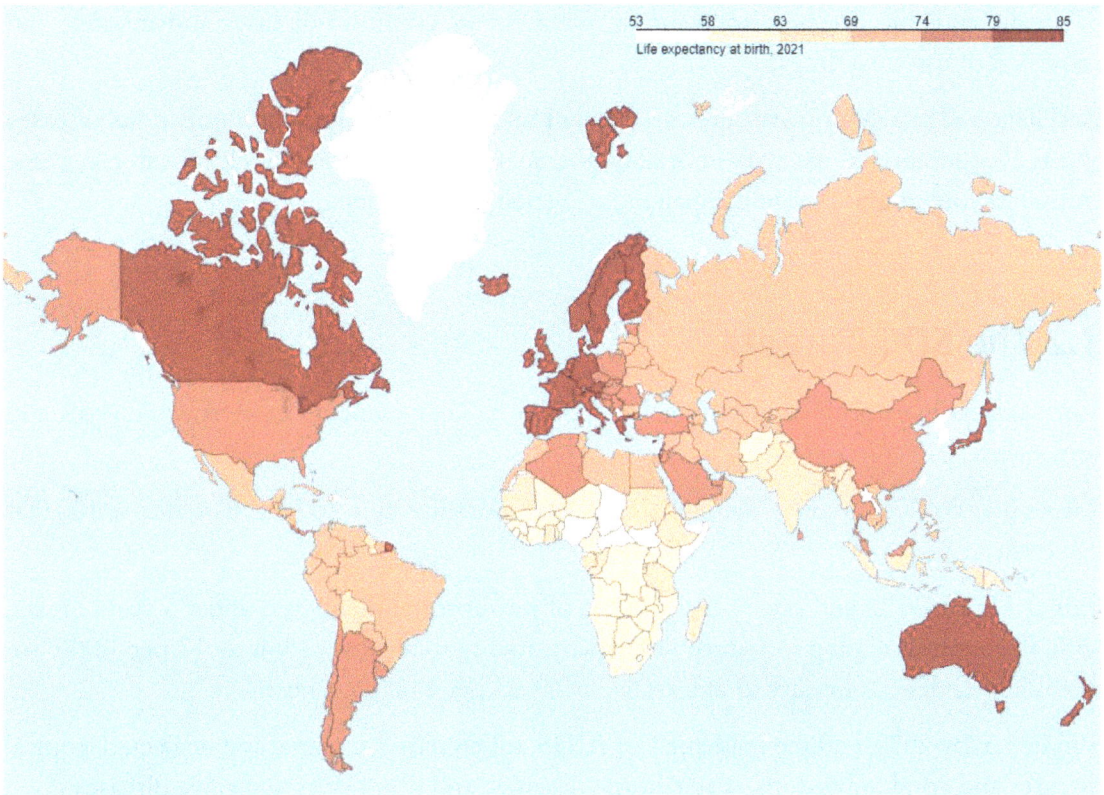

Figure 3.4. Life expectancy at birth 2021. Source: Human Development Index

Public Health

Health Systems

Health systems differ a lot across countries. European countries tend to rely heavily on public healthcare systems like France or the United Kingdom. The United States is primarily privately funded (by the employers and their employees) except for the very poor (Medicaid) and the seniors above 65 (Medicare). Low-income countries often can only afford the rudimentary healthcare system that is sometimes financed by foreign assistance.

Primary Care

Primary care plays an essential role in maintaining the health of a population. According to the Alma Ata ("Declaration of Alma-Ata International Conference on Primary Health Care, Alma-Ata, USSR, 6–12 September 1978," 2004) declaration, primary healthcare:

includes at least: education concerning prevailing health problems and the methods of preventing and controlling them; promotion of food supply and proper nutrition; an adequate supply of safe water and basic sanitation; maternal and child health care, including family planning; immunization against the major infectious diseases; prevention and control of locally endemic diseases; appropriate treatment of common diseases and injuries; and provision of essential drugs;

Excellent and timely primary care can prevent and cure many common infectious diseases and reduce infant and maternal mortality, thanks to the promotion of clean water, hygiene and sanitation, immunization campaigns, and effective medicine.

3.2 The SDG Targets

Some targets have been defined to achieve SDG 3. They combine more specific goals and some actions.

Target 3.1: By 2030, reduce the global maternal mortality ratio to less than 70 per 100,000 live births

Target 3.2: By 2030, end preventable deaths of newborns and children under 5 years of age, with all countries aiming to reduce neonatal mortality to at least as low as 12 per 1,000 live births and under-5 mortality to at least as low as 25 per 1,000 live births

Target 3.3: By 2030, end the epidemics of AIDS, tuberculosis, malaria, and neglected tropical diseases and combat hepatitis, water-borne diseases, and other communicable diseases

Target 3.4: By 2030, reduce by one-third premature mortality from non-communicable diseases through prevention and treatment and promote mental health and well-being

Target 3.5: Strengthen the prevention and treatment of substance abuse, including narcotic drug abuse and harmful use of alcohol

Target 3.6: By 2020, halve the number of global deaths and injuries from road traffic accidents

Target 3.7: By 2030, ensure universal access to sexual and reproductive health-care services, including family planning, information and education, and the integration of reproductive health into national strategies and programmes

Target 3.8: Achieve universal health coverage, including financial risk protection, access to quality essential health-care services, and access to safe, effective, quality, and affordable essential medicines and vaccines for all

Target 3.9: By 2030, substantially reduce the number of deaths and illnesses from hazardous chemicals and air, water, and soil pollution and contamination

Target 3.a: Strengthen the implementation of the World Health Organization Framework Convention on Tobacco Control in all countries, as appropriate

Target 3.b: Support the research and development of vaccines and medicines for the communicable and non-communicable diseases that primarily affect developing countries, and provide access to affordable essential medicines and vaccines in accordance with the Doha Declaration on the TRIPS Agreement and Public Health, which affirms the right of developing countries to use to the full the provisions in the Agreement on Trade-Related Aspects of Intellectual Property Rights regarding flexibilities to protect public health, and, in particular, provide access to medicines for all

Target 3.c: Substantially increase health financing and the recruitment, development, training, and retention of the health workforce in developing countries, especially in the least developed countries and small island developing States

Target 3.d: Strengthen the capacity of all countries, in particular developing countries, for early warning, risk reduction and management of national and global health risks

3.3 How to Improve Health

Healthcare System

Improving health usually depends on a healthcare system that delivers preventive and treatment care to the general population. The healthcare system includes healthcare professionals such as physicians and nurses, hospitals, clinics, pharmacies, medical laboratories, community health centers, government agencies, medical insurance companies, the pharmaceutical industry, and nonprofit organizations.

Healthcare professionals are not always available to treat patients, especially in poor areas, or might not be very motivated because of low pay, poor working conditions, or poor management. Community healthcare workers can provide some of the needed services but need training, economic incentives, and monitoring to reach out and serve a local population.

Mortality Reduction

Improving health to reduce infant and maternal mortality greatly benefits the population. Having proper nutrition, access to water, sanitation, and hygiene (WASH), and affordable healthcare are critical. The prevention and treatment of diseases are also required.

Infection diseases

In low-income countries, many efforts have been focused on preventable infectious diseases such as measles, tuberculosis, and cholera because the cost is relatively modest and solutions are simple. Vaccines, pills, and bed nets (for malaria) can be distributed relatively cheaply. Treatment for HIV is now available with antiretroviral (ARV) therapy (World Health Organization, 2021a). The challenge is to have a distribution network to reach people, educate them, raise their awareness, and encourage adoption.

Non-communicable diseases

As the mortality due to infectious disease decreases and life expectancy increases, there is a relative rise in morbidity due to non-communicable diseases such as cancer, heart disease, stroke, and Alzheimer's disease (World Health Organization, 2020). Changes in diet, a rise in obesity, a growing urban population, and more exposure to all kinds of pollution are contributing to this effect. Better nutrition, living and working conditions, and access to healthcare with early diagnosis and treatment capacities can help address that.

Universal Healthcare

Universal healthcare requires financing, a health workforce, and health system capacities. It is common in many developed countries, with some exceptions like the United States but less so in low-income countries. Countries differ by their coverage (percentage of the population having healthcare) and catastrophic health spending (out-of-pocket expenditure larger than 10% of income)(World Health Organization, 2022). The WHO reports that African countries are worse off with low coverage and high catastrophic spending, and European countries tend to fare better.

Healthcare public expenditures should shift to more prevention and screening services, expand to non-communicable diseases and mental health, and more primary care (World Health Organization, 2022). They should empower healthcare professionals, community health workers, and the population with innovative technology to compensate for the shortage of health system capacities. According to the WHO, the density of doctors in 2014-2020 was 37 per 10,000 in Europe but only 3 per 10,000 in Africa.

Medical Research

Medical research is expensive and tends to be done by research institutions and pharmaceutical companies in developed countries. This also means that the R&D investments are more aligned with the needs of these countries rather than global health. Very little money goes into neglected tropical diseases and vaccines. "Only 1.1% of grants were for neglected tropical diseases and 0.4% for priority diseases on the WHO list of highly infectious (R&D blueprint) pathogens" (Ralaidovy et al., 2020).

It would make sense for developed countries to pool resources to finance R&D for diseases specific to their populations and build manufacturing capabilities to produce essential medicines, generic drugs, medical equipment, and medical supplies with the assistance of established pharmaceutical and medical companies. Smaller, portable, and cheaper medical equipment could be designed locally and more ready to meet the needs of these countries instead of expensive multi-million dollar machines (CT scanner, PT scanner, MRI scanner) targeted at resource-rich health systems. Professionally managed R&D and manufacturing efforts could attract foreign grants and build a sustainable pharmaceutical industry as it exists in India and China.

Health Risk Management

Countries need to prepare emergency response plans to face health risks due to disease outbreaks, pandemics, natural disasters, or conflicts (World Health Organization, 2021b). Each country needs to develop a National Health Emergency Response Operations Plan (NHEROP) that will analyze a public health risk profile and priorities, and available health emergency resources. It also requires early warning systems and developing emergency responses, including action and communication plans.

3.4 What Can AI Do to Improve Health

Prediction

AI can help to predict health in several situations: at the individual level for medical diagnosis and risk assessment, at a community or geographical level for public health surveillance or to address a disease outbreak, and at the molecular level, for drug discovery and development.

Diagnosis

From individual health information such as electronic health records, from health sensors such as a heart or blood pressure monitor, or from medical imaging data such as X-rays or MRI scan images, AI can help diagnose a medical condition. It will typically be done using supervised learning with data from patients with or without particular medical conditions serving training data.

Risk Assessment

Instead of diagnosis, AI can be applied to DNA or other data such as family health records for risk assessment to evaluate the likelihood of developing certain medical conditions during the lifetime or for a given time horizon.

Disease Outbreak and Surveillance

AI can complement epidemiological models to monitor and predict the evolution of disease outbreaks using alternative data such as cell phone data or search query results.

Drug Development

AI can be used for drug development by searching for active molecules that could bind with viruses or improving existing drugs to deal with new variants or viruses. AI can predict the behavior of new molecules or drug configurations. It can also look for combined positive or negative effects with other drugs.

Coordination

Health Policy Planning

AI can help to identify the resources required to care for the health of a population, from adequate housing, food, and sanitation to transportation and distance to healthcare facilities.

In periods of a health crisis, coordination between several actors can be done with AI that could provide information and predict sick individuals and the evolution of a disease.

In a hospital setting, an AI can provide updated checklists to ensure all the required resources are available to care for patients and assist physicians and health professionals.

By monitoring and updating a patient's healthcare records, AI can ensure all drugs and their dosage are appropriate to the patient and are not incompatible when taken together.

Optimization

AI could manage healthcare resources more efficiently by assessing the cost and benefits of interventions, presenting options to patients and their physicians, and providing cost transparency to patients and insurance companies in real time.

At a healthcare system level, AI can help allocate staffing, medical equipment, and beds to maximize health outcomes effectively. In a geographical area, AI can help allocate medical staff and healthcare workers to serve the maximum number of people according to population density, age, gender, health conditions, and distance.

Control

In a clinical care setting, an AI can be connected to sensors and suggest interventions to physicians or alert staff in real time. Though physicians are making medical decisions, an AI can help reduce the number of errors and help reach a diagnosis faster and find an optimal treatment.

AI can help manage inventories of drugs and medical supplies, staff, and beds depending on the flow and diagnosis of incoming patients and local health conditions. AI can also minimize the cost of stay of patients or even the cost of health by suggesting early screening and encouraging preventive medicine.

3.5 Case Studies

Medical Imaging

Machine learning and AI are essential in the field of medical imaging. AI can detect skin or eye conditions, cancer cells, and medical conditions in X-rays, MRIs, or PT-SCANs. Typically, an AI model is trained on a set of labeled images using supervised learning. These images are often specific to a hospital, healthcare system, or country. These images are also particular to the devices used to capture these images.

For instance, McKinney et al. (2020) developed an AI system to screen for breast cancer in mammograms. It used some specific data from the US and the UK. It performs better than a single expert reader with an absolute reduction of 5.7%/1.2% (US/UK) in false positives and 9.4%/2.7% (US/UK) in false negatives. It also generalizes well when trained on UK data and is still successful at dealing with US data.

Still, deploying an AI system to a different set of images is sometimes prone to poor performance. The reason is the distributional shift of the new data relative to the data used to train the model. Azizi et al. (2022) propose a new AI model, REMEDIS (Robust and Efficient Medical Imaging with Self-supervision), for robust medical imaging. Such a model performs well in-distribution (ID) and out-of-distribution (OOD). The aim is to reach data-efficient generalization by improving performance without being specifically retrained on OOD data.

REMEDIS involves three steps. A supervised pretraining phase on non-medical data and a self-supervised pretraining on domain-specific unlabeled medical data to build an encoder for the images, and then supervised fine-tuning on ID labeled medical data to create a classifier. When applied to OOD data, there is an optional supervised fine-tuning, too, or it can be used directly as a zero-shot learning model. The combination of the encoder and classifier gives the final predictor model.

The model is applied and evaluated for six different tasks with their own specific medical imaging data:

Task 1: Dermatology condition classification to identify 26 common skin conditions from digital images.

Task 2: Diabetic macular edema classification to predict central retinal thickness from color fundus photographs taken with a low-power microscope with an attached camera.

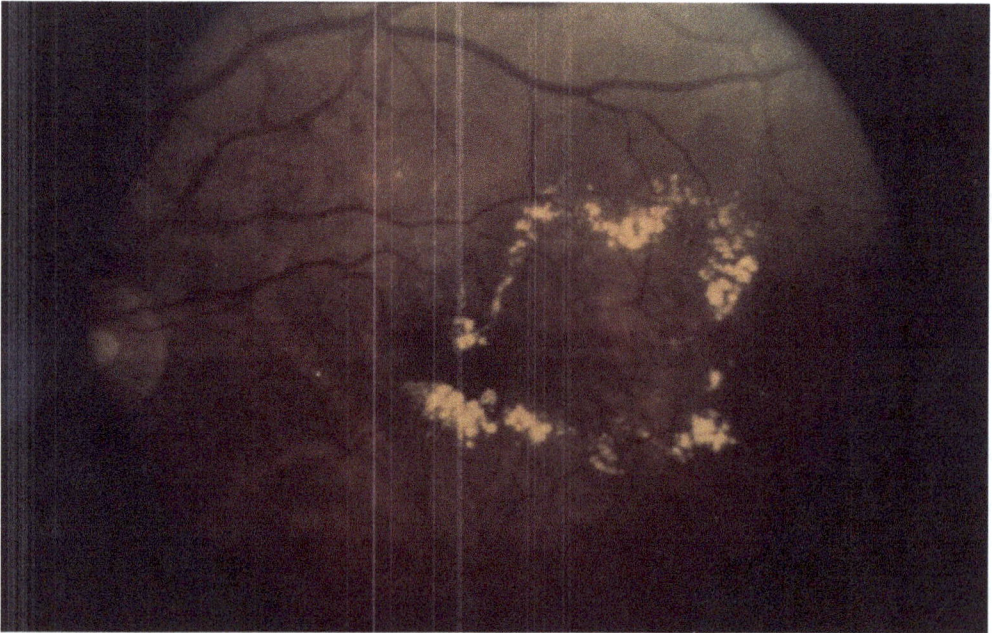

Figure 3.5. Diabetic macular edema. Source: National Eye Institute, National Institutes of Health (photographer credit not given)

Task 3: Chest X-ray classification of chest X-ray images into five common pathologies: atelectasis, consolidation, pulmonary edema, pleural effusion, and cardiomegaly.

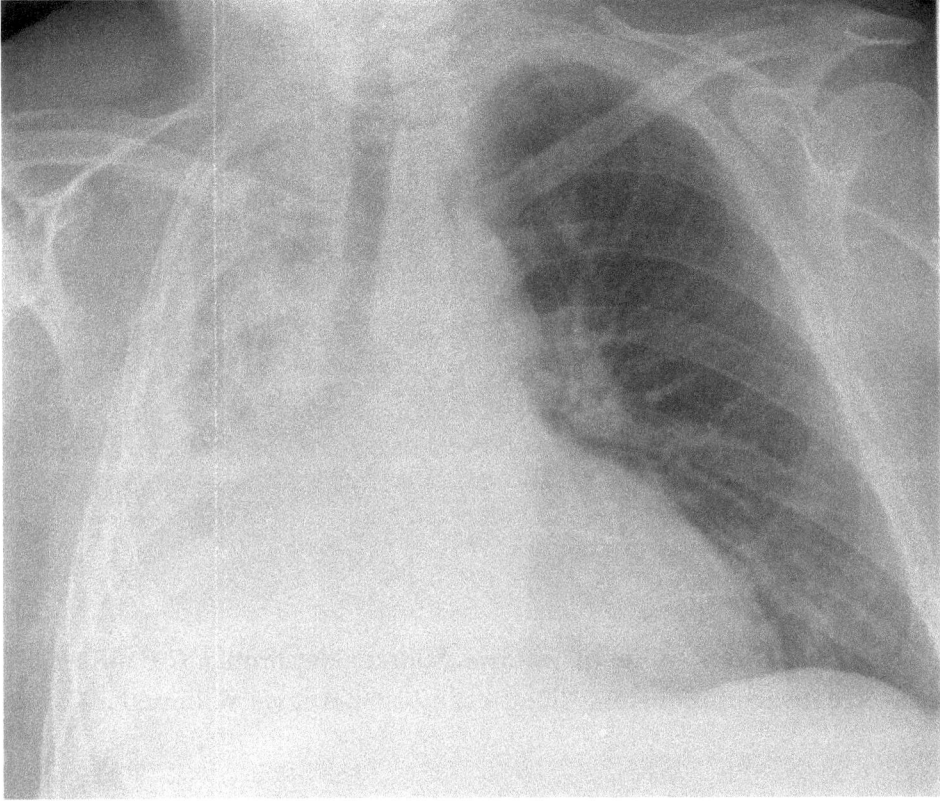

Figure 3.6. Atelectasis. Source: Pabloes at Spanish Wikipedia., CC BY-SA 3.0 <http://creativecommons.org/licenses/by-sa/3.0/>, via Wikimedia Commons

Task 4: Pathology metastases detection to detect cancer metastases in digital whole-slide images of lymph nodes

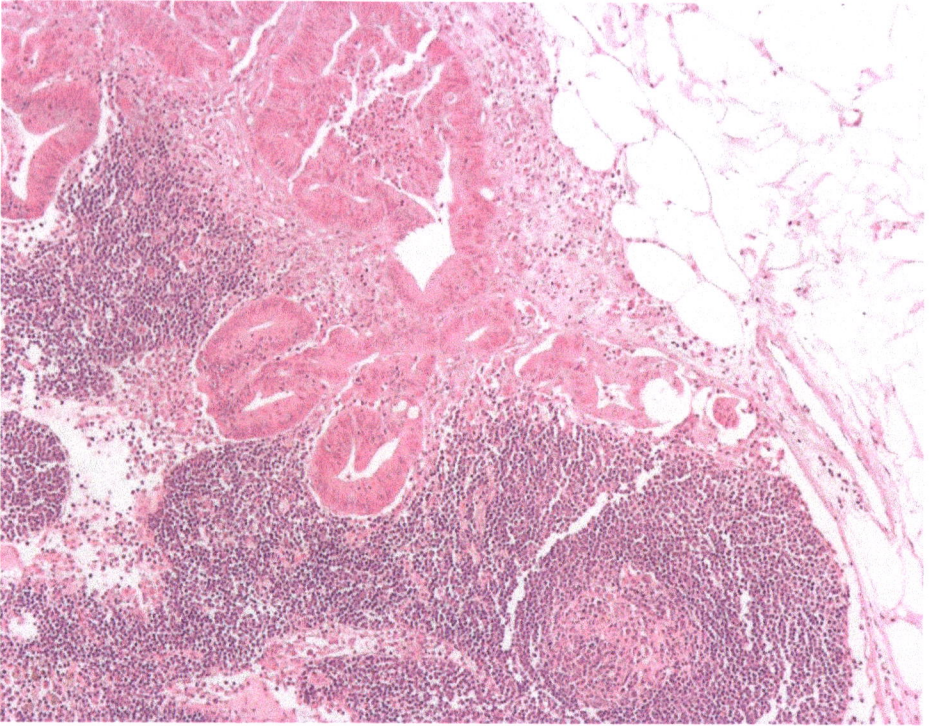

**Figure 3.7. Lymph node metastasis. Source: Nephron, CC BY-SA 3.0
<https://creativecommons.org/licenses/by-sa/3.0>, via Wikimedia Commons**

Task 5: Pathology colorectal survival prediction (5 years) from digital whole-slide images of colorectal tissues histology slides.

Task 6: Mammography classification to predict the occurrence of biopsy-confirmed breast cancer within 39 months after screening.

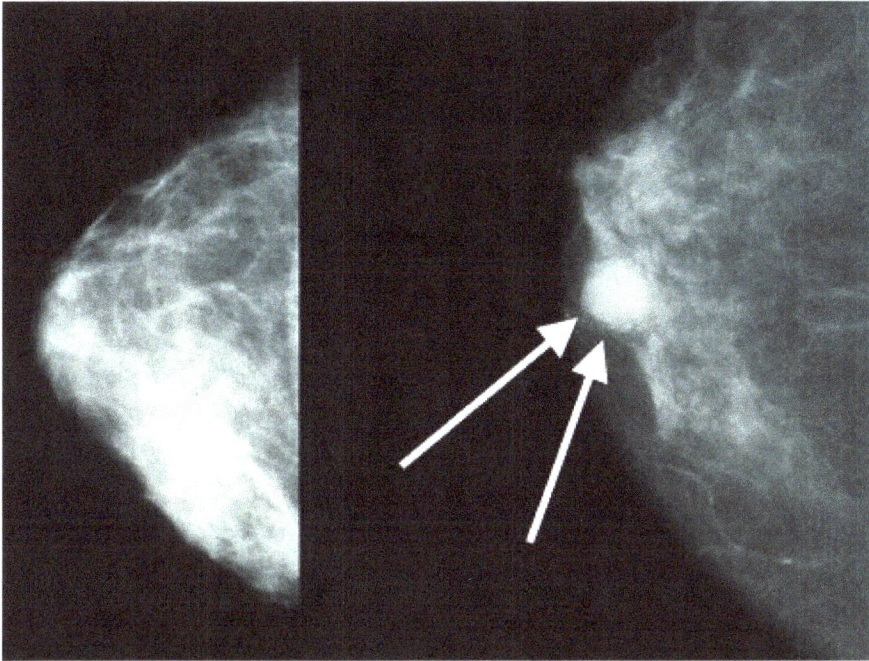

Figure 3.8. Mammograms without (left) and with cancer (right). Source: Bakerstmd, CC BY-SA 4.0 <https://creativecommons.org/licenses/by-sa/4.0>, via Wikimedia Commons

When compared to baseline supervised learning models, REMEDIS improves out-of-distribution performance and data-efficient generalization using 3 to 100 times less labeled data than the benchmarks.

AlphaFold

Proteins make life possible, and understanding how they work is the ultimate goal of biology. These molecules are made of sequences of amino acids and often even combinations of chains of amino acids and take complex three-dimensional (3D) structures that determine how they function.

Protein structure modeling consists in predicting the 3D protein structure from its amino acid sequence. It is a biennial challenge of the Critical Assessment of Techniques for Protein Structure Prediction (CASP) that has been running since 1994. Research teams must submit their model predictions for the structures of over a set of protein targets proposed by CASP. Their models are compared to experimental structures and assessed by their similarity and accuracy.

For CASP14 in the year 2000, AlphaFold from DeepMind (Jumper et al., 2021) outperformed the other submitted models by a high margin. The median root mean squared deviation of its predictions vs. observations were less than one Angstrom, achieving atomic accuracy and much smaller than the next best models at 2.8 Angstrom and above.

In Figure 3.9, AlfaFold gives its 3D prediction on the Chloroplast sensor kinase with a level of confidence. Figure 3.10 provides the predicted aligned error, which indicates, for each residue (an amino acid for a protein) position, the relative position of other residues, with a dark green color indicating low error and light green, high error.

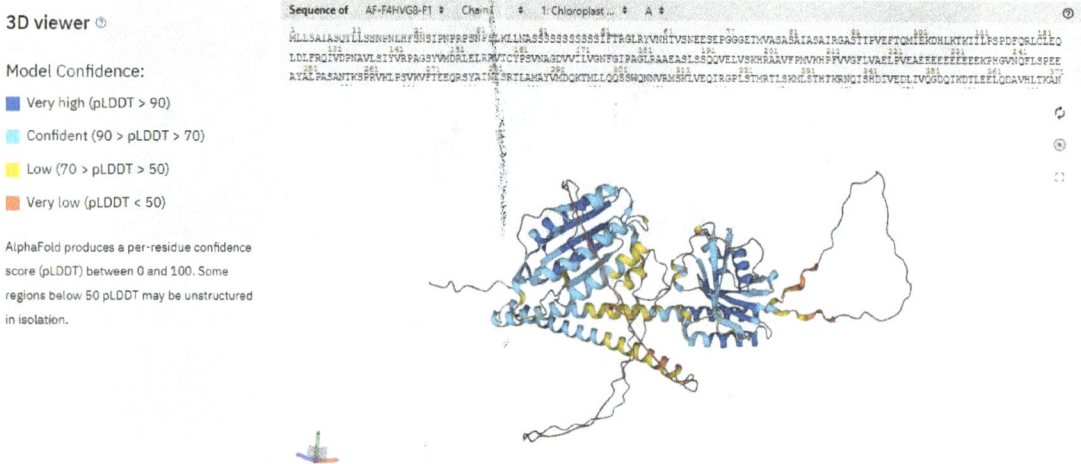

Figure 3.9. Chloroplast sensor kinase, chloroplastic, created with the AlphaFold Monomer v2.0 pipeline. Source: https://alphafold.ebi.ac.uk/entry/F4HVG8

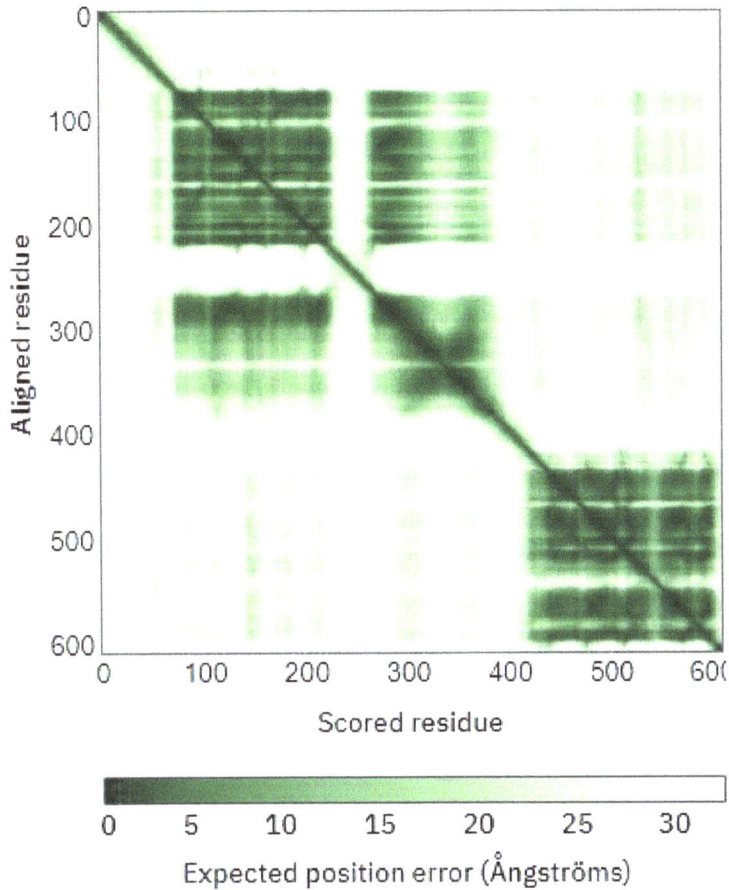

Figure 3.10. Predicted aligned error. Chloroplast sensor kinase, chloroplastic, was created with the AlphaFold Monomer v2.0 pipeline. Source: https://alphafold.ebi.ac.uk/entry/F4HVG8

Proteins are represented in two forms: one tabular form, the MSA (multiple sequence alignment) representations, along with known proteins found in a genetic database, and a pair representation in which each pair of residues appear in a table. These representations are then fed to Evoformer blocks that contain attention-based and non-attention-based components and are progressively transformed by these blocks before going through a structure module that shapes them into a final 3D structure.

DeepMind and the European Molecular Biology Laboratory, European Bioinformatics Institute (Varadi et al., 2022) have released AlphaFold DB, a database of over 360,000 predicted structures from model-organism proteomes. This database was expanded in 2022 to cover 200 million structures covering a large part of the known protein sequences of the human proteome (the set of proteins that can be expressed by the human genome) and of other species.

Covid-19

Wynants et al. (2020) have examined prediction models for diagnosis and prognosis of Covid-19, including models using AI. They looked at 232 models that have been published and peer-reviewed in 169 studies. Using PROBAST (prediction model risk of bias assessment tool) (Wolff et al., 2019), they find that most models have a high or unclear risk of bias and are likely to overestimate their performance. The reasons include a non-representative control population, exclusion of patients, model overfitting, and vague reporting.

They recommend that these studies adhere to the TRIPOD statement (Collins et al., 2015). This includes describing the background and objectives, the source of data, the participants in the study, the outcome, the predictors, the sample size, the statistical analysis methods, the model development, model specification and performance, and a discussion of limitations, interpretation, and implications.

Chapter 4 | Education

> "An investment in knowledge pays the best interest."
>
> Benjamin Franklin

4.1 The State of World Education

Education Trend

Goal 4 is to "Ensure inclusive and equitable quality education and promote lifelong learning opportunities for all." ("Goal 4 | Department of Economic and Social Affairs").

More access to education

Access to primary, secondary, and higher education has improved but is still lower among low-income countries. According to UNESCO (UNESCO, 2021), 20% of children in low-income countries and 10% worldwide (250 million) are out of primary school, and 60% of youth in low-income countries are out of secondary school. The gap is even more significant for higher education.

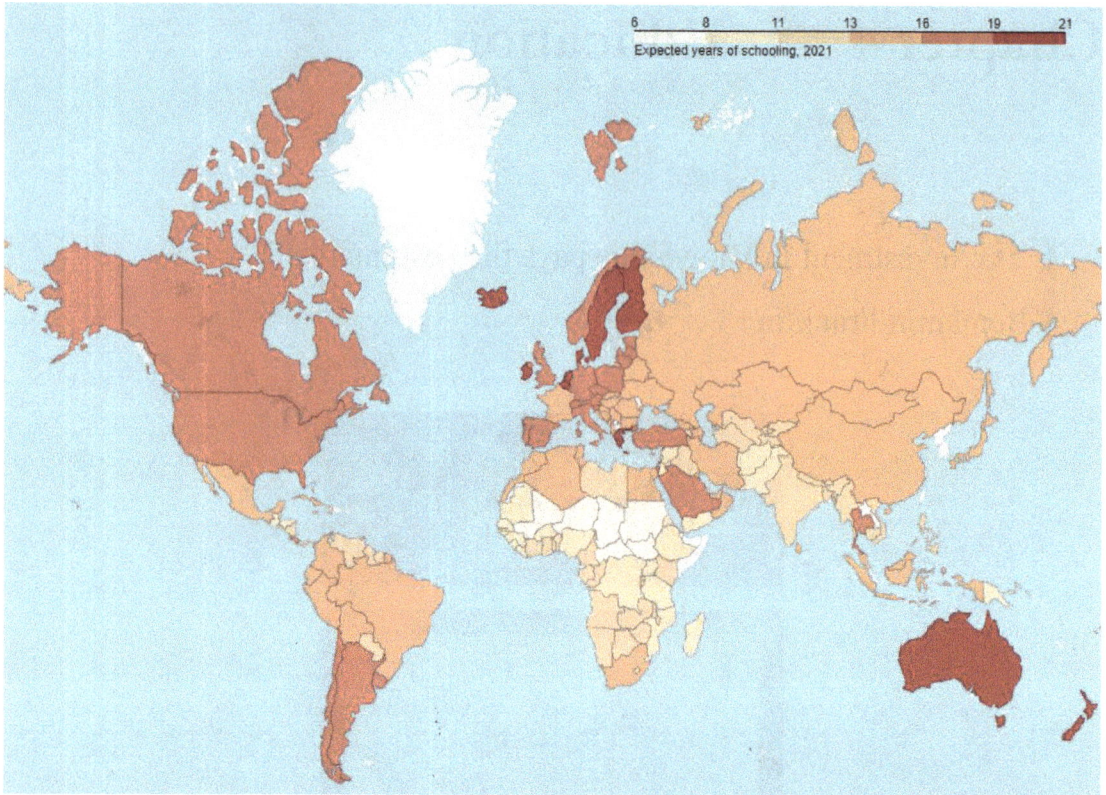

Figure 4.1. Expected years of schooling 2021. Source: Human Development Index

There are also considerable differences in expected years of schooling (Figure 4.1), with some countries at less than three years and richer countries at more than 12 years. Africa, Asia, and Latin America still have relatively low years of schooling.

There are likely different reasons. The population is growing rapidly in some of these regions, and education resources (teachers and infrastructure such as schools and school transportation) are not keeping up. The return to education is further in the future and uncertain, while there might be immediate labor needs, including domestic labor, especially in rural areas. The formal labor market might be underdeveloped, with few job opportunities even with some years of education. In regions with armed conflicts and armed militia, going to school might be very dangerous, especially for young girls. On the supply side, there are not enough teachers, especially in poorer countries, either because of a lack of skills or the economic attractiveness of the profession. Denmark had 253 teaching professionals per 1000 persons under 15 in 2018 vs. 2 per 1000 for Tanzania in 2014 (ILO, 2019).

There is still a gender gap in education in lower-income countries. On average, girls have fewer years of schooling than boys (UNICEF, 2020). In sub-Saharan Africa, in 2018, 22% of girls of primary education age were out of school vs. 17% of boys. In South Asia, it is 8% vs.

6%. The recent Covid pandemic probably worsened with school closure, and girls asked to stay home to provide domestic labor and help their families.

Literacy

According to UNESCO (2021), "An estimated 750 million people worldwide cannot read and write at the basic level of proficiency." Two-thirds of these people are women. The number of illiterate adults has increased in the past fifty years with population growth. Twenty-nine countries have formed the Global Alliance for Literacy ("Global Alliance for Literacy – Member countries | UIL," 2021) to address illiteracy. Many of these countries with low literacy rates are in Africa and Asia. Some are in Latin America and the Caribbean.

Education and income

In general, richer countries have longer average years of schooling. In poorer countries, the average years of education can be deficient such as in sub-Saharan Africa. Countries with more financial resources can afford to invest more in public education, build and maintain schools and pay teachers.

Children of higher socioeconomic status in a country tend to be better educated. The OECD has documented this pattern with its Programme for International Student Assessment ("PISA - PISA," n.d.). PISA assesses the knowledge and problem-solving skills in mathematics, science, and reading of 15-year-old youth. But the differential in economic status is uneven across countries. Some countries or regions are faring better than others, like some large cities in China, and some significant progress has been observed in countries like Singapore.

Digital learning

Education is undergoing digital transformation, especially with remote learning mandated during the Covid-19 pandemic. Digital learning using digital devices such as computers and tablets can provide new opportunities for teaching and learning. However, it is not accessible to all, especially not to millions who lack access to essential services such as electricity and internet, are illiterate, or do not have access to digital devices.

Adult education and lifelong learning

Because of fast technological change, adults need to have access to lifelong learning to acquire and maintain marketable skills and be employable. Education received in college, or high school might become obsolete faster in areas like STEM (Science, Technology, Engineering, and Mathematics). As younger generations become more educated, the older workforce must keep up to remain employable and competitive. It is common for employers to look for skills such as digital marketing, cloud customer relationship management, SEO specialization, or cloud engineering that didn't exist 10 or 20 years ago. Older workers are also dependent on the technology used by their employers. If their employers do not keep up, they risk falling behind.

4.2 The SDG Targets

The Sustainable Development Goal is supported by the following Targets:

Target 4.1: By 2030, ensure that all girls and boys complete free, equitable, and quality primary and secondary education leading to relevant and effective learning outcomes

Target 4.2: By 2030, ensure that all girls and boys have access to quality early childhood development, care, and pre-primary education so that they are ready for primary education

Target 4.3: By 2030, ensure equal access for all women and men to affordable and quality technical, vocational and tertiary education, including university

Target 4.4: By 2030, substantially increase the number of youth and adults who have relevant skills, including technical and vocational skills, for employment, decent jobs, and entrepreneurship

Target 4.5: By 2030, eliminate gender disparities in education and ensure equal access to all levels of education and vocational training for the vulnerable, including persons with disabilities, indigenous peoples, and children in vulnerable situations

Target 4.6: By 2030, ensure that all youth and a substantial proportion of adults, both men, and women, achieve literacy and numeracy

Target 4.7: By 2030, ensure that all learners acquire the knowledge and skills needed to promote sustainable development, including, among others, through education for sustainable development and sustainable lifestyles, human rights, gender equality, promotion of a culture of peace and non-violence, global citizenship and appreciation of cultural diversity and of culture's contribution to sustainable development

Target 4.a: Build and upgrade education facilities that are child, disability, and gender sensitive and provide safe, non-violent, inclusive, and effective learning environments for all

Target 4.b: By 2020, substantially expand globally the number of scholarships available to developing countries, in particular, least developed countries, small island developing States, and African countries, for enrolment in higher education, including vocational training and information and communications technology, technical, engineering and scientific programmes, in developed countries and other developing countries

Target 4.c: By 2030, substantially increase the supply of qualified teachers, including through international cooperation for teacher training in developing countries, especially least developed countries and small island developing States

4.3 How to Improve Education

Primary and Secondary Education

Children should attend primary and secondary schools and benefit from a curriculum and teaching that prepares them to become thoughtful and skillful participants in society and the economy. They need literacy, numeracy, and STEM skills, but also others (The Economist, 2017):

- Interdisciplinary skills

- Creative and analytical skills

- Entrepreneurial skills

- Leadership skills

- Digital and technical skills

- Global awareness and civic education

They require qualified and motivated teachers and parents who prioritize their children's education, including their daughters'. Schools should coordinate with their local communities to ensure the practicality and relevance of their curriculum and teaching. Schools should also receive adequate resources such as teaching materials, textbooks, and access to the internet and digital technologies.

Post-secondary Education

Post-secondary education is necessary to train teachers and people who aspire to take higher-skill jobs. Developed countries should offer scholarships to educate, prepare and facilitate exchanges and knowledge transfers with lower-income countries.

Education should be relevant to the local job market and provide sufficient skills for students to evolve with changes in the job market and create opportunities for themselves. Many workers are self-employed in low-income countries because of a lack of formal job opportunities. Efforts should be focused on favoring legal work arrangements and integrating a young and newly educated workforce, sometimes with apprenticeship and vocational training.

Lifetime Education

Because of rapid technological change, the need for retraining, and many adults who do not have post-secondary education, countries should facilitate lifetime education and provide incentives to people or their current or future employers. Acquired training should be of sufficient quality to get recognized by employers and be valued on the job market with a wage premium.

4.4 What Can AI Do to Improve Education

Prediction

AI can help teachers grade and evaluate homework, papers, and students. An essay can be analyzed automatically by NLP for topics covered, grammar and spelling, logical argumentation, and speed up the evaluation by the teacher. Given the level of a student, the AI can predict future performance and alert the teacher if there is any significant deviation from expectations.

Class participation and discussion in the classroom can be recorded, quantified, and classified to understand the class dynamic and see if some students do not participate as much or have different behavior from the recent past.

AI can help benchmark the effectiveness of teachers, schools, and school districts and compare student performance with predicted performance based on socioeconomic variables, student past performance and characteristics, and available economic and financial resources.

AI can help predict children's school enrollment based on geographical and socioeconomic variables in a country or region. Children in poor and remote areas are less likely to attend school. Weather events such as floods could make some villages inaccessible and schooling much more difficult.

Coordination

AI can help identify the inputs required for good educational outcomes, including the types of activities, the teaching environments, the style of teaching required, and the subjects to be taught. Realtime A/B testing or randomized trials can be implemented across a school system or different classes and analyzed by AI.

Schools tend to be isolated, and more coordination could be done with parents and future employers. Required skills can be analyzed by AI, and the curriculum could be improved with relevant teaching or practical coursework. It would also be possible for companies to set up AI-driven corporate universities to train their employees and recruits.

Optimization

Teaching can be optimized by AI, for instance, with a more personalized curriculum for each student or group of students. AI-driven systems can follow students' progress and adapt to their levels, choosing challenging but possible activities for them to complete.

AI can also optimize the contents of lectures, activities, and the whole learning experience for the students and teachers based on their respective performances and progress. Experienced teachers could be assigned to more challenging classes, for instance, and more advanced students can be given access to more challenging activities.

Control

AI can adjust the curriculum based on feedback from students and teachers and their performance and assessment. Based on significant deviations from expectations, AI can suggest remedies to make the contents easier or more difficult or to add more resources to students who need them. AI can detect student performance anomalies and signal parents, teachers, or administrators to talk and work with the student.

4.5 Case Studies

Tutoring

Conati et al. (2018) provide examples of Intelligent Tutoring Systems (ITS), or AI in education, that use Open Learner Modeling. The ITS runs intelligent pedagogical agents (IPAs), or AI tutors that "can model, predict and monitor relevant learner behaviors, abilities and mental states in a variety of educational activities, and provide personalized help and feedback accordingly."

One class of models is the Open Learner Model (OLM), where users have access to the model's assessment of the student (states and abilities), can cooperate with the model to reach a joint evaluation, or can override a model to reflect their judgments. Users can be teachers or students. In this context, the AI system must be explainable so that users can understand and interact with it.

The authors give two examples in the first category of models, called scrutable models. The first one is the TARDIS model, developed to coach young people for job interviews (Porayska-Pomsta et al., 2014). It collects information from virtual job interviews and visualizes the assessment for the learner and human practitioners. In the second example taken from Long and Aleven (2017), the students are offered self-assessment tools to evaluate their knowledge that can be compared to some correct problem-solving strategies. The students can then self-reflect on their performance and assessment. The last example is an editable OLM (Basu et al., 2017). Learners can choose tasks and strategies to solve a problem, and the system analyzes and assesses the learner's choices compared to suboptimal or desired strategies. The steps are presented in direct-acyclic graphs that the learner can modify.

Minerva

Minerva (Lewkowycz et al., 2022) is an AI model that can perform quantitative reasoning and solve mathematical and STEM problems without access to external tools. It is built on the PaLM model, a large language model from Google (Chowdhery et al., 2022).

Question: A line parallel to $y = 4x + 6$ passes through $(5, 10)$. What is the y-coordinate of the point where this line crosses the y-axis?

Model output: The line is parallel to $y = 4x + 6$, which means that it has the same slope as $y = 4x + 6$. Since the line passes through $(5, 10)$, we can use the point-slope form of a line to find the equation of the line:

$$y - 10 = 4(x - 5)$$
$$y - 10 = 4x - 20$$
$$y = 4x - 10$$

Now that we have the equation of the line, we can find the y-coordinate of the point where the line crosses the y-axis by substituting $x = 0$ into the equation:

$$y = 4 \cdot 0 - 10 = \boxed{-10}.$$

Figure 4.2. Minerva solved a multi-step problem. Source: https://ai.googleblog.com/2022/06/minerva-solving-quantitative-reasoning.html

The model starts with a pretrained PaLM decoder model and then is fine-tuned on a training set of 38.5B tokens taken from 1.2M arXiv papers in LATEX format and web pages containing mathematics (expressions in MathJax format). The objective is to predict the subsequent tokens (up to 512) from the previous 1024 tokens (autoregressive objective).

The model is evaluated on three datasets: MATH, a dataset of middle school and high school math problems; GSM8k, a dataset of grade school word math problems; MMLU-STEM, a dataset of multiple-choice questions in Science, Technology, Engineering, and Mathematics, and OCWCourses, based problems found in MIT Open Courses in STEM. The model is usually promoted with some samples of questions and answers and is run several times to produce several solutions. The result consistent with the majority of the answer is the final one.

The Minerva model with 540B parameters and majority voting for the answer performs the best of the MMLU-STEM dataset with an accuracy of 75%. It performs the worst on the

OCWCourses dataset. It still outperforms previous models. The model still makes mistakes due to incorrect reasonings and calculations. Interestingly, the model is not simply memorizing the answers from the training set but is coming out with its reasoning.

Codex

Codex (Chen et al., 2021) is a GPT language model specialized in generating code. It is fine-tuned on Python code available publicly on GitHub. It also powers the commercial GitHub product, GitHub Copilot, to assist in writing code (Figure 4.3).

```ts
#!/usr/bin/env ts-node

import { fetch } from "fetch-h2";

// Determine whether the sentiment of text is positive
// Use a web service
async function isPositive(text: string): Promise<boolean> {
  const response = await fetch(`http://text-processing.com/api/sentiment/`, {
    method: "POST",
    body: `text=${text}`,
    headers: {
      "Content-Type": "application/x-www-form-urlencoded",
    },
  });
  const json = await response.json();
  return json.label === "pos";
}
```

Figure 4.3. Example of GitHub Copilot. Source: https://github.com/features/copilot

Codex's task is to generate the Python code for a function given a string of descriptions of its functionality (Python docstrings). A human reading the docstring should be able to know what the function is doing. Codex is trained to do the same. Codex is fine-tuned from a GPT model with 12B parameters.

For each problem represented in a docstring, Codex generates several code samples. If any of the code samples passes a series of unit tests, the problem is considered solved. Codex is evaluated on 164 handwritten programming problems (the HumanEval dataset). If Codex is allowed to run 100 code solutions, it finds at least one solution that passes the unit tests for most of these problems.

Chapter 5 | Work, Gender Equality, and Inequalities

"No society can surely be flourishing and happy, of which the far greater part of the members are poor and miserable."

Adam Smith

5.1 The State of World Work

Goal 8 of the SDG is to "promote sustained, inclusive and sustainable economic growth, full and productive employment and decent work for all." It consists of labor participation, unemployment, and working conditions. ("Goal 8 | Department of Economic and Social Affairs").

The latest 2021 SDG report notes the worsening of the youth and women's labor participation. The Covid-19 pandemic made the situation worse in 2020. Participation in these groups is very low, and unemployment is exceptionally high in less developed countries. In 2019, the proportion of youth not in education, employment, or training for young men was 14% and more than doubled to 31% for young women.

Work Trend

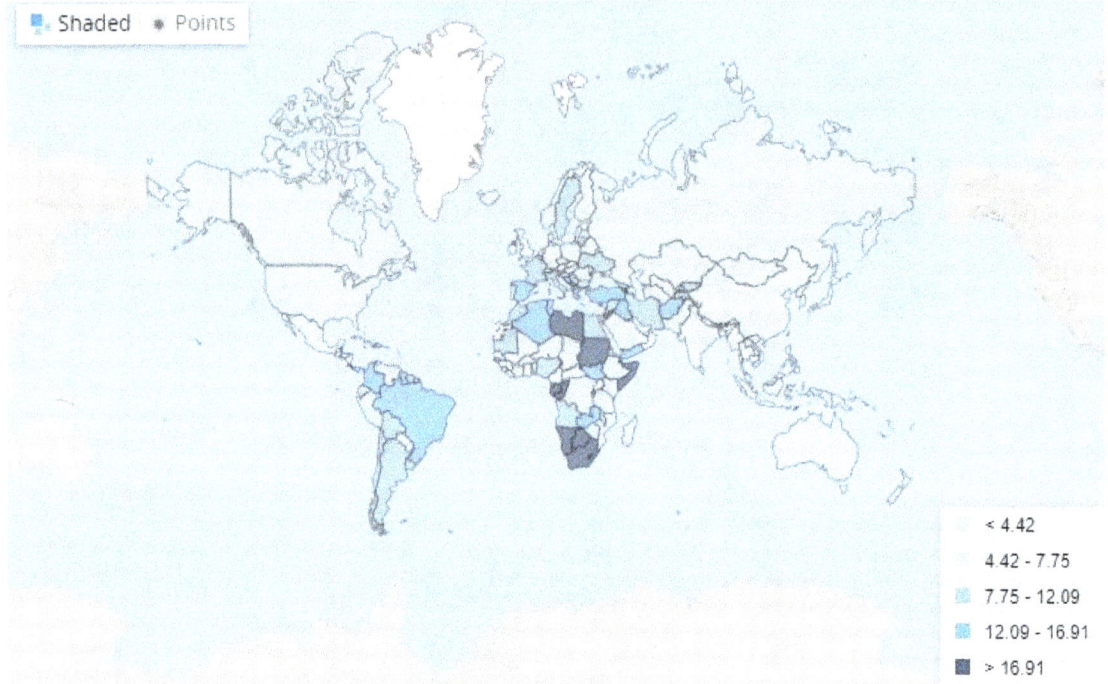

Figure 5.1. 2021 Unemployment, total (% of total labor force) (modeled ILO estimate) by country

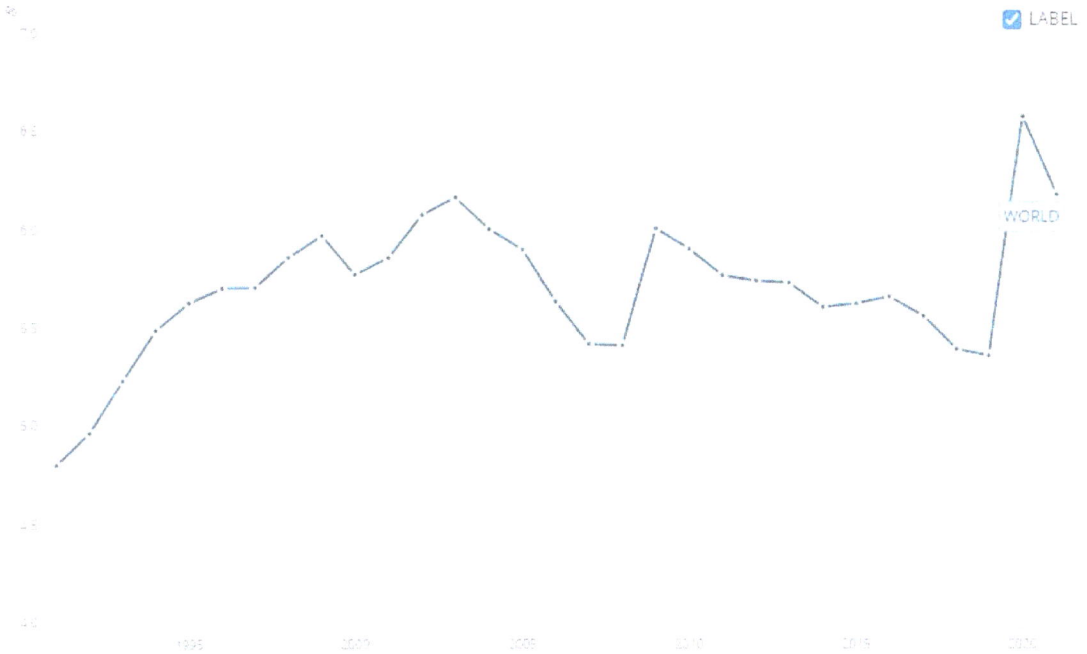

Figure 5.2. 2021 World unemployment, total (% of the total labor force) (modeled ILO estimate)

Unemployment is a common statistic to track progress in the job market. However, it is imperfect because it follows only people who are actively looking for jobs and not people who are out of the labor force but would be open to work. A person might not be actively looking for a job if no work is available, for instance, in agriculture outside the harvest season.

Unemployment tends to be higher in developing countries and is correlated with poverty but is an imperfect measure of the availability of productive employment and work opportunities. The reason is that many people are self-employed or work for other family members because they do not find wage jobs and are too poor to offer not to work (Fields, 2019). The kind of work that they do is of very low productivity, such as being a street vendor or a smallholder farmer growing vegetables and selling them in the market. The income they make is often not sufficient to lift them out of poverty. The ILO calls this work situation vulnerable employment. Usually, the poorer the country, the larger the share of vulnerable employment. Even though this is a form of employment, it is really a sign of a lack of good job opportunities.

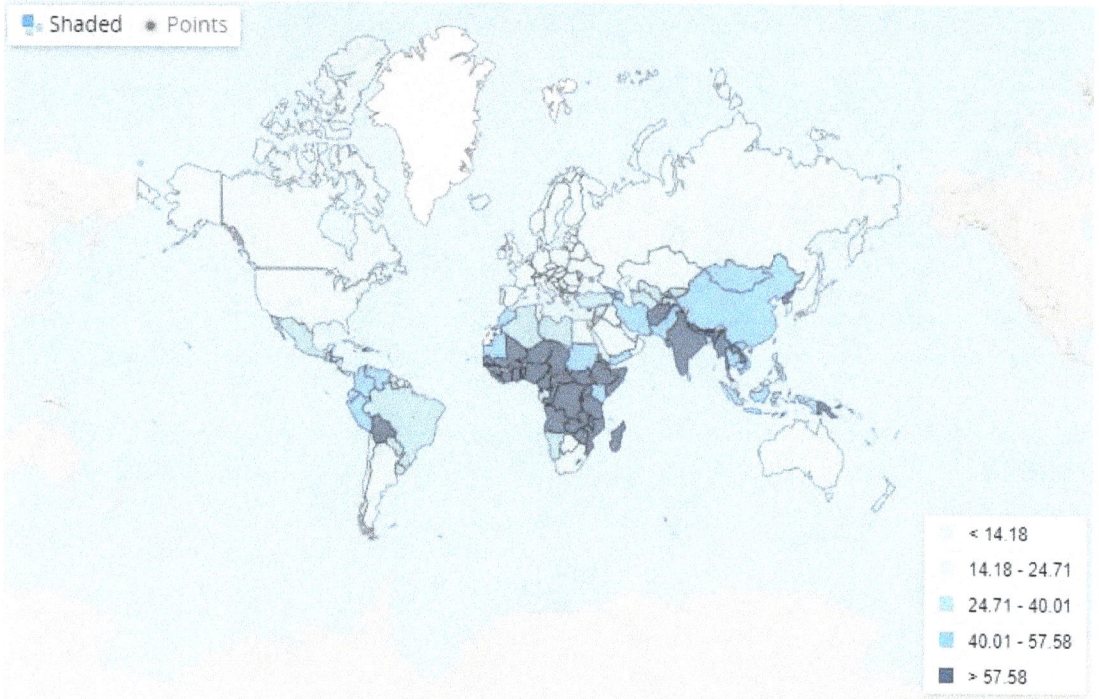

Figure 5.3. 2021 Vulnerable employment, total (% of the total labor force) (modeled ILO estimate) by Country

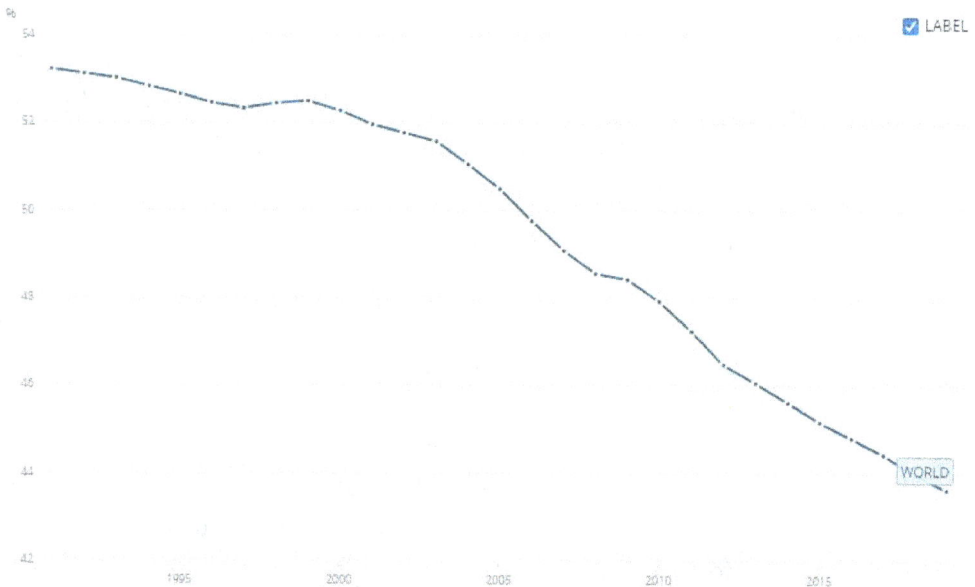

Figure 5.4. 2021 World vulnerable employment, total (% of the total labor force) (modeled ILO estimate)

The pandemic has affected workers in developing countries more as their governments didn't financially support their populations as generously as in developed countries (World Employment and Social Outlook, 2022).

Lack of health and education hinder work and productive employment though it is not uncommon to see much unemployed youth with postsecondary degrees. This is a case of mismatch in the labor market where these young graduates do not find firms that could use or need their skills, are not willing or are too small to invest in their practical education to complement a less valuable university education, or do not have the technical, managerial, organizational size and expertise to employ them productively, or are protecting employed but less-educated older workers from competition.

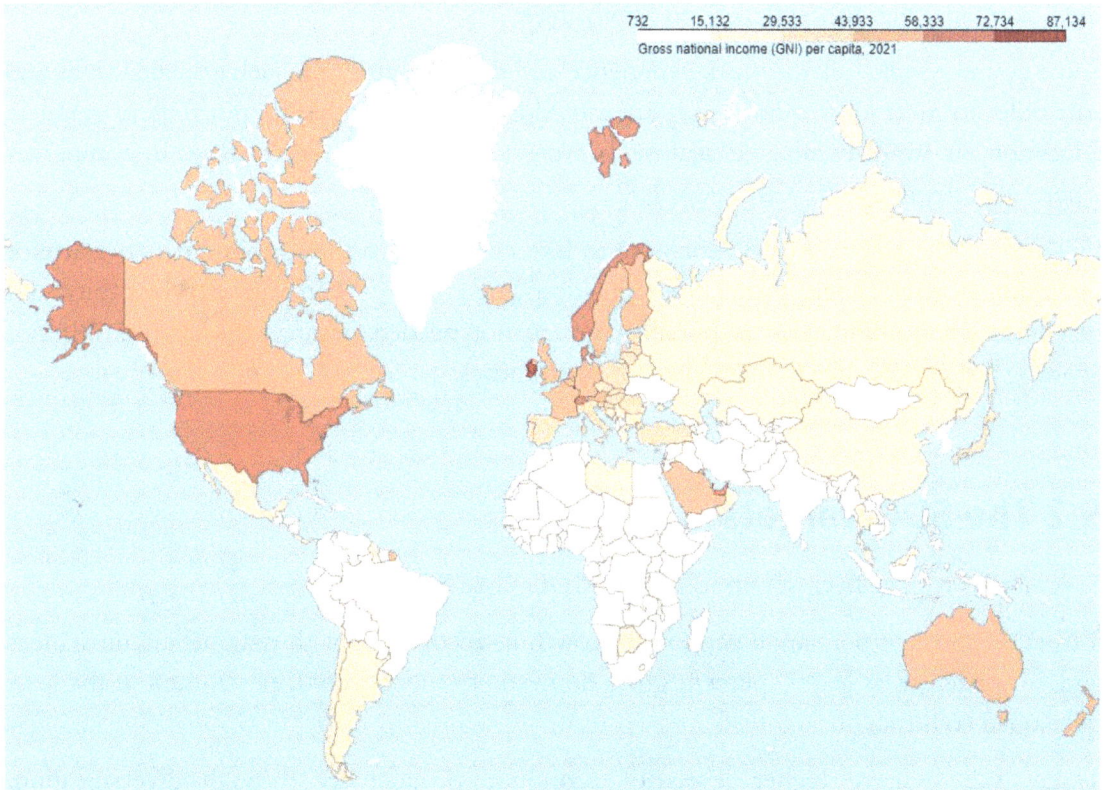

Figure 5.5. Gross National Income (GNI) per capita, PPP 2017. Source: Human Development Index

Youth Unemployment

Youth unemployment tends to be higher than adult unemployment. According to the ILO (2020), the number of youth (15 to 24 years old) participating in labor has decreased from 568 million to 497 million despite the increase in the world population. One reason is the increase of young people, with most women not in employment, education, or training (NEET).

The youth's low labor participation has several plausible causes:

Some young women are not encouraged to work in some countries, like in the Middle East, or have to stay home to provide unpaid domestic labor, or cannot rely on society to help them combine their professional and family lives.

Some young people lack the work experience and the relevant skills, such as digital skills and soft skills, to meet job requirements, are too educated for jobs that do not require graduate education, or are discriminated against to protect the jobs of older workers in companies where seniority and loyalty are rewarded.

Financially, they might be too expensive to hire compared to their productivity because of minimum wage and social protection regulations, are at risk of being replaced by capital and machines when automation is possible, or are not needed because the economy is not growing fast enough like in many developed countries.

5.2 The SDG Targets

Several targets have been set up to achieve SDG Goal 8:

Target 8.1: Sustain per capita economic growth in accordance with national circumstances and, in particular, at least 7 percent gross domestic product growth per annum in the least developed countries

Target 8.2: Achieve higher levels of economic productivity through diversification, technological upgrading, and innovation, including through a focus on high-value added and labor-intensive sectors

Target 8.3: Promote development-oriented policies that support productive activities, decent job creation, entrepreneurship, creativity, and innovation, and encourage the formalization and growth of micro-, small- and medium-sized enterprises, including through access to financial services

Target 8.4: Improve progressively, through 2030, global resource efficiency in consumption and production and endeavor to decouple economic growth from environmental degradation, in accordance with the 10-year framework of programs on sustainable consumption and production, with developed countries taking the lead

Target 8.5: By 2030, achieve full and productive employment and decent work for all women and men, including for young people and persons with disabilities, and equal pay for work of equal value

Target 8.6: By 2020, substantially reduce the proportion of youth not in employment, education, or training

Target 8.7: Take immediate and effective measures to eradicate forced labor, end modern slavery and human trafficking, and secure the prohibition and elimination of the worst forms of child labor, including recruitment and use of child soldiers, and by 2025 end child labor in all its forms

Target 8.8: Protect labor rights and promote safe and secure working environments for all workers, including migrant workers, in particular, women migrants, and those in precarious employment

Target 8.9: By 2030, devise and implement policies to promote sustainable tourism that creates jobs and promotes local culture and products

Target 8.10: Strengthen the capacity of domestic financial institutions to encourage and expand access to banking, insurance, and financial services for all

Target 8.a: Increase Aid for Trade support for developing countries, in particular, least developed countries, including through the Enhanced Integrated Framework for Trade-Related Technical Assistance to Least Developed Countries

Target 8.b: By 2020, develop and operationalize a global strategy for youth employment and implement the Global Jobs Pact of the International Labour Organization

5.3 How to Improve Work

There is a direct correlation between unemployment and economic growth. So higher economic growth, such as in the US or in China, should improve labor markets. Youth unemployment and the low labor participation of women preceded Covid-19, however. Better education, child care, on-the-job training, and direct money transfers are typically recommended. For instance, a woman might have to stop working to care for young children or elderly parents because her household cannot afford paid care.

5.4 What Can AI Do to Improve Work

AI could help thanks to:

- AI-powered education platforms to educate and train workers

- AI-assisted care to look after children or parents

- AI-powered job market and application platforms to match job seekers and employers

- AI-powered targeted welfare system to assist financially potential workers in need

Prediction

AI can help assess and predict a candidate's job performance or a fit for a role. AI can predict a company's performance as an employer in terms of job satisfaction, job compensation and benefits, and career growth and advancement. AI can recommend job candidates to companies or companies to job candidates.

AI can predict labor and skill shortages in different industries, regions, or countries depending on the market and economic conditions. AI can predict surplus labor, future layoffs, and redundancies by companies, sectors, regions, or countries. AI can also run the analysis by skill sets, age groups, education levels, professions, and other criteria. AI can also predict who needs assistance to find or fill a job (child care, transportation, healthcare).

Coordination

AI can help plan to acquire the skills required for specific jobs and industries or set up teams with the best-combined skills. AI can help employers to develop and train their employees for necessary skills. AI can be a personal career coach or an intelligent assistant to HR executives.

AI can operate an internal or external job matching platform to match supply and demand and account for individual and business circumstances. AI could benchmark wages and benefits to ensure that employees are fairly and competitively compensated. AI could help monitor all career opportunities, advancements, and progressions and make the workplace more transparent and fair, especially for underrepresented groups.

Optimization

AI can help optimize the working environment to make employees more productive by keeping schedules, allocating employee time and tasks more efficiently, taking notes in meetings, analyzing data and documents, preparing intelligent documents, and generating reports.

AI can help build optimal teams with the proper resources to undertake new projects. AI could help make agile development and business practices more streamlined and more efficient. AI could work as a scrum master or agile coordinator and prepare all the agile reporting and documentation automatically.

Control

AI can work as an avatar of employees to attend virtual meetings, for instance, in different time zones or regions on their behalf, take notes, communicate and report back. An AI can also work as a personal assistant. Another AI can work as a personal coach, a health assistant, a financial and benefit planner, or a work-life balance assistant.

AI can control the time employees and employers spend on different tasks and suggest improvements, such as reducing the frequency of meetings or travels. AI can control the quality of work delivery, sales cycles, customer interactions and product feedback, randomized business trials and experiments, and read through all past business interactions to guide new product development, innovations, and ideas.

5.5 The State of World Gender Equality

Goal 5 of the SDG is to "achieve gender equality and empower all women and girls"

Women are underrepresented in political institutions. They are victims of child marriage and violence. Women do a lot of unpaid household and care work. ("Goal 5 | Department of Economic and Social Affairs").

Gender equality is an important goal for human development and justice. In many countries, girls do not have equal access to education. Some get married very young and bear children with a high risk of mortality. They spend a lot of time on unpaid labor to take care of their home and their family. Even when they are educated, they still face discrimination in the job market or suffer from a gender pay gap. During the recent pandemic, many women had to drop out of the workforce to take care of their children because of school closures. Women are also more often victims of domestic violence and violence in general.

The sources of gender inequality are complex. According to Springer Nature ("What are the origins of gender inequality? | For Researchers | Springer Nature," n.d.), "the creation of gender inequality is a subtle, life-long, and partly unconscious process, fuelled, among others, by implicit cognitions about the role of men and women in society, and gendered stereotypical pictures."

There are attempts to quantify gender inequality. The United Nations ("Human Development Report 2020," 2020) follows the progress in gender equality using the Gender Inequality Index (GII). The GII is constructed from three dimensions. Each dimension covers several indicators:

- Reproductive health: maternal mortality ratio, the adolescent birth rate

- Empowerment: female and male population with at least secondary education, female and make shares of parliamentary seats

- Labor market: female and male labor force participation rates

The GII differs across countries and tends to be concentrated in poorer countries but not always. European countries such as The Netherlands, Denmark, Sweden, Norway, and Germany tend to score high. Poorer countries going through armed conflicts tend to do very poorly, such as Yemen, Afghanistan, Niger, and Congo. Women are often the first victims in times of crisis.

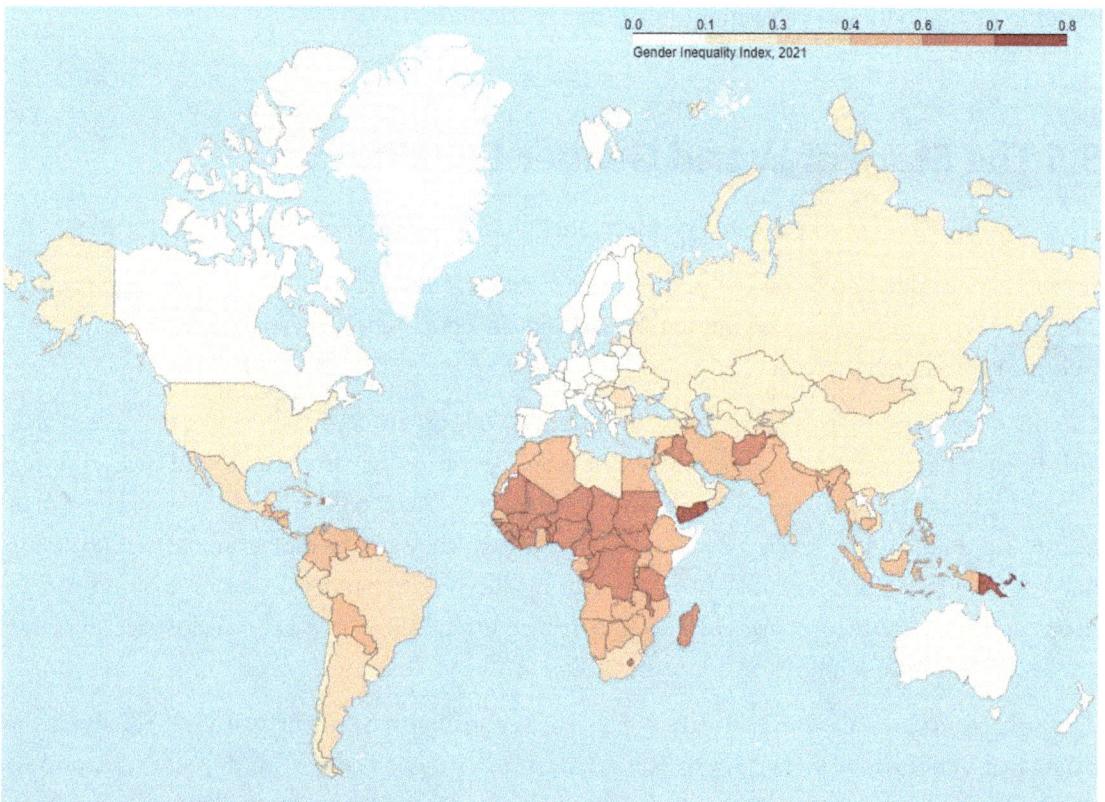

Figure 5.6. Gender inequality index. Source: United Nations

The GII for the world (Figure 5.7) has improved (decreased) over time, but progress is uneven across countries, especially in Africa and the Middle East. It tends to worsen in countries like Iraq or Yemen when political instability prevails.

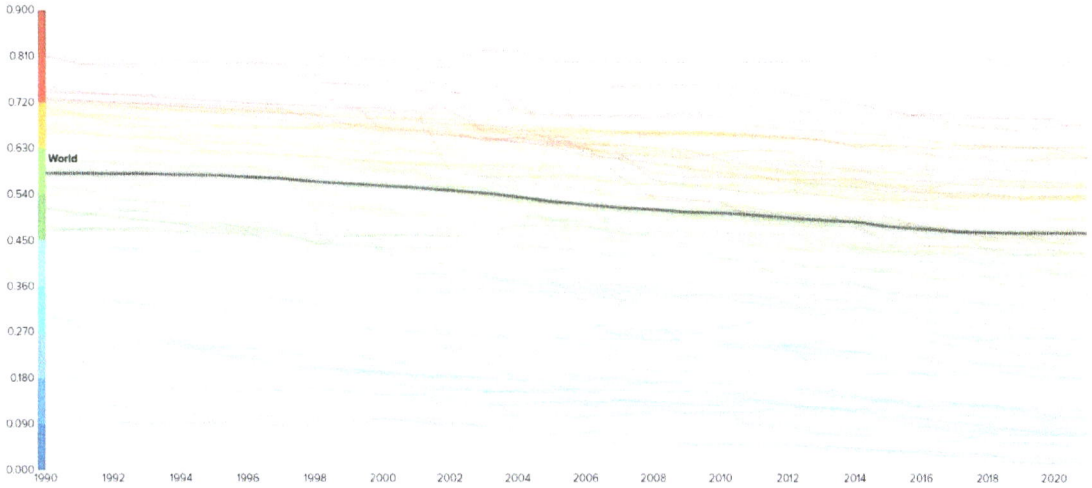

Figure 5.7. Global gender inequality index 1990-2021. Source: https://hdr.undp.org/data-center/thematic-composite-indices/gender-inequality-index#/indicies/GII

A helpful statistic is the female labor income share in each country. It tends to be low in the same region where the GII is high. A low labor share does not necessarily mean that women are not compensated equally but that women tend to have more junior positions or leave the workforce early once they have children, like in Japan or South Korea.

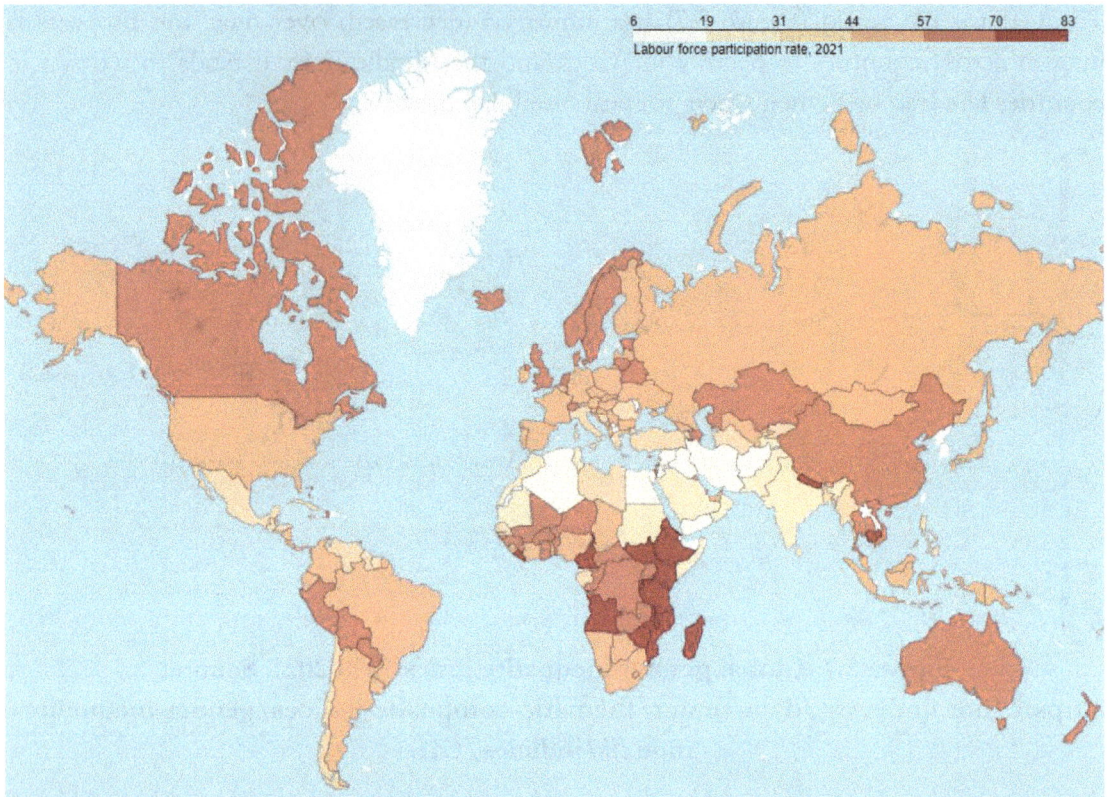

Figure 5.8. Female labor income shares across the world in 2021. Source: United Nations

5.6 The SDG Targets

Several targets have been defined to reach the goal of reducing gender inequality:

Target 5.1: End all forms of discrimination against all women and girls everywhere

Target 5.2: Eliminate all forms of violence against all women and girls in public and private spheres, including trafficking and sexual and other types of exploitation

Target 5.3: Eliminate all harmful practices, such as child, early and forced marriage, and female genital mutilation

Target 5.4: Recognize and value unpaid care and domestic work through the provision of public services, infrastructure, and social protection policies, and the promotion of shared responsibility within the household and the family as nationally appropriate

Target 5.5: Ensure women's full and effective participation and equal opportunities for leadership at all levels of decision-making in political, economic, and public life

Target 5.6: Ensure universal access to sexual and reproductive health and reproductive rights as agreed in accordance with the Programme of Action of the International Conference on Population and Development and the Beijing Platform for Action and the outcome documents of their review conferences

Target 5.a: Undertake reforms to give women equal rights to economic resources, as well as access to ownership and control over land and other forms of property, financial services, inheritance, and natural resources, in accordance with national laws

Target 5.b: Enhance the use of enabling technology, in particular information and communications technology, to promote the empowerment of women

Target 5.c: Adopt and strengthen sound policies and enforceable legislation for the promotion of gender equality and the empowerment of all women and girls at all levels

5.7 How to Improve Gender Equality

Changing cultural and social attitudes is an essential step to improving gender equality. Still, it is difficult to implement if political, religious, cultural, and business leaders are not committed to this goal. To see women's opportunities in other countries or to see women in leadership positions can inspire people in less progressive countries to aim for gender equality.

Investing in health (Chapter 3) and education (Chapter 4) for women is critical to addressing gender inequality. Reducing the maternal mortality rate and discouraging child marriage can help young women be healthy and able to develop and acquire skills. Education is also vital as it will open economic opportunities for women and allow them to be more autonomous. If a woman is not literate, obtaining official documents and having civic, legal, and property rights will be more difficult.

Access to the labor market to earn a living and financial autonomy is also essential for improved gender equality. When the responsibility for raising the children is not shared equally, women have more difficulties finding or keeping a financially rewarding job. The provision of childcare and pediatric healthcare could facilitate such an adjustment.

5.8 What Can AI Do to Improve Gender Equality

Prediction

AI can help measure and predict gender inequality and gender unequal treatment such as schooling, domestic work, and the pay gap. AI can predict the return to investment in girls and women and the economic and social loss of not doing it.

AI can analyze and predict the impact of hiring and interview practices, public policies, institutions, laws, and regulations on gender equality. For instance, by law, some jobs might not be open to women, or physical requirements have been calibrated for men. Some employment practices might be discriminatory against women, for instance, by forcing very long work hours incompatible with having a family and young children or not having access to childcare.

Coordination

AI could identify the drivers of gender inequality and the gender pay gap and assess and coordinate them to benefit women. For instance, better health and education, reproductive rights, a higher legal age for marriage, and more accessible and affordable childcare could help more women's participation in labor markets.

Optimization

AI could help design more inclusive hiring practices that could increase the hiring of women. The same can be done for more women's career promotion and work practices. Facilitating more work-at-home arrangements with the help of AI could encourage more women to join the workforce.

AI can optimize the resources (health, education, laws and regulation, reproductive rights, and childcare infrastructure) to reduce gender inequality and guide investment decisions in the drivers of gender inequality.

Control

AI can monitor gender inequality in a country, a region, or a company and suggest changes or improvements in public policy or business policy that could reduce gender inequality with an assessment of the economic cost and benefit. For instance, companies that do not sufficiently consider hiring women compared to their peers could be asked to dedicate more resources to reducing gender inequality.

5.9 The State of World Inequalities

Goal 10 is to "reduce inequality within and among countries" ("Goal 10 | Department of Economic and Social Affairs").

The report ("The World Inequality Report 2022 presents the most up-to-date & complete data on inequality worldwide," n.d.) presents the income distributions within and among countries. Figure 5.9 shows the Top 10%/Bottom 50% income gap across the world in 2021 by country. The higher the ratio, the more unequal a country is. The Middle East, Africa, South Asia, and South and Central Americas have the worst income inequalities. Europe and Australia have more income equality.

Perfect equality is probably not realistic and even desirable. The most productive people should probably work and be rewarded more like the most talented sports athletes should be able to compete at the highest level. It would not make sense to randomly select people in the world population to form an elite NBA team. Even for a regular job position, a candidate is assessed, and the hiring company selects the best one. The reason is that in the marketplace, the consumer will choose the best product and not any product randomly and will not value all the products equally.

Even outside of an economic environment, like in the world of art or ideas, not everyone is treated equally. A public intellectual might write a book that becomes a bestseller; another might sell very few copies. An artist might have his paintings exhibited at the Metropolitan Museum of Art or the Louvre Museum, but the vast majority do not. It would be strange to put random artworks selected from all the artists who have ever lived or who are alive.

Inequality is often seen in monetary terms, but in other settings, inequality could be intangible. It can be a title, a rank, a degree of prestige or freedom, or the number of followers on social media. A tenured professor has much more prestige, freedom, and security than an adjunct lecturer. Academics compete for this level of prestige, security, or freedom. Being free to pursue some academic interest while being paid is very valuable but is not given to everyone.

Even though inequality is not bad, per se, excess inequality is probably harmful if it concentrates too much power in a few hands, captures the institutions (Chapter 13), and has an excessive political influence on the government that could harm the majority of the people. It is problematic in a democracy, where the principle of one person having one vote becomes one dollar, one vote, because of the importance of political donations to run for office.

Figure 3 *Top 10/Bottom 50 income gaps across the world, 2021*

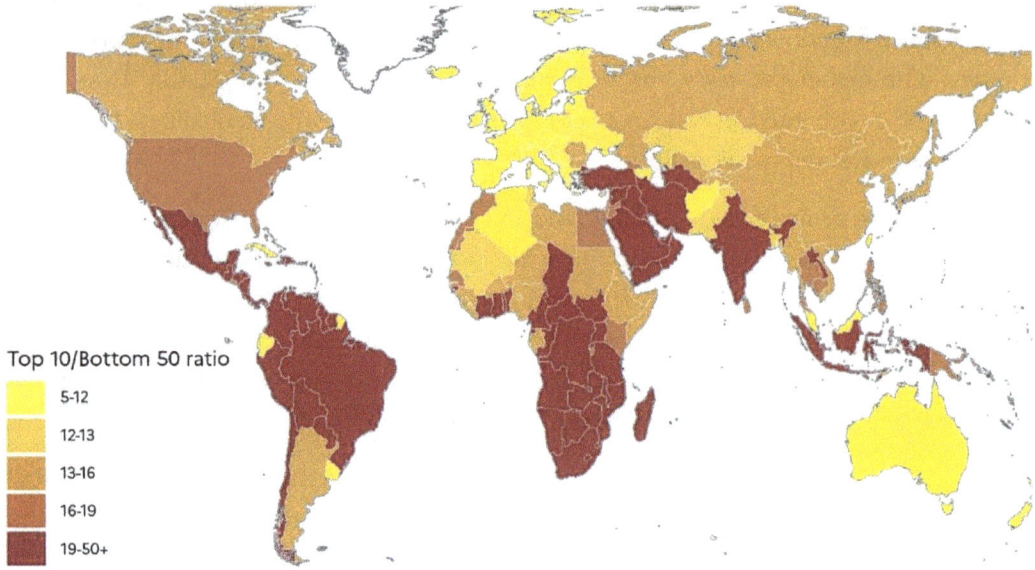

Interpretation: *In Brazil, the bottom 50% earns 29 times less than the top 10%. The value is 7 in France. Income is measured after pension and unemployment payments and benefits received by individuals but before other taxes they pay and transfers they receive.* **Source and series:** *wir2022.wid.world/methodology.*

Figure 5.9. Top 10/Bottom 50 income gap across the world, 2021

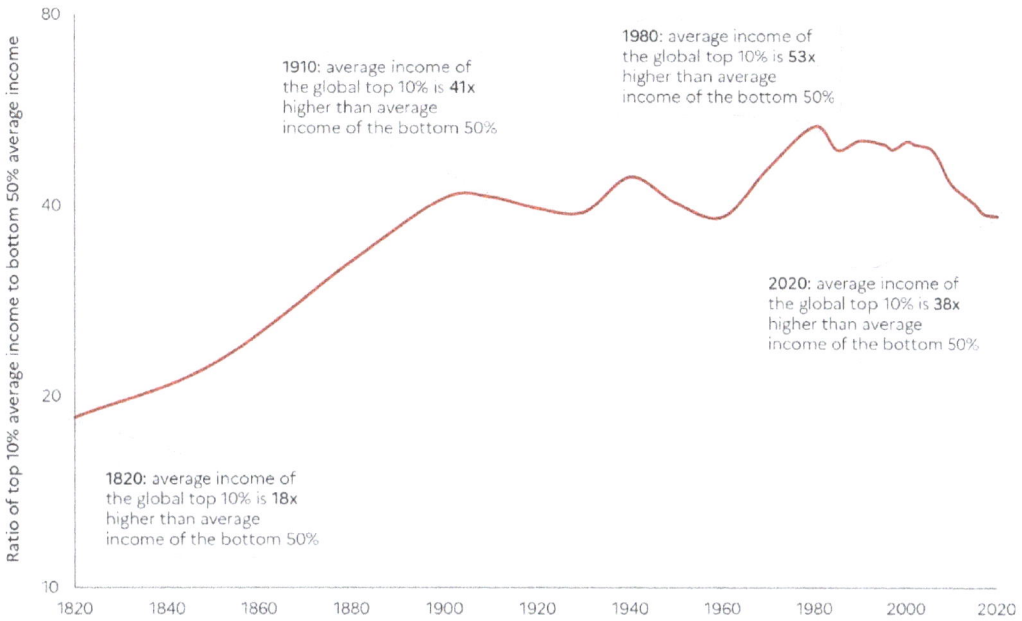

Figure 5 *Global income inequality: T10/B50 ratio, 1820-2020*

1910: average income of the global top 10% is 41x higher than average income of the bottom 50%

1980: average income of the global top 10% is 53x higher than average income of the bottom 50%

2020: average income of the global top 10% is 38x higher than average income of the bottom 50%

1820: average income of the global top 10% is 18x higher than average income of the bottom 50%

*Interpretation: Global inequality, as measured by the ratio T10/B50 between the average income of the top 10% and the average income of the bottom 50%, more than doubled between 1820 and 1910, from less than 20 to about 40, and stabilized around 40 between 1910 and 2020. It is too early to say whether the decline in global inequality observed since 2008 will continue. Income is measured per capita after pension and unemployment insurance transfers and before income and wealth taxes. **Sources and series:** wir2022.wid. world/methodology and Chancel and Piketty (2021).*

Figure 5.10. Top 10/Bottom 50 income gap across the world, 1820-2020

The historical trend has been a decrease in world inequality but an increase in certain countries, as documented by World Inequality Report ("The World #InequalityReport 2022 presents the most up-to-date & complete data on inequality worldwide," n.d.). This is probably not a simple coincidence. The reduction of world inequality is explained mainly by the rise of China and, to some extent, India. The emergence of a middle-class in China has benefited from China becoming an export champion and the de facto factory of the world.

Trade theory predicts that labor in a capital-abundant country like the United States gets hurt when the country trades with a labor-abundant country like China, even though both countries benefit globally (the economic pie is bigger). On the contrary, it does not predict that the pie is shared equally between capital and labor. Therefore a redistribution is required to spread the economic gain more equally. A more egalitarian society with more progressive taxation is doing some useful redistribution.

Technology is also a great factor in inequality. Using more technology is like trading with a foreign country where labor is highly productive (can work 24 hours a day, does not need to get paid, never goes on strike). The effect of labor on countries using a lot of technology is negative, at least in the short run, and increases inequality. In the long run, one hopes that labor will relocate to jobs that compete with technology but complement technology.

There is an increase in inequality within countries. There are more refugees and migrants to escape poverty. Remittance costs are high.

5.10 The SDG Targets

The Sustainable Development Goal is supported by the following Targets:

Target 10.1: By 2030, progressively achieve and sustain income growth of the bottom 40 percent of the population at a rate higher than the national average

Target 10.2: By 2030, empower and promote the social, economic, and political inclusion of all, irrespective of age, sex, disability, race, ethnicity, origin, religion or economic or other status

Target 10.3: Ensure equal opportunity and reduce inequalities of outcome, including by eliminating discriminatory laws, policies, and practices and promoting appropriate legislation, policies, and action in this regard

Target 10.4: Adopt policies, especially fiscal, wage, and social protection policies, and progressively achieve greater equality

Target 10.5: Improve the regulation and monitoring of global financial markets and institutions and strengthen the implementation of such regulations

Target 10.6: Ensure enhanced representation and voice for developing countries in decision-making in global international economic and financial institutions in order to deliver more effective, credible, accountable, and legitimate institutions

Target 10.7: Facilitate orderly, safe, regular, and responsible migration and mobility of people, including through the implementation of planned and well-managed migration policies

Target 10.a: Implement the principle of special and differential treatment for developing countries, in particular, least developed countries, in accordance with World Trade Organization agreements

Target 10.b: Encourage official development assistance and financial flows, including foreign direct investment, to States where the need is greatest, in particular, least developed countries, African countries, small island developing States, and landlocked developing countries, in accordance with their national plans and programmes

Target 10.c: By 2030, reduce to less than 3 percent the transaction costs of migrant remittances and eliminate remittance corridors with costs higher than 5 percent

5.11 How to Reduce Inequalities

Reducing inequalities can be achieved by lifting the poorer groups in a population. These groups often include women and children. Anything that helps reduce gender inequality, such as improving their education and giving them better access to the job market, will reduce inequalities.

Offering more equal opportunities for all people, especially when they are children, is also essential. Evidence in the United States shows that growing up in a better neighborhood makes a difference in children's outcomes (Bergman et al., 2019). Economists Ann Case and Angus Deaton (Case and Deaton, 2021) document a big difference in health and socioeconomic outcomes for college and non-college graduates. Better allocation of resources, such as in public health and education across neighborhoods, geographical areas, and socio-economic classes, would offer better economic opportunities for all. It is also crucial that the quality of these public services need to meet some minimum standards to benefit the less advantaged groups.

For many reasons, equal opportunities will not lead to equal outcomes. Some individuals or groups might have a very positive outcome, and some others a very negative outcome as success and failure can depend on not only skills and efforts but also luck or bad luck. Financial transfer and partial redistribution might be warranted as social insurance to compensate or help groups with bad outcomes. For instance, workers who are displaced by trade or technology and who can move to better jobs because of housing costs could benefit from public help.

How wealth was created matters too. As suggested by Professor Aghion (Aghion et al., 2021), wealth made thanks to innovation is probably less problematic than wealth derived from monopolistic and natural resource rents. The latter might be taxed more heavily or be controlled by the State but not captured by a narrow group of people. If individuals exercise influence through monopolistic companies, better economic regulations such as anti-trust regulations would be necessary.

Economists (Hoffmann et al., 2020) have examined inequality across different countries. They show that inequality is often a policy choice. Inequality in France, as measured by the Gini coefficient, is less than in the United States, for instance. Choices such as the provision of universal healthcare and free secondary and public education can alleviate inequality in a country.

Institutions can be influenced by individuals with great wealth to protect or benefit them at the expense of the general population. Laws can be written to favor them or their companies and deter new entrants in their industries, taxes might not be paid, and political and philanthropic donations might provide them with excess control on public decisions. Therefore better political accountability and transparency of political decision-makers could reduce inequality by benefiting the larger population instead of a narrow group of influential people.

5.12 What Can AI Do to Reduce Inequalities

We discussed how AI could help deliver health and education and alleviate poverty. We focus here on tools more specific to inequality.

Prediction

AI can help predict inequality. It is already possible to follow wealth and income inequality in the United States with high-frequency tools such as ("Realtime Inequality," n.d.). This would be useful to simulate the impact of different public policies on inequality.

In particular, AI can help predict tax revenues and analyze any shortfalls due to underreporting or shifting taxes to more tax-friendly states or countries. AI can help detect tax fraud and improve tax yield.

Coordination

AI could identify the drivers of inequality and assess and coordinate them to benefit everyone. Available education, health facilities, and basic public services can be compared across different wealth and income groups.

In case of economic shock, AI could help identify the zones requiring relief efforts and coordinate the needs of these affected areas.

Optimization

AI could help design a more efficient tax system that could maximize tax revenues while minimizing economic distortions and tax evasion.

AI can optimize the resources (financials, people including educators, health professionals, public safety officers, and infrastructure) allocated to reduce inequality and guide investment decisions in the drivers of inequality.

Control

AI can suggest and compare decisions that should be taken to the decisions taken by politicians or government agencies and quantify the loss of inequality globally and by income and wealth groups or other subgroups. Decisions could include an increase or decrease in taxation, cash transfers and subsidies, vouchers, or changing laws and regulations that hinder income mobility.

AI can monitor inequality and suggest changes or improvements in policy that would favor a reduction in inequality with an assessment of the economic cost and benefit. For instance, schools that do not sufficiently improve the prospects of poor students could be asked to revise their strategy.

5.13 Case Studies

Work

In Peng et al. (2022), the authors examine to what extent AI can affect human decisions in evaluating candidates. They run some experiments to study hybrid decision systems where humans get recommendations from AI and see how it affects their decisions, in particular accuracy and bias. They compare the results for human-only, model-only, and hybrid systems.

The task is to consider the professional bio of a candidate (anonymous and no gender indication) and assign it an occupation (e.g., lawyers, paralegals, teachers). They have a dataset of 397,907 bios with 28 occupations.

They present eight bios and one occupation and ask online workers to identify four bios that belong correctly to that occupation. They do the same with the AI systems that run a deep neural network (DNN) or a simpler bag of words model (BOW). They also use a random model. For the hybrid model, they give the AI predictions to the online workers before they make their own decisions. They then calculate their performance with the true positive rate (TPR), the proportion of bios correctly assigned to the correct occupation, and the difference in TPRs between women and men.

	Human	Random	H+R	DNN	H+DNN	BOW	H+BOW
attorney							
paralegal	+			+		+	+
physician				+			
surgeon			−	−		−	−
professor							
teacher	+						

Figure 5.11. Bias (ΔTPR = TPR women - TPR men) across conditions for tested occupations

They find (Figure 5.11) that the hybrid system Human + DNN presents no significant biases relative to Human only or DNN only and to the BOW system. It is unclear, however, that these results would generalize, but there do not seem to be simple extrapolation rules on the bias.

Gender Inequality

Feldman and Peake (2021) discuss bias in machine learning and propose an end-to-end bias mitigation framework. They define four bias metrics for group fairness (different groups receive the same model class predictions): Statistical Parity Difference, Equal Opportunity Difference, Average Odds Difference, and Disparate Impact.

Statistical Parity Difference is the difference in class prediction between two groups. Equal Opportunity Difference is the difference in class prediction between two groups when the groups belong to the correct class. Average Odds Difference is the average difference between the false positive rate between two groups and the false positive rate between the groups. The last metric, the Disparate Impact, is similar to Statistical Parity Difference but uses a ratio instead of the difference in class prediction between two groups.

They discuss three types of bias mitigation algorithms: pre-processing by changing the data distribution, in-processing with constrained model training, and post-processing with constrained model prediction. The in-processing step involves an adversarial network that tries to uncover the variable of interest (e.g., gender).

They use the Adult dataset from the UCI Machine Learning Repository to study these algorithms and a deep learning model. The task is to classify the income level based on individual characteristics. They found in their experiments that Statistical Parity Difference was the lowest with post-processing only. Still, the end-to-end mitigation with the three processing steps works best for Equal Opportunity Difference and Average Odds Difference.

Inequalities

Korinek and Stiglitz (2017) examine the effect of technological change and AI on inequalities. They discuss the relationship between technological change and welfare and its impact on human workers, especially when the technology is designed to replace labor.

If markets are perfect and agents do not know their role in the economy, they will want to be fully insured against technological change, and technology benefits all. If agents know their roles (workers, capitalists, or innovators), but redistribution is costless, technology can still benefit all. If redistribution is costly, some individuals might lose out on technological change.

If markets are imperfect, for instance, there is imperfect information, or some industries are concentrated, there is no guarantee that technology can benefit all, even after redistribution. For example, suppose innovators earn extra rents on their innovations (thanks to monopoly or enforcement of intellectual property rights). In that case, they might make workers worse by lowering their wages and enriching the entrepreneurs or changing the labor demand and other factors.

They discuss technological unemployment caused by wages that do not adjust and make labor too expensive or by workers who cannot find jobs fast enough as technology replaces work. They also look at the impact of superhuman artificial intelligence and the potential of increasing inequalities. Superhuman AI might control more scarce resources and push human labor below the subsistence level.

Chapter 6 | Cities and Communities

> "whether in London's ornate arcades or Rio's fractious favelas, whether in the high-rises of Hong Kong or the dusty workspaces of Dharavi, our culture, our prosperity, and our freedom are all ultimately gifts of people living, working, and thinking together— the ultimate triumph of the city."
>
> Edward L. Glaeser

6.1 The State of World Cities and Communities

Goal 11 is to "make cities and human settlements inclusive, safe, resilient and sustainable" ("Goal 11 | Department of Economic and Social Affairs,").

Cities and Communities Trend

A rising urban population

The world population is increasingly living in cities. According to the UN (World urbanization prospects, 2019), 55 percent of the world's population lived in urban areas in 2018, from 30 percent in 1950. The urban population is expected to reach 68 percent by 2050, with the most significant increase in Asia and Africa (Figure 6.1).

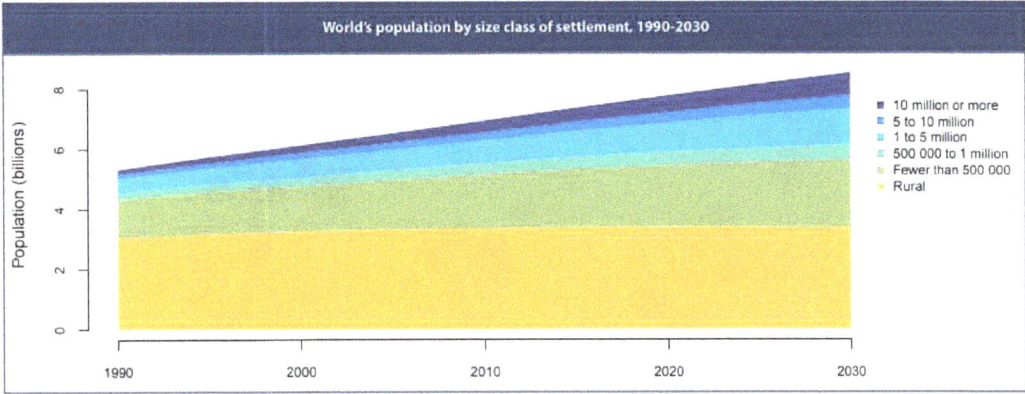

Figure 6.1. World's population by size of the settlement, 1990-2030. Source: United Nations, The World's Cities in 2018

By 2030, the most prominent cities will come primarily from low and middle-income countries (Figure 6.2). The largest city will be Delhi in India, overcoming Tokyo, Japan, reflecting the different demographic trends.

The world's ten largest cities in 2018 and 2030			
City size rank	City	Population in 2018 (thousands)	City	Population in 2030 (thousands)
1	Tokyo, Japan	37 468	Delhi, India	38 939
2	Delhi, India	28 514	Tokyo, Japan	36 574
3	Shanghai, China	25 582	Shanghai, China	32 869
4	São Paulo, Brazil	21 650	Dhaka, Bangladesh	28 076
5	Ciudad de México (Mexico City), Mexico	21 581	Al-Qahirah (Cairo), Egypt	25 517
6	Al-Qahirah (Cairo), Egypt	20 076	Mumbai (Bombay), India	24 572
7	Mumbai (Bombay), India	19 980	Beijing, China	24 282
8	Beijing, China	19 618	Ciudad de México (Mexico City), Mexico	24 111
9	Dhaka, Bangladesh	19 578	São Paulo, Brazil	23 824
10	Kinki M.M.A. (Osaka), Japan	19 281	Kinshasa, Democratic Republic of the Congo	21 914

Figure 6.2. The world's ten largest cities in 2018 and 2030. Source: United Nations, The World's Cities in 2018

The mega-cities will be mainly in the south among the developing countries, thanks to favorable demographics and rural-urban migration (Figure 6.3).

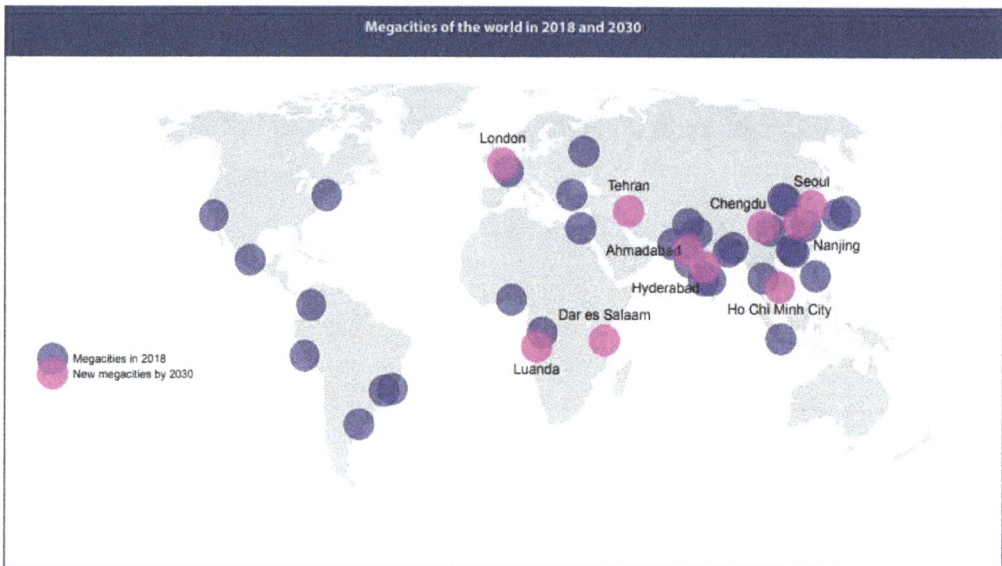

Figure 6.3. Megacities of the world in 2018 and 2030. Source: United Nations, The World's Cities in 2018

As a country develops, the life expectancy of the urban population increases, and higher wages in manufacturing and services in urban areas attract migrants from rural areas. According to ("BiodiverCities by 2030: Fostering nature-positive urban development | IUCN Urban Alliance," n.d.), $70 trillion of economic activity, or 80% of the 2019 World GDP, was generated in cities. Their share of GDP is expected to increase with the rising urban population.

As more people live in cities, they require housing, infrastructure (clean water, sanitation, waste management, energy, roads, public lighting, transportation), goods, and essential services (food markets and retail stores, education and leisure, and healthcare). In lower-income and middle-income countries, some large cities are overwhelmed and cannot adequately accommodate the increased population forcing the poorest to live in slums. In higher-income countries, cities do not grow as fast and even see their population stagnate or shrink.

Urban areas can bring many benefits, such as higher wages, education, job and business opportunities, and leisure activities, but also costs such as higher cost of living, lack of housing, traffic congestion, crime, and pollution.

Environmental impact

As the rising world population is increasingly living in cities, urban areas need to expand and become significant consumers of energy and producer of pollution (cities are the source of 75% of greenhouse gas emissions ("BiodiverCities by 2030: Fostering nature-positive urban development | IUCN Urban Alliance," n.d.)), due to housing and office development, construction, transportation, private consumption, and business activities. Beyond the direct footprint of cities, there is a large impact on the environment due to the disposal of waste and untreated wastewater, air pollution, and the reduction in green spaces, forests, and biodiversity (cities contribute to 11-16% of global biodiversity loss ("BiodiverCities by 2030: Fostering nature-positive urban development | IUCN Urban Alliance," n.d.)), and natural habitats.

Investments in climate change

According to the Climate Policy Initiative ("The State of Cities Climate Finance," n.d.), cities also need to prevent the damage of climate change: storm and wind, extreme precipitation, flood and sea level rise, chemical change, water scarcity, mass movement, extreme temperatures, and wildfire. They need to invest in urban mitigation of climate change, dual uses, and urban adaptation.

For mitigation, they invest in sustainable transport (metro, trams, electric vehicles and buses, bicycles), building infrastructure and energy efficiency, renewable energy generation, general urban development and management, and waste and wastewater management.

To adapt to climate change, they invest in water and wastewater management, disaster risk management, urban development management, infrastructure, energy, and other built environment, sustainable transportation, agriculture, forestry, natural resource management, coastal protection, building infrastructure, and energy efficiency. The level of financing is still very far from what is required to address the impact of climate change fully.

6.2 The SDG Targets

The Sustainable Development Goal is supported by the following Targets:

Target 11.1: By 2030, ensure access for all to adequate, safe, and affordable housing and basic services and upgrade slums

Target 11.2: By 2030, provide access to safe, affordable, accessible, and sustainable transport systems for all, improving road safety, notably by expanding public transport, with special attention to the needs of those in vulnerable situations, women, children, persons with disabilities and older persons

Target 11.3: By 2030, enhance inclusive and sustainable urbanization and capacity for participatory, integrated, and sustainable human settlement planning and management in all countries

Target 11.4: Strengthen efforts to protect and safeguard the world's cultural and natural heritage

Target 11.5: By 2030, significantly reduce the number of deaths and the number of people affected and substantially decrease the direct economic losses relative to the global gross domestic product caused by disasters, including water-related disasters, with a focus on protecting the poor and people in vulnerable situations

Target 11.6: By 2030, reduce the adverse per capita environmental impact of cities, including by paying special attention to air quality and municipal and other waste management

Target 11.7: By 2030, provide universal access to safe, inclusive, and accessible green and public spaces, in particular for women and children, older persons, and persons with disabilities

Target 11.a: Support positive economic, social and environmental links between urban, per-urban, and rural areas by strengthening national and regional development planning

Target 11.b: By 2020, substantially increase the number of cities and human settlements adopting and implementing integrated policies and plans towards inclusion, resource efficiency, mitigation and adaptation to climate change, resilience to disasters, and develop and implement, in line with the Sendai Framework for Disaster Risk Reduction 2015-2030, holistic disaster risk management at all levels

Target 11.c: Support least developed countries, including through financial and technical assistance, in building sustainable and resilient buildings utilizing local materials

6.3 How to Improve Cities and Communities

Equitable and Sustainable Cities

Mahendra et al. (2022) suggest seven sectoral transformations (energy, housing, water, sanitation, land management, transport, and the informal economy) beneficial to cities:

- Design and deliver basic infrastructure services such as water, sanitation, transport, and energy to the vulnerable populations that have good coverage, are of quality, and are affordable

- Partner with alternative service providers such as community-based organizations to increase access to municipal services

- Collect and use data to gain local insights

- Recognize and support informal workers: give them legal rights, economic and social rights, access to core infrastructure services, social protection, and representation

- Finance and subsidize to fill gaps in core services

- Develop urban planning to improve infrastructure services and land use

- Transform governance and institutions to build diverse coalitions and alignment

Only building affordable housing might not satisfy the local communities if they are far from job opportunities and essential services such as schools and transportation.

Nature-based solutions

Cities and communities need to adopt more nature-based solutions. They include having more green space, tree coverage, parks, rivers, and water ponds to improve air quality, water quality, biodiversity, and human health and reduce motorized traffic and urban heat. Cities can also become more resilient to natural disasters such as flooding and climate change (Global Platform for Sustainable Cities, 2021)

6.4 What Can AI Do to Improve Cities and Communities

Prediction

AI can help predict demand for municipal services such as sanitation, drinkable water, energy, public transportation, public schools, and housing with a growing urban population and migration. AI can help predict tax revenues and potential revenue shortfalls based on economic activity, tax rates, tax collection, and compliance.

AI can predict environmental variables such as air pollution, greenhouse gas emissions, water quality, the volume of waste disposals, and their effects on population well-being using sensors, surveys, social media, citizen reporting, and information on population, households, transportation, energy and water consumption, business and economic activities.

Coordination

AI can help to plan cities and communities and the services they provide to their residents. AI can identify drivers influencing specific outcomes and benefits and coordinate the different city departments that need to be involved. For instance, poor student performance could be due to the school, housing, family circumstances, long transportation time, malnutrition, or poor health that would need coordination from education, housing, social services, health, and transportation departments. New urban development will also need coordination from several departments and services that AI can help set up.

AI can also assist in coordinating a shared economy by identifying where resources are available such as a private car, some extra food, or some tools, and matching them with potential users or consumers.

Optimization

AI can optimally allocate resources to reach goals defined by the city or community. AI could calculate the cost and benefits of each option and choose the most effective course of action. To limit crime, AI could optimize teams of police officers and mental health professionals to work together to be dispatched to maximize their impact. AI could help optimize shelter, social services, and healthcare resources to care for vulnerable populations.

Control

AI can control urban traffic and automatically enforce common infractions such as speeding or illegal parking. AI can also manage property and business tax collections, customer services, and customer assistance. AI can control autonomous public vehicles such as trains and buses and can control the availability of shared modes of transportation. AI can maintain and irrigate trees, plants, and flowers in public spaces. AI can also maintain roads, public spaces, and buildings.

6.5 Case Studies

Transportation in Cities

Iyer (2021) presents a survey on intelligent transport systems in smart cities. These systems are divided into traffic management, public transportation, safety management, and manufacturing and logistics.

In traffic management, the main goal is to avoid congestion. AI can predict congestion and suggest alternative routes to vehicles. AI can guide traffic lights to manage traffic flows in real-time by predicting traffic using cameras or vehicle sensors. AI can help optimize traffic patterns and design better routes. For cities adopting congestion pricing, AI can help adjust prices in real-time to reflect the congestion cost and move traffic to off-peak periods.

In public transportation (trains, metros, tramways, buses), AI can predict traffic, and public transportation usage, inform users and passengers, and help optimize routes, schedules, and driving patterns. AI can allow optimal refueling or charging and predictive maintenance by sending alerts to drivers, technicians, and fleet managers.

In safety management, AI can assist drivers in limiting fatigue, provide some autopilot or remote control capabilities, and be used as an early warning system to prevent collisions, vehicle or driver failures, or passenger endangerment.

In manufacturing and logistics, AI can leverage data generated by sensors in vehicles or vehicle parts or by suppliers to predict and optimize production and delivery. AI can be used for inspection and quality control, and quality monitoring. AI can uniform users for optimal vehicle servicing and maintenance schedules.

Decision-Making

Wagner and de Vries (2019) document that AI can be used for urban development and land management decision-making. AI simulates urban growth, classifies land use and urban areas, and performs specific prediction tasks such as traffic or crime forecasting.

In a simulation, AI can be combined with cell or grid-based modeling to simulate urban growth, land use, and emergency management such as flooding and extreme weather events. Transition rules for cell use can be estimated with historical data and used to generate simulated urban development scenarios. Multi-agent systems can be combined with cell models for more complex interactions and simulations.

AI can be used for the classification of land use using satellite data as well as for monitoring urban development changes. Urban heat can also be monitored using satellite sensors, and in wartime, urban destruction and migration can also be documented.

AI can predict traffic from cameras and sensors on roads or vehicles. AI can also be used for crime prediction and monitoring using CCTV or information collected by the public or police forces.

Internet of Things (IoT) and Artificial Intelligence (AI) for Smart Cities

China has been at the cutting edge of building smart cities. (Wang et al., 2021) looks at implementing AI for smart cities in China and cites ten challenges:

1. Lack of infrastructure: this is the topic of Chapter 11

2. Insufficient funds or capital: this is the topic of Chapter 14

3. Cybersecurity and data risks

4. Smart waste and hygiene management: this is the topic of Chapter 12

5. Lack of professionals

6. Managing energy demands: this is the topic of Chapter 8

7. Managing transportation: this is explored in (Iyer 2021)

8. Environmental risks: this is the topic of Chapters 7, 9 and 10

9. Managing public health and education: this is the subject of Chapters 3 and 4

10. Lack of trust in AI and IoT

Cybersecurity and data risks are concerns in smart cities as they require a lot of data to function. Hackers can target data centers and city infrastructures for ransomware or sabotage. Hospitals and power utilities are especially vulnerable to these attacks as their patients and users can be exposed to severe risks.

The lack of professionals trained in cybersecurity, IoT, and AI is also a constraint for cities, especially in poorer countries. Cities need to partner with technology companies to develop smart city projects but will have to build in-house expertise to remain in control.

Lack of trust in AI and IoT is also a hindrance to developing smart cities. Trustworthy AI needs to respect privacy and the law, be unbiased, be safe, and respect fundamental human rights and values as it is proposed, for instance, by the (European Commission, 2021).

There are clear concerns about surveillance, face recognition devices, DNA collection, and phone tracking, as documented by Qian et al. (2022). Problems are not only in China but also in other countries. In 2020, Toronto abandoned a smart city project led by Sidewalk Labs, part of Google, due to concerns about privacy (Stouhi, 2022).

PART II CLIMATE AND ENERGY

Chapter 7 | Climate Change

> "What is the use of a house if you haven't got a tolerable planet to put it on?"
>
> Henry David Thoreau

7.1 The State of World Climate

The related SDG, Goal 13, is to "take urgent action to combat climate change and its impacts." ("Goal 13 | Department of Economic and Social Affairs"). The general strategy has been to focus on mitigation, i.e., reducing greenhouse gas emissions, adaptation, i.e., making the world more resilient to climate change, and on finance, to help countries to invest and pay for all of it.

World Climate Trend

A Warming Climate

Climate change is the most significant existential risk that threatens humanity. Since the industrial revolution, the global average temperature has risen because of greenhouse gas emissions such as CO2 and methane. The scientific consensus is now that global warming is due to human activities.

The influential UK-based Nicholas Stern report (Stern, 2006) concluded that "climate change could have very serious impacts on growth and development" and "climate change demands an international response, based on a shared understanding of long-term goals and agreement on frameworks for action." It recommends to "take strong action [..] to avoid the worst impacts of climate change."

Increased population and rising standard of living have historically increased energy consumption and generated more greenhouse gas emissions per capita in countries such as China, the US, India, Russia, Japan, and in Europe and Asia.

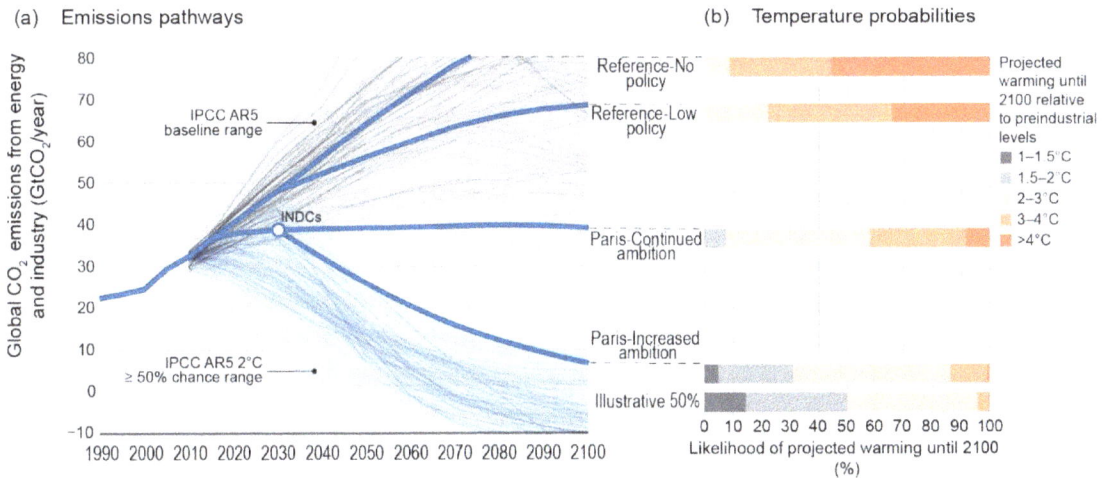

Figure 7.1. Projected global CO2 emissions from energy and industry. Source: This panel, "Emission Pathways," is an adapted figure provided by Jae Edmonds. The original figure is found in: A.A. Fawcett, G.C. Iyer, L.E. Clarke, J.A. Edmonds, N.E. Hultman, H.C. McJeon, J. Rogeli, R. Schuler, J. Alsalam, G.R. Asrar, J. Creason, M. Jeong, J. McFarland, A. Mundra, and W. Shi, 2015: Can Paris pledges avert severe climate change? Science, 350 6266,1168-1169. The figure version presented here was adapted from the original as follows: For panel #1, The faint lines representing the emissions trajectories were removed. For panel #2, The Illustrative 50% likelihood projection was removed from the bottom of the chart., Public domain, via Wikimedia Commons

Industrial manufacturing, energy production, agriculture, land use, farming and deforestation, and transportation all contribute to greenhouse gas emissions (Figure 7.2) and the general warming of the planet, with hazardous consequences for humankind and the environment.

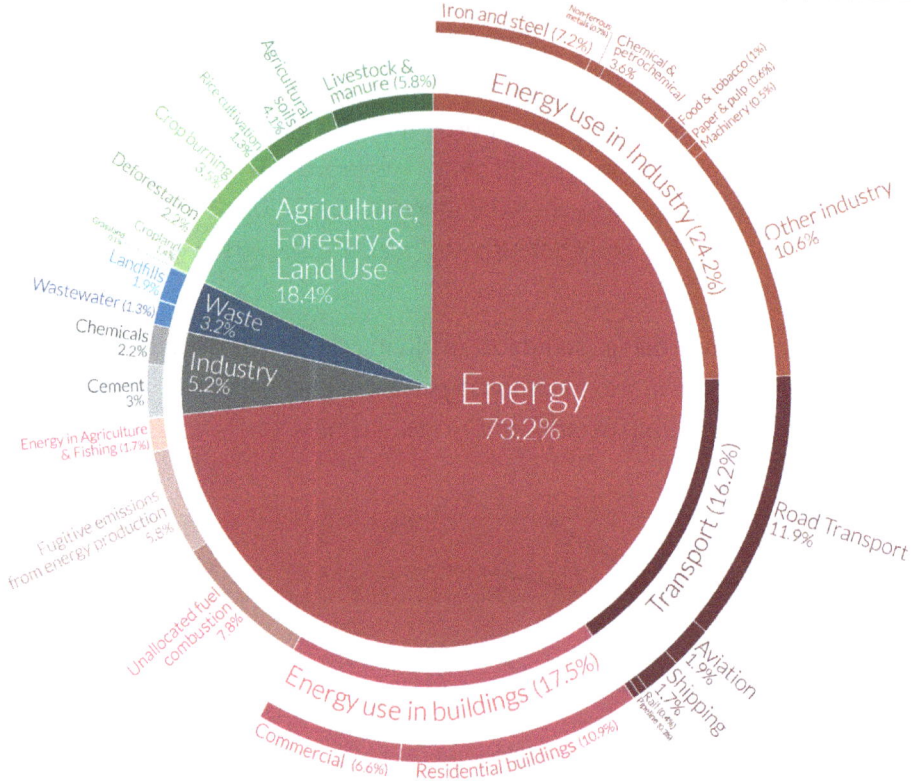

Global greenhouse gas emissions by sector
This is shown for the year 2016 – global greenhouse gas emissions were 49.4 billion tonnes CO_2eq.

Figure 7.2. GHG emissions mostly come from Energy use (73.2%), Agriculture, Forestry & Land (18.4%), and Industry (5.2%) Use in 2016

Serious consequences include extreme weather events, drought, rising sea levels, floods, disease, or food shortage. They have been well-documented in the work of many climate scientists and synthesized by the Intergovernmental Panel on Climate Change.

Paris Agreement

In 2015, 193 countries adopted the Paris Agreement ("The Paris Agreement | UNFCCC," n.d.), an international treaty on climate change that covers climate change mitigation, adaptation, and finance. To reduce the effects of climate change, they agree to limit the temperature increase to 1.5°C compared to the pre-industrial age and to be net-zero in terms of greenhouse gas emissions by 2050.

Countries need to come up with their climate action plans called National Determined Contributions (NDCs) that they need to revisit every five years with more ambitious plans and long-term low greenhouse gas emission development strategies, which are long-term NDCs. At the 2021 United Nations Climate Change Conference, the parties met in Glasgow to update their NDCs. As a result, they pledged to revisit the emission reduction plans in 2022, phase down coal, and provide climate finance for developing countries.

The NDCs still fall short of the efforts required to achieve the 1.5°C limit and net-zero emissions by 2050. Covid-19 has cut the level of greenhouse gas emissions but at a tremendous economic cost. Achieving the long-run emission targets is still a work in progress and might not even be possible.

The Intergovernmental Panel on Climate Change (IPCC)

The IPCC is an organization based in Geneva that informs governments about the science and impact of climate change. It was founded in 1988 and is endorsed by the United Nations. It includes governments and scientists of 195 countries.

The IPCC publishes several assessment reports every 5-7 years, written by leading scientists on a consensus basis with the approval of their governments. In each piece, the experts review evidence from statistics, data, models, or observations in the scientific literature. The evidence is then analyzed and assigned confidence levels and likelihood probabilities. It is a slow process but is fully backed by each government.

The most recent one, the sixth assessment report, is being published in 2021-2022 and gives some valuable insights on the impacts and project risks from climate change on ecosystems and human societies and infrastructures. It finds the following evidence:

Climate change through rising temperature, heatwaves, wildfires, droughts, extreme weather events, rising sea levels, and floods already has an observed impact on terrestrial, freshwater, and ocean ecosystems, on cities and infrastructure, health and wellbeing, water security and food production.

Climate change risks due to an increased global temperature, such as increased frequency and magnitude of extreme weather events, will affect low-lying coastal systems, terrestrial and ocean ecosystems, critical physical infrastructure, networks and services, living standards and equity, human health, food security, water security, and peace and migration (representative key risks).

Some observed adaptations in natural and human systems to climate change remain small, incremental, reactive, and insufficient to avoid climate change impacts. Barriers to adaptation include "limited resources, lack of private sector and citizens engagement, insufficient mobilization of finance (including for research), lack of political leadership, limited research and/or slow and low uptake of adaptation science, and low sense of urgency." Some adaptation options are no longer available when the temperature goes beyond 1.5°C.

Climate Resilient Development (CRD) which includes adaptation to reduce climate change risks, mitigation by reducing greenhouse gas emissions, enhanced biodiversity, and achieving the SDGs, is required to address climate change. CRD can work through the energy, industry, urban and infrastructure, land and ecosystems, and societal systems with the appropriate policies.

7.2 The SDG Targets

The Sustainable Development Goal is supported by the following Targets:

Target 13.1: Strengthen resilience and adaptive capacity to climate-related hazards and natural disasters in all countries

Target 13.2: Integrate climate change measures into national policies, strategies, and planning

Target 13.3: Improve education, awareness-raising, and human and institutional capacity on climate change mitigation, adaptation, impact reduction, and early warning

Target 13.a: Implement the commitment undertaken by developed-country parties to the United Nations Framework Convention on Climate Change to a goal of mobilizing jointly $100 billion annually by 2020 from all sources to address the needs of developing countries in the context of meaningful mitigation actions and transparency on implementation and fully operationalize the Green Climate Fund through its capitalization as soon as possible

Target 13.b: Promote mechanisms for raising capacity for effective climate change-related planning and management in the least developed countries and small island developing States, including focusing on women, youth, and local and marginalized communities * Acknowledging that the United Nations Framework Convention on Climate Change is the primary international, intergovernmental forum for negotiating the global response to climate change.

7. 3 How to Improve the Climate

Mitigation

Climate mitigation is the topic of the Working Group III of the IPCC Sixth Assessment Report ("Climate Change 2022," n.d.). The report lists several mitigation options grouped by categories: Energy, Agriculture, Forestry and Land Use, Buildings, Transport, Industry, and Others (Figure SPM.7 of the report). It does into details of each sector:

Energy

Energy is the largest sector contributing to greenhouse gas emissions and should be the priority focus to have a chance to mitigate the effect of climate change. In the next chapter (Chapter 8), we discuss the different options to address climate change in the energy sector. Wind and solar energy play a huge role in contributing to reducing greenhouse gas emissions. Phasing out of fossil fuels, especially coal, is critical, with no new construction of coal-fire plants and no new field exploration of sources of oil and gas.

Agriculture, Forestry and Land Use (AFLU)

Reduced conversion of forests and other ecosystems and carbon sequestration in agriculture have the most significant potential contribution to net emission reduction in 2030.

Reduced conversion of forests and other ecosystems (wetlands, peatlands, grasslands, savannas) means the end of deforestation, especially the tropical forests, and land restoration and reforestation. Carbon sequestration in agriculture is made possible thanks to soil management and agroforestry.

AFLU policies depend on a lot of factors, but the regulation of land use, sufficient economic incentives, efficient governance, technology, and data are significant.

Transport

In transportation, the most significant contributor is the transition to electric vehicles and more energy-efficient modes of transportation in urban areas, such as public transit, bicycles, shared mobility, and walking. Biofuels, synthetic fuels, and hydrogen could also be, at one point, sources of energy in aviation and shipping.

Industry

In the industrial sector, production could be made more sustainable and more energy-efficient thanks to electrification, renewable energy, biofuels, material substitution, hydrogen reduction processes, carbon capture use and storage, direct air carbon capture, research and development, and a more circular value chain.

Urban Systems

Cities can move to more electrification, material, and energy efficiency, public transportation, more energy-efficient buildings, better urban planning and design, less commute between homes and jobs, and more Nature-based solutions (green roofs, trees, parks, and ponds).

Carbon Pricing

Economists Blanchard and Tirole (2021) agree that carbon should be priced so agents account for the social cost of CO_2 emissions in their economic decisions. This can be done through a carbon tax or a trading mechanism of emission rights. A carbon tax could be levied at consumption (downstream) or production (upstream), and a border adjustment should be adopted so that production does not move outside the country imposing the tax. Some of the tax revenues could be earmarked to compensate losers of the transition, for instance, rural inhabitants with no alternatives but to use their cars to commute.

Adaptation

The IPCC report on adaptation (Pörtner et al., 2022) suggests several climate responses and adaptation options:

Climate defense

Many adaptation measures are described for food and agriculture (Chapter 2), health (Chapter 3), land and water ecosystems (Chapters 9 and 10), urban systems (Chapter 6), infrastructure (Chapter 7), and energy systems (Chapter 8).

Other risks

Disaster risk management, warning systems, and social safety nets should be adopted to make society more resilient to climate change and risk sharing.

7.4 What can AI do to improve the climate

Prediction

Based on satellite observations and remote sensors, AI can help predict and measure greenhouse gas emissions. AI can build more granular climate models to predict local changes in CO_2 concentration. AI can predict the impact of climate change on sea level, lang masses, coastal areas, ocean-atmospheric interactions, weather patterns, temperature, and humidity.

AI can help on the demand and supply sides of the energy markets. Section 8.4 of Chapter 8 provides information and energy.

In Agriculture, Forestry, and Land Use, AI can help predict the different land uses and changes from satellite imaging and predict the impact on CO_2 emissions and absorptions. AI can predict which area, crop, and farming methods will be more resilient to climate change. AI can help indicate food waste and the CO_2 content of food production.

In Transportation, AI can predict energy consumption and greenhouse gas emissions of different modes of transportation. In public transit, AI can be used to indicate the required capacity and the final demand.

In Industry, AI can predict greenhouse gas emissions from the inputs, materials, and energy used along the value chain for different industrial processes. AI can help in reporting climate change impacts on business operations.

For Urban systems, AI can predict energy consumption, greenhouse gas emissions, pollution level, and temperature increases for different urban planning scenarios and configurations, including transportation, buildings, housing, offices, and businesses.

Coordination

Across the different sectors (Energy, Agriculture, Forestry and Land Use, Transport, Industry, and Urban systems), AI can identify the other factors influencing greenhouse gas emissions and quantify their impacts. AI can then help coordinate policymakers' efforts to reduce greenhouse gas emissions. Measures can include phasing out some carbon or energy-intensive modes of production or reducing energy demand by investing in more energy efficiency.

Other efforts can be at the planning stage. For instance, putting offices close to housing and schools in urban planning will reduce commuting time and transportation use. Charging stations and reserve batteries must be placed optimally to serve electric vehicle users.

Optimization

Across the different sectors (Energy, Agriculture, Forestry and Land Use, Transport, Industry, and Urban systems), AI can optimize the outputs and services to minimize greenhouse gas emissions. Some of this optimization can be done through carbon taxes and carbon pricing. AI can help determine the appropriate level for all agents to internalize the cost of greenhouse gas emissions. AI can optimize devices such as machines, cars, batteries, and even living and working spaces to be more energy efficient.

Control

AI can help manage energy markets to guarantee sustainable energy supply by controlling energy suppliers and network access. AI can also control energy bidding systems to reliable source energy at the lowest cost. AI can also decide to take out or add more suppliers or consumers to reduce market imbalances.

In Agriculture, Forestry, and Land Use, AI can control autonomous machines to cultivate and harvest crops, raise, feed, and care for livestock, monitor forests and illegal logging, and change land use.

In Transportation and Urban Systems, AI can help control autonomous vehicles and transportation systems to reduce congestion, and energy consumption, minimize travel time and meet the demand of users. AI could dynamically change prices to shift loads or encourage more sharing in case of high congestion on roads. AI can control the functioning of buildings, in particular their air conditioning and heating systems.

In Industry, AI can control the production and distribution process and even the whole value chain to minimize the climate impact and reduce waste. AI can control an entire value chain to make it operate circularly and encourage recycling and reuse.

Rolnick et al. (2019) provide other examples of AI and climate change.

7.5 Case Studies

Measuring Carbon Flux

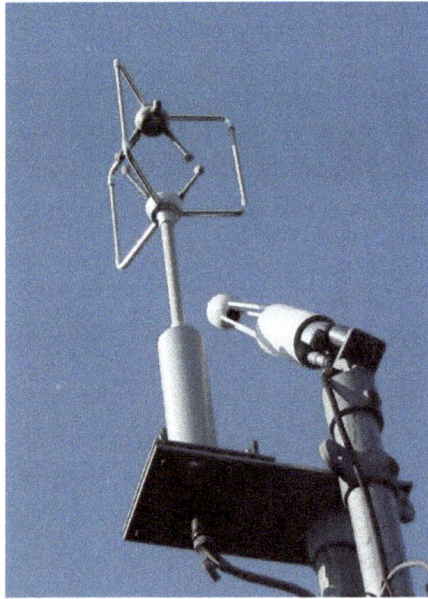

Figure 7.3. Eddy covariance tower. Source: Veedar at English Wikipedia, Public domain, via Wikimedia Commons

A standard method to measure gas and energy exchanges between land and water areas and the atmosphere is to use the eddy covariance technique, which uses a ground anemometer (to measure wind speed) and an analyzer (to measure gas concentration). Networks of measurement sites, such as FLUXNET, provide global coverage (Baldocchi, 2014) but need to be upscaled to the regional and international levels.

Tramontana et al. (2016) introduce FLUXCOM, a set of machine learning models that can predict the fluxes (CO_2: gross primary production (GPP), terrestrial ecosystem respiration (TER), net ecosystem exchange (NEE) or the net CO_2 exchange with the atmosphere, energy: latent heat (LE), sensible heat (H), and net radiation (Rn) or the difference between incoming and outcoming energy radiation) measured by eddy covariance sites. The authors explore remote sensing data only and remote sensing data and meteorological data as predictors and use an ensemble of machine learning models (tree-based methods, regression splines, neural networks, and kernel methods).

The remote sensing data come from the MODIS (Moderate Resolution Imaging Spectroradiometer) sensors ("MODIS Web," n.d.) ("ORNL DAAC MODIS SUBSETS," n.d.). They include Land Surface Temperature, the Vegetation Index and Enhanced Vegetation Index, the Leaf Area Index, the fraction of absorbed photosynthetic active radiation, Bidirectional Reflectance Distribution Function (BRDF)-corrected surface, the Normalized DifferenceWater Index, and the Land Surface Water Index. The meteorological data include air temperature, global radiation, vapor pressure deficit, and precipitation. They find that these models "have shown a high capability to predict CO_2 and energy fluxes, particularly the across-site variability and the mean seasonal cycle, with a general tendency towards increasing performance in the following order: NEE, TER, GPP, LE, H, and Rn." Much research has been done to improve these models using other remote sensing data from LANDSAT and other satellites and has been refined to particular areas such as drylands (Barnes et al., 2021).

Evaporation

Koppa et al. (2022) use machine learning to help predict terrestrial water evaporation (E) at scale. It is an essential variable in the water cycle, vegetation cycle, and extreme weather and climate change modeling. Instead of focusing on E directly, they focus on the transpiration stress of plants S, the limit of plant transportation when water is scarce, as it ensures better physical consistency and interpretability of results. It is there a hybrid method that combines pure machine learning (like FLUXCOM) and a model of the evaporation process ("GLEAM | Global Land Evaporation Amsterdam Model," n.d.). The evaporation process model uses precipitation, meteorological data on evaporation, stress, and soil data on moisture to calculate potential evaporation.

The model's inputs that predict S are derived from networks of eddy covariance towers and plant transpiration measurement stations: plant available water, vegetation optical depth, vapor pressure deficit, air temperature, incoming shortwave radiation, and atmospheric CO_2 concentration.

They find that this hybrid approach outperforms processed-base models and pure machine learning models, especially in the forested (tall vegetation) regions in the northern latitude. This approach can reduce overfitting, reduce computation time, and improve accuracy.

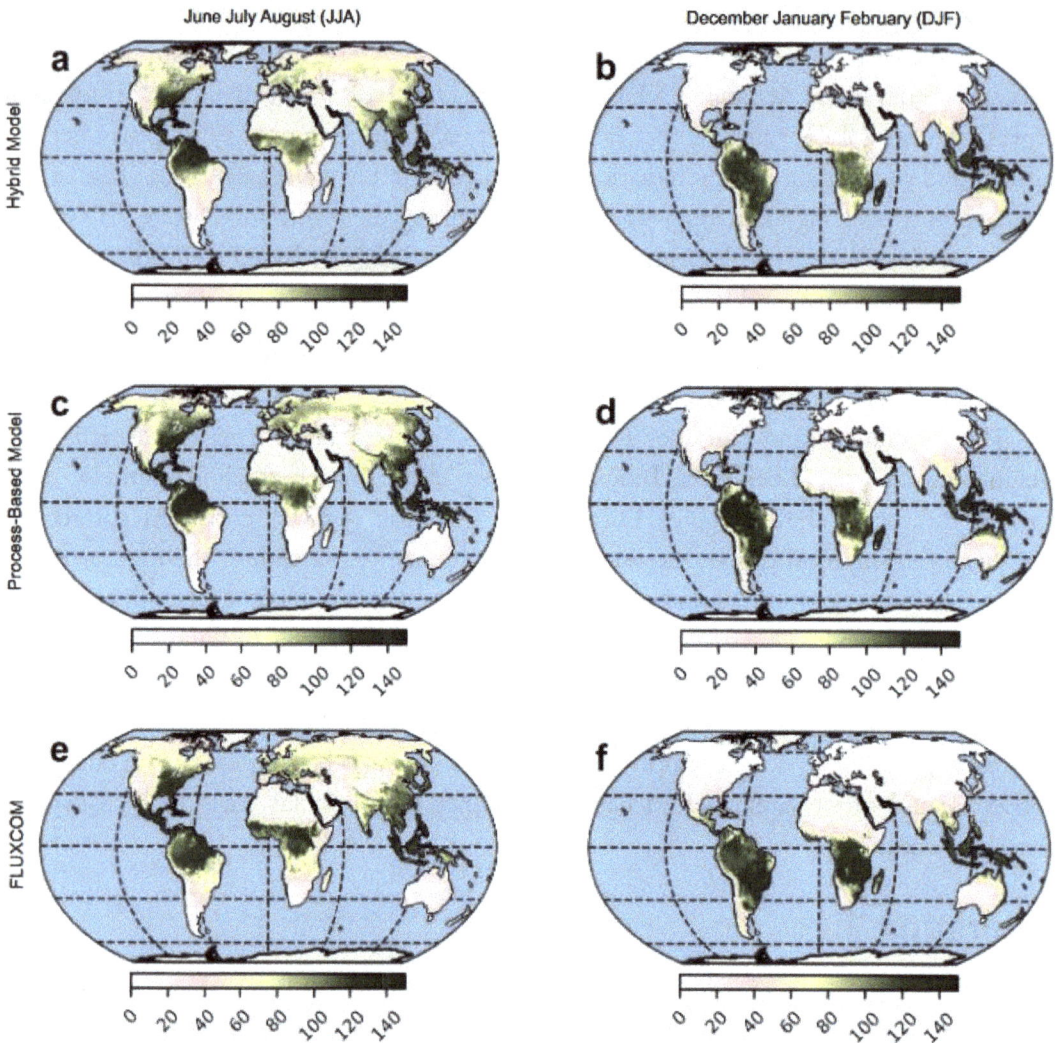

Figure 7.4. Comparisons of evaporation predictions between hybrid, process-based model and FLUXCOM. Source: (Koppa et al., 2022)

Carbon Capture

Yan et al. (2021) survey machine learning applications in carbon capture, utilization, and storage (CCUS). It is an essential but controversial component of a plan to address climate change. It is controversial because the technology is far from mature and can only capture a minimal quantity of CO_2. It is, however, necessary for some sectors, such as steel and cement, where CO_2 emissions cannot be avoided.

They divide the applications into five categories that we discuss briefly:

Absorption

CO_2 absorption is the process of CO_2 being captured into a solvent. AI can help predict CO_2 capture levels and rate of absorption of CO_2 in solvent-based absorption reactions using data from process simulators. AI can also study carbon solubility in different solutions and the thermodynamics of solvent-based carbon capture. AI can also predict produced materials' physical and thermodynamic properties and screen for solvents.

Adsorption

CO_2 adsorption is the process of CO_2 being captured onto a surface, the adsorbent. AI can help screen, discover, optimize, and synthesize adsorbents such as Metal-Organic Frameworks (MOF) with suitable properties. AI can help predict the adsorption properties and structures of some surfaces.

Combustion

Oxy-fuel combustion is a combustion process involving pure oxygen instead of air and produces CO_2 ready for capture. AI can help optimize, monitor, and control the combustion process. It can, for instance, monitor the combustion by surveilling the image of the flame. AI can also help to optimize Chemical looping combustion, where a metal oxide on a moving bed provides the oxygen for combustion.

Transportation

AI can help optimize, monitor, and measure the flow of captured CO_2 in pipelines. In particular, it can help predict the mass flow rate, density, and gas volume fraction of CO_2 in different phases. Using imaging and sensors, AI can also help detect leakages and anomalies in transportation pipelines.

Storage and utilization

AI can help predict CO_2 behavior in storage, such as its solubility, trapping in low permeable zones, residual trapping thanks to capillary forces, and mineral trapping with a chemical reaction. AI can also help detect leakages from storage.

CO_2 can be used by injection in oil fields to extract more oil and be stored underground (enhanced oil recovery or EOR). AI could optimize the process and forecast oil production with this EOR process. An AI model can be an alternative or proxy to a full-blown numerical model and optimize a full CO2-CCUS and EOR process and reservoir behavior.CO2 can also be converted into materials and mineralized to turn into concrete. AI can help predict and optimize the durability and characteristics of these materials.

Chapter 8 | Energy

> "Energy is the only universal currency: one of its many forms must be transformed to another in order for stars to shine, planets to rotate, plants to grow, and civilizations to evolve."
>
> Vaclav Smil

8.1 The State of World Energy

Goal 7 is to "Ensure access to affordable, reliable, sustainable and modern energy for all." ("Goal 7 | Department of Economic and Social Affairs").

Energy Trend

Energy is used in all sectors of the economy: industry (industrial processes, manufacturing), construction and infrastructure building (cement production, road construction), power generation (from coal fire, natural gas turbine, or nuclear plants, renewable energies), transportation (ground, sea, air transportations with gasoline, diesel fuel, jet fuel, electricity), buildings (heating, air-conditioning, hot water), agriculture and food production, services, etc. Without energy and innovations such as the steam engine, electricity generation and distribution, modern steelmaking, and the combustion engine, humanity would have been stuck in the pre-industrial age and remained dependent on low-productivity agriculture. There would be no manufacturing, mass production, internal trade, and global supply chains.

Energy use is increasing with economic development. Richer countries tend to consume much more energy per capita than poorer countries, and countries such as China have increased their energy consumption as they become more developed. Still, hundreds of millions of people do not have access to a reliable source of energy, such as an electricity grid, and use low-tech solutions such as wood burning for heating and cooking, damaging their health and the environment.

Composition of Energy Production

Energy sources tend to be mostly fossil fuels: coal, natural gas, oil, and biomass, and release greenhouse gas emissions such as CO_2 or methane CH_4 when they are burnt to generate heat and pressure and be converted to energy. Other sources that do not emit greenhouse gas are nuclear fission and renewable energies produced by solar photovoltaic panels, wind turbines, and hydroelectric dams. Some forms of energy are consumed directly, such as gasoline in a car engine, or are converted to electricity.

Coal and Biomass

Coal is the most polluting and carbon-intensive energy source but is widely available in countries like India and China that need a lot of energy to grow. Coal is primarily used in electricity generation though it is also used in steel production. In electricity generation, it can be replaced by natural gas, which is cleaner in terms of CO_2, nuclear power, and renewable energy, such as wind and solar photovoltaic (PV), which do not emit CO_2. Still, according to the IEA, 200GW of coal-fired plants have been approved and will be added by 2030 in their Announced Pledge Scenario (APS), mainly in China, India, and Southeast Asia. Coal-fired plants can be equipped with Carbon capture, utilization, and storage (CCUS), but the cost is still very high (IEA, 2021a).

Biomass includes wood, wood processing wastes, and agricultural and biological wastes (U.S. Energy Information Administration, 2022). Coal-fired plants can be retrofitted to burn biomass instead of coal, such as the Drax plant in the United Kingdom. Biomass still emits CO_2, but growing forests could reabsorb the CO_2. This is, however, controversial as it takes a long time for forests to absorb CO_2 (Ravilious, 2020).

Oil and Natural Gas

Natural gas emits less CO2 than coal when used to produce electricity. Technologies such as combined cycle gas turbines can efficiently generate power, and cogeneration can create both power and heat. A limitation of natural gas is that it is not easy to transport and needs costly infrastructure (pipelines or LNG terminals). Many countries need to import it from geopolitically unreliable countries. It is not the case for the United States, but it is for Europe, which needs to import from Russia or Algeria in addition to the United Kingdom and Norway.

Oil is the primary liquid fuel source and has many uses, from transportation, petrochemical manufacturing, heating, and power generation. It is relatively easy, safe, and cheap to transport internationally on oil tankers and is relatively energy efficient. Like natural gas, it emits CO2 and exposes countries to international markets and geopolitical risk (OPEC and Russia). It also needs refineries to transform into gasoline and other products. Oil and gas extraction also generates flaring and methane leaks that harm the environment (Myers, 2022).

Nuclear Power

Nuclear power is advantageous in terms of energy independence, greenhouse gas emissions, and stable base load electricity generation. Still, many countries do not plan to add capacities and are even closing nuclear plants, such as Germany or the United States. Countries such as France, China, and the United Kingdom will expand and replace their aging nuclear plants. The traditional arguments against nuclear power are safety, risk of air and water contamination, and nuclear waste disposal. More recently, the cost of nuclear power generation has been higher than natural gas and renewable energy (wind and solar). Research is ongoing on other types of nuclear power, such as nuclear fusion and small and modular power plants.

Renewable Energy

Renewable energy sources include hydropower, wind turbines, solar photovoltaic, geothermal, and biomass. Wind power and solar PV have become very competitive against fossil fuels and nuclear power. Their costs have decreased over the past 20 years, and many countries have ambitious plans to expand the use of renewable energy. The European Commission targets 45% of renewables in the energy mix in Europe. There are still some issues to address, such as energy storage and the variability of electricity production, for instance, at night when solar PVs do not function.

Cost of Energy Production

All these sources have direct costs such as extraction and transportation costs but also indirect costs that economists call negative externalities. Burning coal generates a lot of air pollutants, such as fine particles and greenhouse gasses, such as CO2, CO, or CH4, that cause excess mortality and global warming. The benefit is that coal is relatively cheap and abundant in countries such as China and India, making them less reliable for imports.

Universal Access to Energy

The world has made progress in giving access to energy in the form of electricity to most countries' populations (90%). In certain countries like Africa, electrification is a challenge as the cost of building a grid might be prohibitive with a low ability of the consumers to pay. The cost of PV and solar panels increased during the Covid pandemic due to disruption in supply chains and higher world inflation.

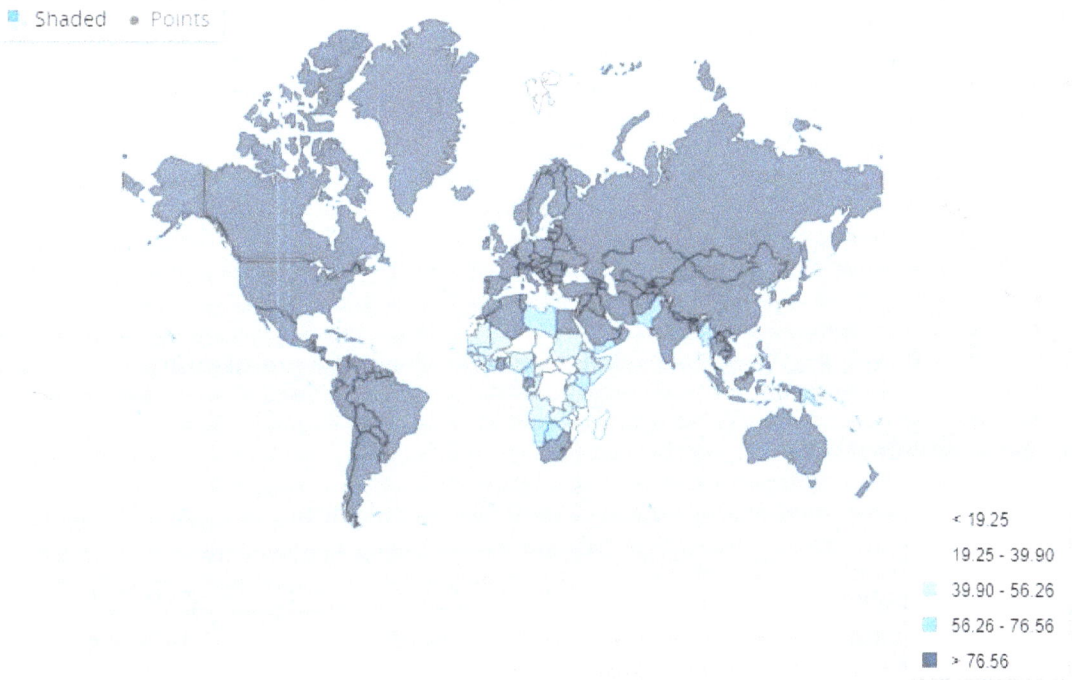

Figure 8.1. Access to electricity (% of the population) by country in 2020

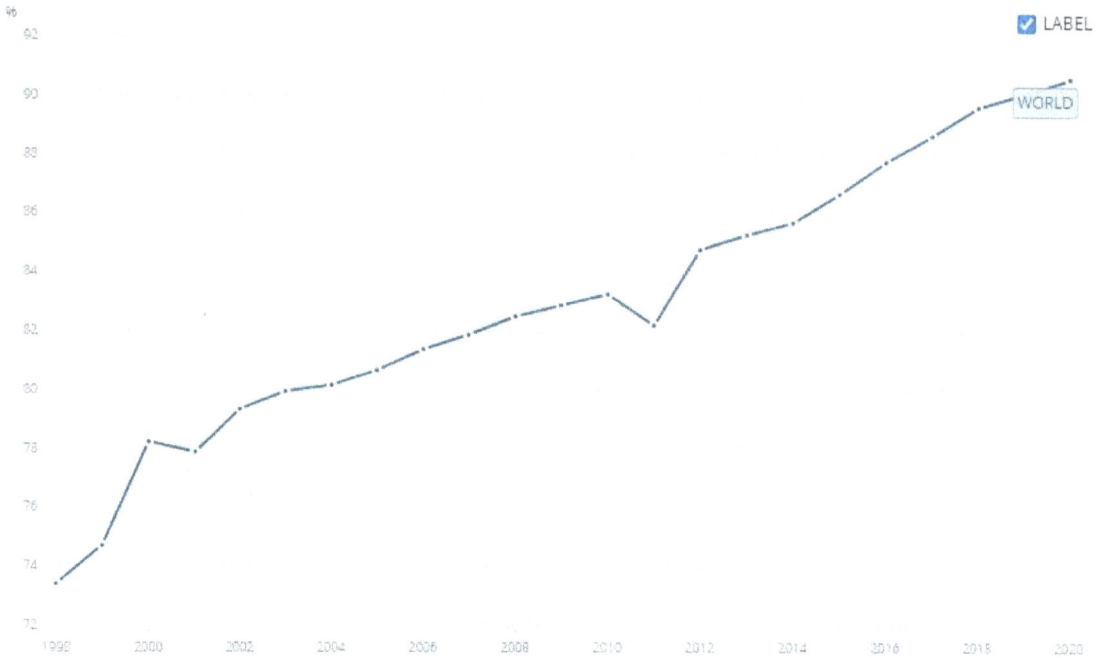

Figure 8.2. World access to electricity (% of the population)

Energy Efficiency

The IEA plans to improve energy efficiency in its Net Zero Emission scenario. This includes better fuel economy for cars, material efficiency in industry, better energy management of buildings, retrofitting, and more robust standards for appliances. The design of cities, more public transportation, the integration with nature, and a more sustainable economy should also contribute to gains in energy efficiency.

Clean Energy Transition

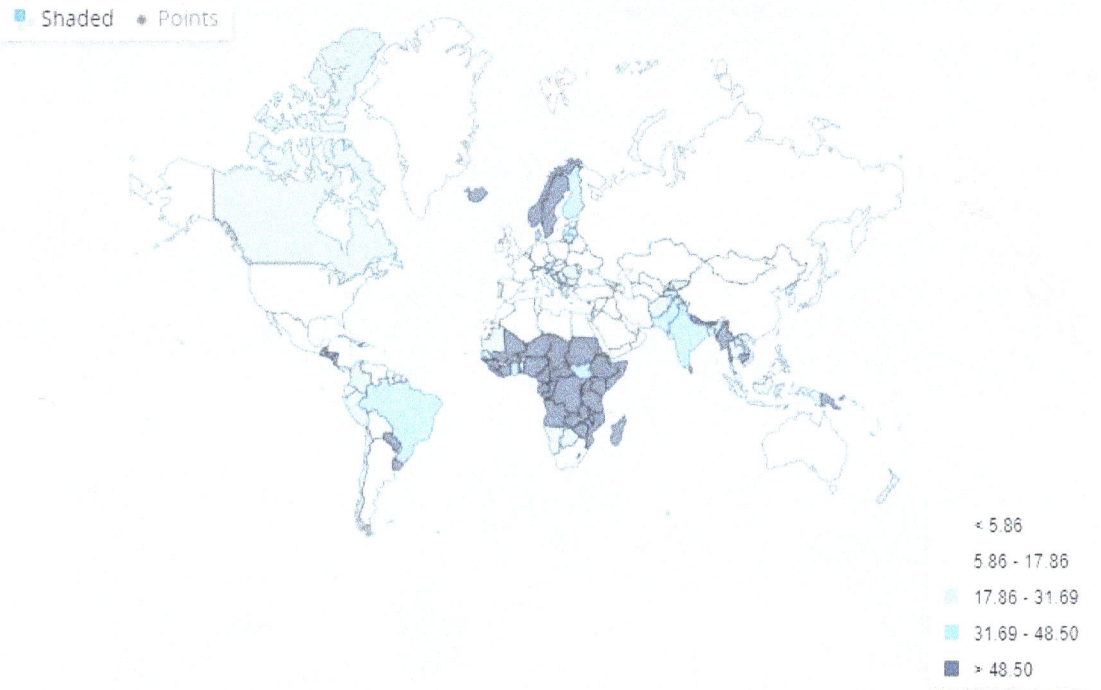

Figure 8.3. Renewable energy consumption (% of total final energy consumption) by country in 2018

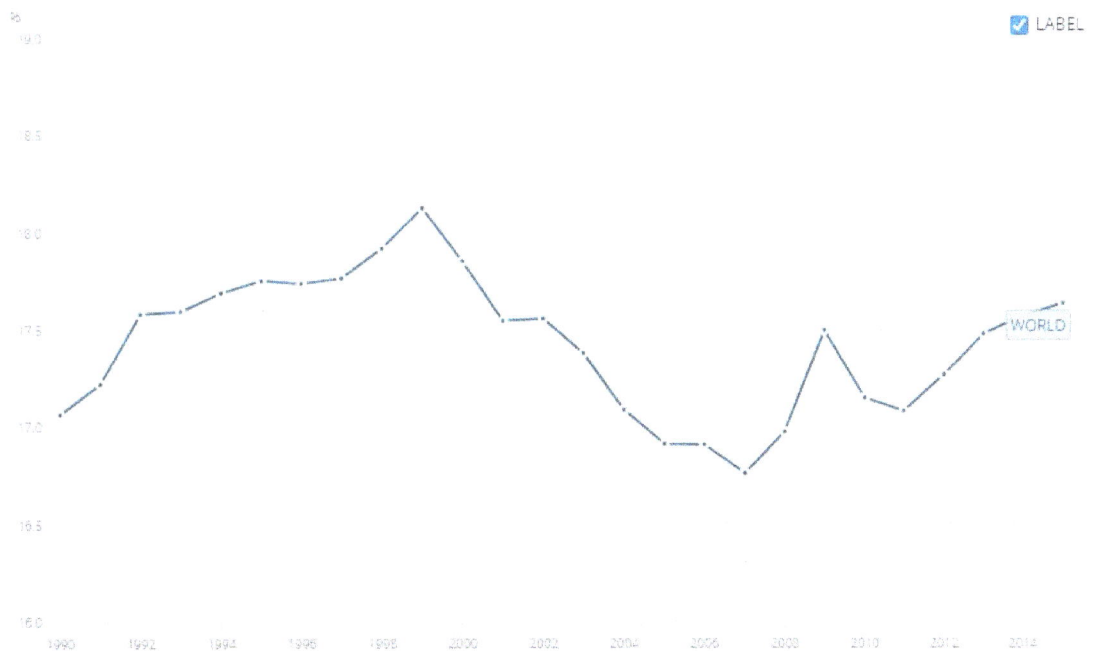

Figure 8.4. World renewable energy consumption (% of total final energy consumption)

The energy sector (IEA, 2021b)needs to go through a massive transition towards a low greenhouse gas emission one because of a rising population with increased energy demand but also the 1.5°C and net zero objectives to address climate change. A successful transition requires the phasing out of coal, cut in methane emissions, less reliance on oil and gas, expansion of renewable energy and low-emission fuels, clean electrification (from wind turbines and solar Photovoltaics), adoption of electric vehicles, better energy efficiency, and innovation in clean energy technologies.

8.2 The SDG Targets

The Sustainable Development Goal is supported by the following Targets:

Target 7.1: By 2030, ensure universal access to affordable, reliable, and modern energy services

Target 7.2: By 2030, increase substantially the share of renewable energy in the global energy mix

Target 7.3: By 2030, double the global rate of improvement in energy efficiency

Target 7.a: By 2030, enhance international cooperation to facilitate access to clean energy research and technology, including renewable energy, energy efficiency, and advanced and cleaner fossil-fuel technology, and promote investment in energy infrastructure and clean energy technology

Target 7.b: By 2030, expand infrastructure and upgrade technology for supplying modern and sustainable energy services for all in developing countries, in particular least developed countries, small island developing States, and land-locked developing countries, in accordance with their respective programmes of support

8.3 How to Improve the Production and Consumption of Energy

The International Energy Agency (IEA, 2021c) has shown a pathway to reach net zero by 2050 and limit the temperature increase to 1.5°C. The plan is ambitious and requires a significant change in the world energy mix with a massive expansion of renewable energy. It also depends on some technological innovations such as large-capacity batteries for energy storage, hydrogen electrolyzers, carbon capture, utilization, and storage (CCUS).

The IEA proposes a set of priority actions:

- Governments need to set milestones on the pathway to net zero. Milestones include no new coal plants, no new oil and gas fields approved, phasing out of coal plants in advanced countries by 2030, no new internal combustion engine cars sales by 2035, and net zero emissions electricity by 2040.

- Increase investments in clean energy and energy infrastructure to 5 trillion dollars per year by 2030.

- Address energy security risks, in particular, the growing dependency on critical minerals and increased concentration of oil production.

- Reinforce international cooperation by accelerating innovation, developing international standards, and coordinating to scale up clean technologies needs.

The IEA points out that the existing policies scenario and the scenario, including the announced pledges by the governments, still fall short of the necessary efforts to be on the pathway to net zero in 2050.

Energy efficiency in all sectors (energy supply, buildings, appliances, industry, transportation), electrification of end-uses (electric cars, batteries, and others), and a significant shift to renewable energy (hydrogen, wind and solar, biomass, and modern bioenergy, biofuel) and other sources such as nuclear are three critical components to net zero. Improvement of CCUS technologies, hydrogen production, and preventing leaks from oil and gas extraction (IEA, 2021b) will also help.

8.4 What Can AI Do to Improve the Production and Consumption of Energy

Prediction

On the supply side, AI can help locate energy sources, such as the best places to set up wind farms or solar PV installations. In fossil fuel production, AI can help detect methane leakages and reduce pollution.

AI can help predict energy production and cost based on inputs and factors such as weather and climate. Solar PV will be based on sun exposure, wind farms on the weather and cloudiness, and natural gas depend on energy market prices and transportation costs. AI can also predict greenhouse gas emissions using sensors and satellite imaging data.

On the demand side, AI can help predict the demand of different sectors based on economic activity, weather, and seasonality. For instance, the temperature will drive the demand for electricity due to air-conditioning units in the summer and the need for heating fuel or gas in the winter.

Coordination

AI can identify the factors driving supply and demand in energy markets. AI can help with planning capacities for energy supply based on future demand or the energy mix of supply. Intermittent producers could be complemented with less intermittent ones or with complementary ones.

Optimization

AI can optimize short-term production and demand in energy markets. AI can help with operations and maintenance schedule optimization. AI can optimize the cost of energy-intensive production processes or the production of independent producers. AI can help optimize the energy production and distribution value chain and identify cost efficiency opportunities.

Control

AI can help control short-term production and demand in energy markets. AI can monitor and control the inputs, outputs, and overall operations for efficiency, safety, and security. AI can automatically ramp up production from stand-by operators to meet peak demand or cut production if demand falls or requires energy storage. AI can help operate the power grid and avoid power congestion. AI can be used for real-time energy pricing to account for demand-supply imbalance and appropriately price the cost of greenhouse gas emissions and pollution (surge pricing, for instance).

8.5 Case Studies

Power Grid

Kruse et al. (2021) use explainable AI to quantify, predict and explain power grid frequency in three European areas (Continental Europe, the Nordic area, and Great Britain). Stability of the power grid frequency is necessary for the good functioning of the power grid, the management of supply and demand, and the prevention of electricity blackouts. Even though AI is promising for grid management due to the increased availability of load and frequency data, the black box nature of some models could present some security risks and require explainability.

They evaluate four hourly indicators of power grid frequency: maximum frequency deviation within the hour (nadir), the rate of change of frequency (RoCoF), the mean square deviation (MSD) from 50 Hz, and the integrated frequency deviation (integral). They use the following features: the day-ahead load forecast, day-ahead scheduled generation, day-ahead wind and solar power forecast, day-ahead electricity prices, actual load and actual generation per production type, ramp features (slope), for daily forecast errors, and indicators of times, weekdays and months from 2015 to 2019.

They use the XGBoost model (Chen and Guestrin, 2016), a boosting algorithm that adds a new tree at each fitting iteration. The tree is selected to minimize a loss function. Each iteration improves the fitting of the training data. The loss function includes some gradient terms (first and second order terms) and regularization terms (to limit the size of the trees and prevent overfitting). The splitting at each different node is then decided on an enhanced score based on the loss function that measures the quality of the split.

For explainability, they use the SHAP (SHapley Additive exPlanations) framework (Lundberg and Lee, 2017). SHAP values show the impact of each feature on the output as well as the global importance of each feature. Figure 8.5 shows the SHAP values of several features on the mean square deviation (MSD) in the different regions and the model prediction vs. the actual data.

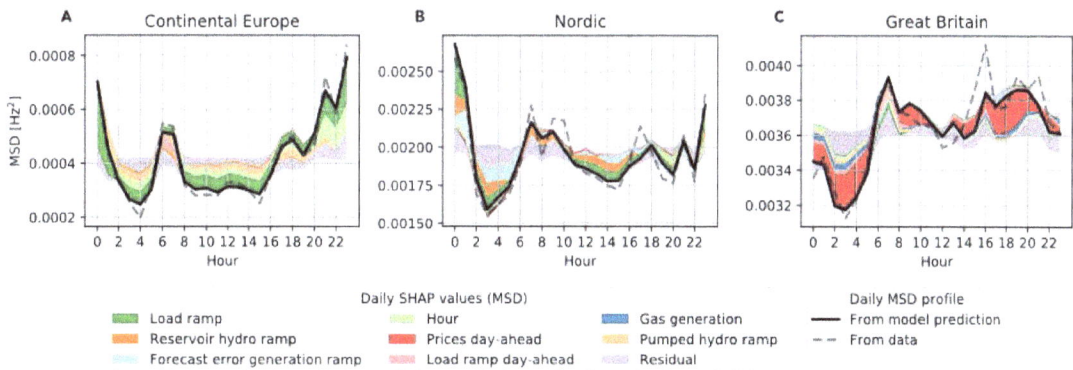

Figure 8.5. Daily SHAP values (MSD). Source: (Kruse et al., 2021)

Energy Demand Response

Antonopoulos et al. (2020) review papers from 2009 to 2018 using AI in energy demand response. They focus on how users change their demand on the electric power system based on price, incentive, or contractual signals they receive. A high price will lower the demand. More incentives would increase the demand for some periods.

They identify six application areas: load and price forecasting, load scheduling and control at the aggregator level, load scheduling and control at the consumer level, design of pricing and incentive schemes, and load and customer segmentation.

Load forecasting

AI can help forecast load demand. It can include baseline load demand without demand response incentives and flexibility forecasting that incorporates the effect of signals on the demand. Demand can be at the aggregator level (wholesale) or domestic level (retail customers, residentials, buildings). AI models can be regressions, support vector machines, and neural networks.

Price forecasting

To complement load forecasting, AI can help with price forecasting on the demand side at the aggregator or consumer level. Based on demand bids and past prices, prices can, for instance, be forecasted accurately. These forecasts can be used to design price incentives.

Load scheduling and control at the aggregator level

AI can help optimize and control the optimal load of a portfolio of assets when interacting with the grid, system operators, and a demand response system. The objective could be to maximize profits or minimize losses.

Load scheduling and control at the consumer level

At the consumer level, AI can help schedule and control energy management systems (EMS). The EMS have to optimize in the face of the demand response signals and consumer demand, preference, and costs. EMS can account for other factors, such as environmental pollution.

Design of pricing and incentive schemes

AI helps design the optimal dynamic scheme based on price elasticity and consumer demand, or the difference between expected and realized consumption. Prices, incentives, and contracts can be designed optimally to maximize a provider's profits.

Load and customer segmentation

AI can help identify different customer groups to segment markets and differentiate demand response schemes between these groups. Load data, bid-offer data, and consumer characteristics are factors that can segment customers and receive different demand responses.

Fusion Energy

Nuclear fusion is the process of making hydrogen isotopes (deuterium and radioactive tritium) fuse and form helium atoms and create energy. They form a plasma heated at very high temperature and pressure thanks to magnetic fields. The plasma has to be confined in a Tokamak reaction chamber in the shape of a torus (Figure 8.6) and kept in place with magnetic controllers.

Figure 8.6. Tokamak à Configuration Variable (TCV). Source: CRPP-EPFL, Association Suisse-Euratom, CC BY-SA 4.0 <https://creativecommons.org/licenses/by-sa/4.0>, via Wikimedia Commons

Degrave et al. (2022) use Deep Reinforcement Learning (RL) to manage these controllers. The particular RL method (Figure 8.7) used is an Actor-Critic algorithm (MPO, maximum a posteriori optimization), with a Critic network that evaluates a value function based on the final objective on the plasma (e.g., shape, see ("Plasma shaping," 2022)) or stabilization of position and location, and plasma conducted current) and a Policy network that makes real-time decisions on the magnetic control coils based on the environment, such as sensors.

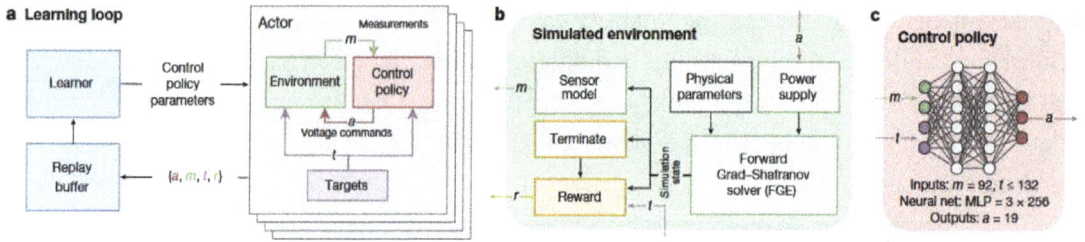

Figure 8.7. Reinforcement Learning architecture. Source: (Degrave et al., 2022)

Learning is done on a simulator, and control is done on real hardware. They find that their model can accurately control the characteristics of the plasma in real-world experiments with the Tokamak à Configuration Variable (TCV) (a research nuclear fusion reactor based at EPFL, Switzerland). They could also successfully control new plasma configurations with, for instance, the presence of droplets.

PART III NATURE

Chapter 9 | Land Ecosystems

> "To reconnect with nature is key if we want to save the planet."
>
> Jane Goodall

9.1 The State of Land Ecosystems

Goal 15 is to "protect, restore and promote sustainable use of terrestrial ecosystems, sustainably manage forests, combat desertification, and halt and reverse land degradation and halt biodiversity loss." ("Goal 15 | Department of Economic and Social Affairs").

Land Ecosystems Trend

Economic development has proceeded since the industrial revolution without much regard for the state of Nature. Even though Nature has been a source of raw materials, biofuels, fresh water, soil, and food for humans and has provided invaluable ecosystem services such as climate, air quality, freshwater, and ocean acidity regulation, it has deteriorated under human use with an ever-increasing world population. It has been domesticated with resource extraction, deforestation, human land-use change, agriculture, and urban development. The loss of biodiversity, natural habitats, and pollution of air, water, and soil are indicators of the severe impact of human activity on Nature.

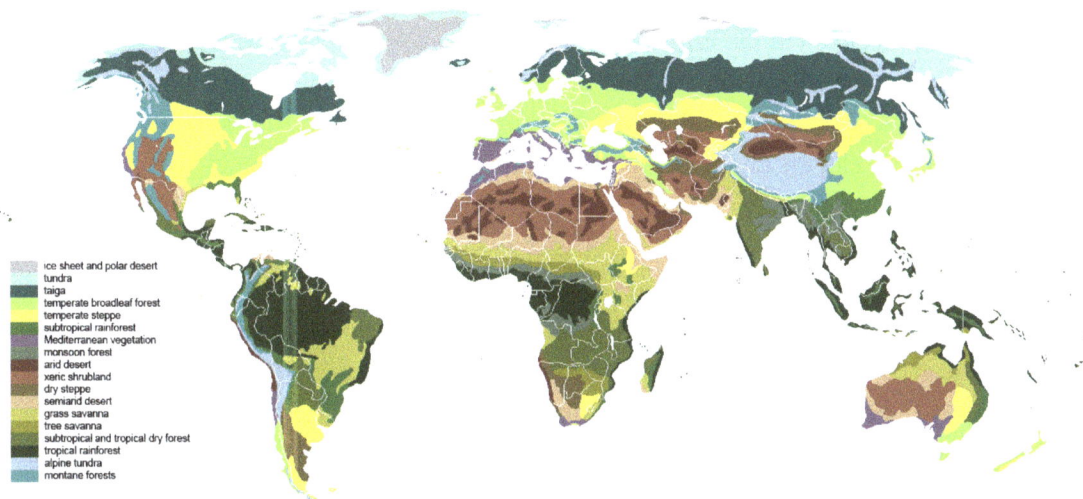

Figure 9.1. Biomes. Source: By Ville Koistinen (user Vzb83) - the blank world map in Commons and WSOY Iso karttakirja for the information, CC BY-SA 3.0, https://commons.wikimedia.org/w/index.php?curid=1700408

In the IPBES Global Assessment Report (IPBES, 2019), experts have recognized the vital role of Nature in providing ecosystem function and services to humans, but also that it has been deteriorating, especially in the last 50 years. Transformative changes would be required to reverse these trends and reach the goals of the 2050 Vision for Biodiversity ("Towards the vision 2050 on biodiversity," 2019).

According to (United Nations Convention to Combat Desertification, 2022), 44 trillion dollars of GDP originates from natural capital and nature services. They include climate, water, air regulations, disease and pest control, waste decomposition, and leisure amenities. They are, however, overexploited and depleted by humankind.

Natural habitat and biodiversity

Natural habitat has declined with human development and exploitation of natural resources. Agricultural lands, human settlements, towns, and cities have encroached on or replaced forests, grasslands, and other natural ecosystems. Lakes, rivers, wetlands, and coastal areas are also affected by human activities, especially pollution and contamination (see Chapter 10).

As a result, the number and variety of animals, plants, and insects are shrinking and are replaced by crops and livestock that are much less diverse. Any disappearance of natural species also affects the food chain downstream (prey) or upstream (predators). For instance, a species that does not face any more predators will multiply and over-consume its food (smaller prey, insects, fruits, grass, or plants). Introducing alien species can also disturb an ecological system and cause long-term damage to native species.

Biodiversity has declined in the last 50 years. According to the IPBES (2019), 25% of species of studied plants and animals are at risk of extinction. The biomass of wild mammals has decreased by 82% since prehistory. Drivers of extinction include land and sea use change, direct exploitation, climate change, pollution, and invasive alien species.

Deforestation

The land has been used for agriculture and cleared of forests, replaced by crops and animal farming with a considerable loss of biodiversity and CO_2 absorption capacity. Deforestation and forest degradation continue in favor of agriculture. According to (FAO, 2022a), there are around 4 billion hectares of forests worldwide, and only one-third is primary forest (naturally regenerated and untouched by humans). Four hundred twenty (420) million hectares have been lost to land use, and the rate of deforestation has been 10 million hectares per year from 2015 to 2020. The WWF (WWF, 2019) estimates that more than half of the vertebrate forest population has disappeared.

Desertification and land degradation

The overexploitation of soil, water, and vegetation has led to desertification and land degradation (United Nations Convention to Combat Desertification, 2022). According to United Nations (United Nations Convention to Combat Desertification, 2022), 20 to 40% of the land is degraded because of unsustainable land use and an economic growth model that favors extraction of natural resources rather than nature conservation. The objective is Land Degradation Neutrality (LDN) with no net increase in land degradation and maintenance of sustainable land use.

9.2 The SDG Targets

Twelve targets have been defined to reach SDG 15.

Target 15.1: By 2020, ensure the conservation, restoration, and sustainable use of terrestrial and inland freshwater ecosystems and their services, in particular forests, wetlands, mountains, and drylands, in line with obligations under international agreements

Target 15.2: By 2020, promote the implementation of sustainable management of all types of forests, halt deforestation, restore degraded forests and substantially increase afforestation and reforestation globally

Target 15.3: By 2030, combat desertification, restore degraded land and soil, including land affected by desertification, drought, and floods, and strive to achieve a land degradation-neutral world

Target 15.4: By 2030, ensure the conservation of mountain ecosystems, including their biodiversity, in order to enhance their capacity to provide benefits that are essential for sustainable development

Target 15.5: Take urgent and significant action to reduce the degradation of natural habitats, halt the loss of biodiversity and, by 2020, protect and prevent the extinction of threatened species

Target 15.6: Promote fair and equitable sharing of the benefits arising from the utilization of genetic resources and promote appropriate access to such resources, as internationally agreed

Target 15.7: Take urgent action to end poaching and trafficking of protected species of flora and fauna and address both demand and supply of illegal wildlife products

Target 15.8: By 2020, introduce measures to prevent the introduction and significantly reduce the impact of invasive alien species on land and water ecosystems and control or eradicate the priority species

Target 15.9: By 2020, integrate ecosystem and biodiversity values into national and local planning, development processes, poverty reduction strategies, and accounts

Target 15.a: Mobilize and significantly increase financial resources from all sources to conserve and sustainably use biodiversity and ecosystems

Target 15.b: Mobilize significant resources from all sources and at all levels to finance sustainable forest management and provide adequate incentives to developing countries to advance such management, including for conservation and reforestation

Target 15.c: Enhance global support for efforts to combat poaching and trafficking of protected species, including by increasing the capacity of local communities to pursue sustainable livelihood opportunities

9.3 How to Protect Land Ecosystems

The FAO (FAO, 2022b) is proposing key response options grouped into four areas:

- Adopting inclusive land and water governance:

  This includes collaboration and shared governance between stakeholders and sectors, developing coordinated and coherent policies and approaches by avoiding fragmentation and power imbalances and improving coordination between sectors (land, water, agriculture, environment, finance), strengthening and harmonizing land and water tenure systems, effectively engaging all stakeholders, improving employment, livelihoods and gender equity, and undertaking governance analysis.

- Implementing integrated solutions at scale:

  This includes integrated land management, incentives to maintain ecosystem services, integrated water resources management, integration of food, water, energy, ecosystem services (nexus approach), addressing climate change impacts, sustainable soil management, using Nature-based solutions, agroecological approaches, agroforestry systems, and crop-livestock systems.

- Embracing innovative technologies and management:

  This includes sustainable soil management, rainfed agricultural production, better water productivity, harvesting rainwater, better water use efficiency, water accounting, and auditing, modernizing irrigation systems, better water storage, protecting groundwater, limiting pollution by nutrients and fertilizers, reducing the use of pesticides and contaminants, reducing the salinity of water and soil, more research in crops and biotechnologies, adopting ICTs and big data, reducing food loss and waste, promoting sustainable diet and circular economy.

- Investing in long-term sustainability:

  This includes more climate financing from international finance institutions for water, agricultural, and land projects, Nature-based solutions, more equity in irrigation projects, innovative, responsible project and resource management and governance with better data, communication, and technology, engaging farmers in the land, water, and agricultural sustainability efforts.

  To preserve biodiversity, the IUCN maintains a red list of endangered species ("The IUCN Red List of Threatened Species," n.d.). It provides peer-reviewed scientific information on the status and risk of extinction of over 100,000 species and subspecies.

9.4 What Can AI Do to Protect Land Ecosystems

Prediction

AI can help monitor, predict, and classify land use from satellite observations and sensors. AI can predict crop yield and health. AI can indicate water and soil nutrient quality and deficiency. AI can help identify human settlements, disaster zones, drought, and flooding areas. AI can help monitor the water cycle, evaporation, and cloud formation and predict rainfalls. AI can help monitor the carbon cycle and identify emissions and absorptions of greenhouse gases. AI can help monitor biodiversity and species at risk of extinction. AI can monitor the temperature of large land masses and predict areas susceptible to drought, desertification, and wild forest fires.

Coordination

AI can help coordinate resources for land, forest, and biodiversity conservation and restoration by identifying the factors that can cause degradation. AI can help plan for the consequences of crop failures and natural disasters. AI can identify and guide resources to reach vulnerable human populations because of a lack of food and water or forced displacements. AI can coordinate efforts to fight against illegal poaching or illegal land use.

Optimization

AI can help optimize the use of land and inputs such as fertilizers, irrigation systems, and types of crops to maximize crop yield and alternative land use while being sustainable. For a forest, AI can optimize the characteristics of trees to cut to ensure the replenishment of future trees. AI can help optimize a local animal population to keep a healthy balance between prey, predators, and the entire ecosystem.

Control

Autonomous AI agricultural machines can help in farming and harvesting. AI can help with feeding, managing, caring for, and diagnosing crops and livestock animals and with predictive maintenance of farming machinery. AI can control irrigation systems, and in a closed environment, such as in a greenhouse or a vertical farm, it can contain all the components of precision farming.

9.5 Case Studies

Dynamic World

Dynamic World is a near real-time model of global land use land cover use (LULC) (Brown et al., 2022). It leverages the satellite imaging data of Sentinel 2, Google Earth Engine (Gorelick et al., 2017), and Google Cloud to produce LULC data at high frequency, high resolution, and globally consistent fashion.

Figure 9.2. Sentinel 2 Multispectral Instrument Data. Catskills, NY. Source: https://dynamicworld.app/explore

Figure 9.3. Dynamic World. Catskills, NY. Source:
https://dynamicworld.app/explore

The model uses Sentinel-2 Level 2 A Surface Reflectance imagery data as training data paired with masked and normalized Sentinel-2 Level 1 C Top of Atmosphere reflectance images. The images are preprocessed to remove the effect of cloudiness and shadows.

The model objective classifies land use into nine classes: water, trees, grass, flooded vegetation, crops, shrub, scrub, built area, bare ground, and snow and ice. Annotators are employed to label the images. Twenty-five experts in photo interpretation or remote sensing and 45 non-experts participated in interpreting 4,000 tiles and 20,000 tiles, respectively. The minimum area was 50m by 50m.

The classification model is a fully convolutional neural network and gives probabilities of belonging to each class. Dynamic World can then process new Sentinel 2 images in 45mn and produce a new LULC image every 14.4 seconds.

Such near real-time land cover use data can provide a lot of information about water usage and evaporation, flooding, urban expansions, deforestation, agricultural expansion, and the state of glaciers, which help monitor climate change, agriculture, or urban development.

Extinction risk

Biodiversity is critical for preserving nature, and it is threatened by species extinction while the human population keeps growing and consuming more land, water, and natural resources. Zizka et al. (2022) developed the IUCNN model to assess the extinction of a species based on the Red List of the International Union for the Conservation of Nature ("The IUCN Red List of Threatened Species," n.d.). Each species can be classified into five categories: least concern (LC), near threatened (NT), vulnerable (VU), endangered (EN), and critically endangered (CR).

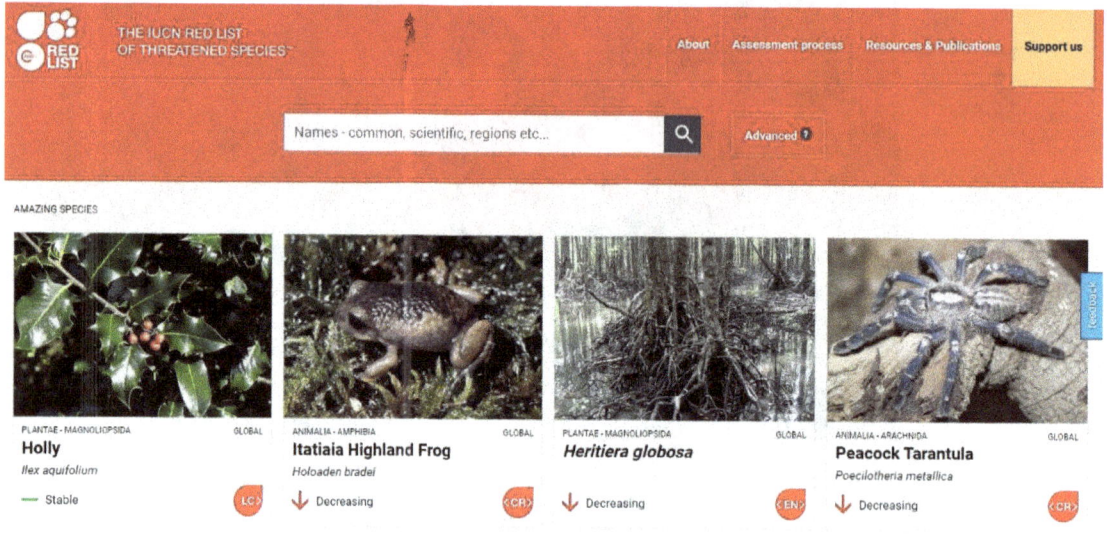

Figure 9.4. The IUCN Red List of threatened species website. Each species is assigned a class (least concern (LC), near threatened (NT), vulnerable (VU), endangered (EN), and critically endangered (CR)). Source: https://www.iucnredlist.org/

IUCNN implements four models using fully connected neural networks (nn) or convolutional neural networks (cnn): cnn-class (convolutional neural networks+classification), nn-class (neural networks+classification), bnn-class (Bayesian neural networks+classification), and nn-reg (neural networks+regression).

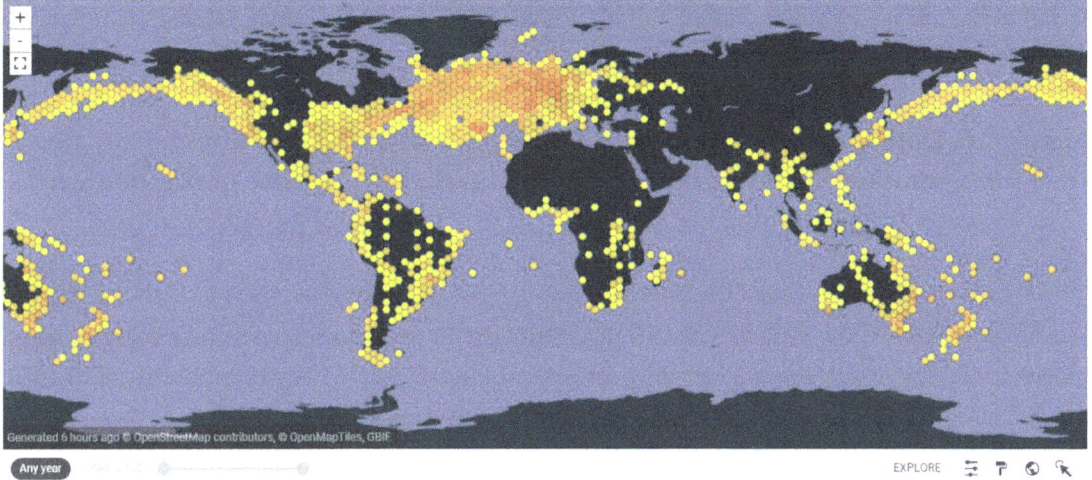

Figure 9.5. Occurrences of Anthocerotophyta. Source: GBIF, Global Biodiversity Information Facility https://www.gbif.org/

Features can include geographical data with position (longitude, latitude range) and the number of occurrences (Figure 9.5) that will feed into a CNN or quantitative and categorical data such as biome type, climate variables, human footprint impacts, and traits that will feed into a neural network model.

The authors find these models perform well when applied to orchids, especially for the binary case of not threatened vs. possibly threatened. For the complete classification, nn-class and nn-reg have mixed results; bnn-class and nn-class perform better.

Wildfire Prediction

Wildfires are very damaging to human safety, human health, and climate change. Predicting the risk and spread of wildfires should be very valuable. Huot et al. (2022) propose the 'Next Day Wildfire Spread' dataset that helps predict the spread of wildfires.

The dataset contains historical wildfires in the US aggregated in Google Earth Engine (Gorelick et al., 2017) and feature variables such as elevation, wind direction, wind speed, minimum temperature, maximum temperature, humidity, precipitation, drought index, vegetation, population density (a proxy for anthropogenic activity), and energy release component (composite fuel moisture index) at 1km resolution. Figure 9.6 shows an example of this data.

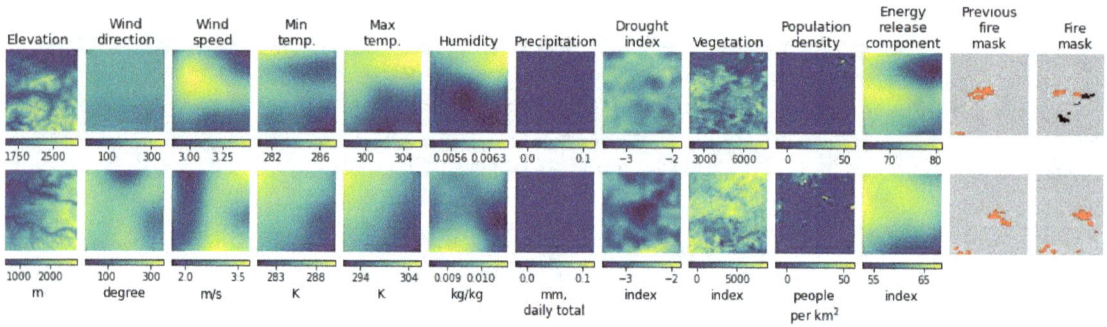

Figure 9.6. Data from the 'Next Day Wildfire Spread' dataset. 64 km x 64 km area at 1 km resolution. Temp: temperature. Fire mask: the presence of fire. Source: https://www.kaggle.com/datasets/fantineh/next-day-wildfire-spread

The authors apply these data to a next-day wildfire prediction model based on a convolutional autoencoder for image segmentation (presence of fire or not). They compare the model to two base models, a logistic regression model and a random forest.

They use the Area Under the Curve (AUC) for the Precision-Recall curve as a metric to compare the model. They find that the neural network model performs the best, followed by the random forest and the logistic regression. The model performs better with an AUC above 50% with an eight times coarser resolution.

Chapter 10 | Water Ecosystems

"The sea, the great unifier, is man's only hope. Now, as never before, the old phrase has a literal meaning: we are all in the same boat."

Jacques Yves Cousteau

10.1 The State of World Clean Water

Goal 6 is to "ensure availability and sustainable management of water and sanitation for all." ("Goal 6 | Department of Economic and Social Affairs").

Clean Water Trend

Freshwater is a product of the water cycle (Figure 10.1) and is used by nature. Freshwater is, however, becoming a scarce resource because of increased population, urbanization, water exploitation and pollution in developed countries, and drought in some low and middle-income countries. Clean water is sourced from groundwater or processed by water-treating plants but is not always accessible in all regions, countries, towns, and cities.

Water is used for human services (drinking, sanitation, health), as input to food and agriculture, and for leisure activities (United Nations, 2021a). 69% of global water usage is for agriculture, with higher use where irrigation is adopted. Agriculture is also a significant source of water pollution because excess nutrients contaminate groundwater, rivers, and coastal areas. Pollution is also due to industry and untreated wastewater.

Water usage is increasing with economic development and is increasingly used for energy, industry, and human usage. The risk of water shortage is possible and will be affected by excess water consumption, water pollution, drought, and climate change, especially in the more arid areas or in some months of the year.

Integrated water resource management is critical when the water is shared among different stakeholders and sometimes even countries. A river can be used by farmers for irrigation, by an electric utility company exploiting a dam, fishermen, and the public for leisure activities. Better water management is possible with less waste and less waste in food and agriculture.

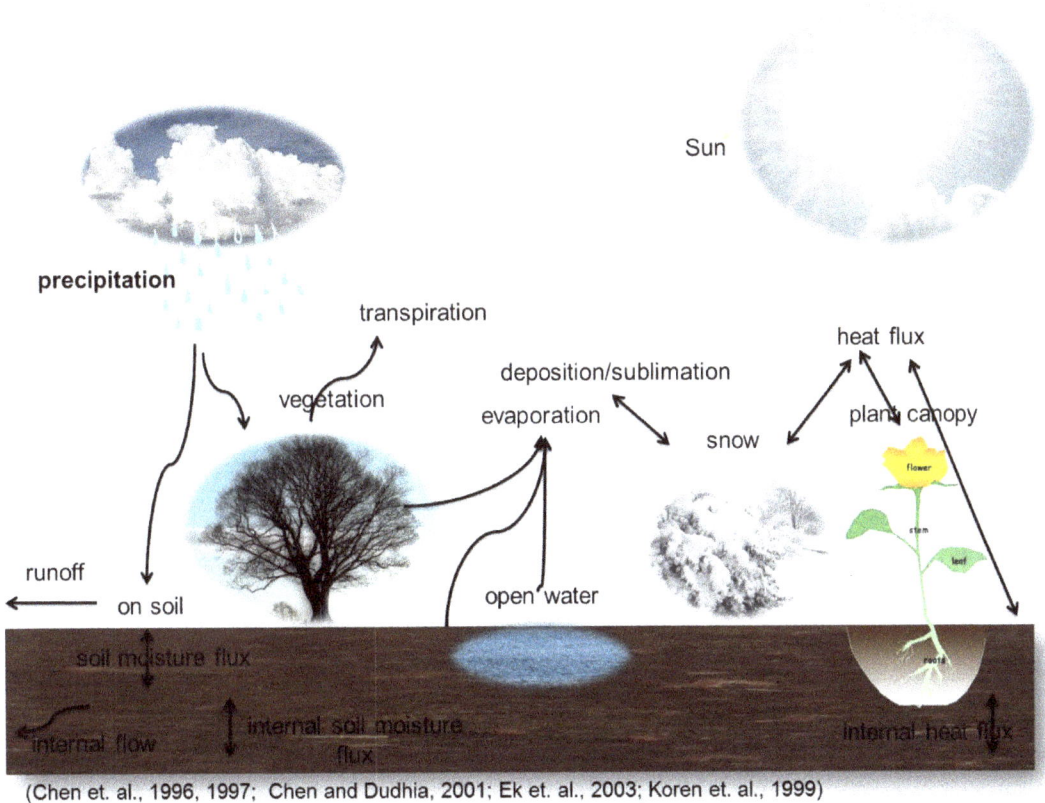

(Chen et. al., 1996, 1997; Chen and Dudhia, 2001; Ek et. al., 2003; Koren et. al., 1999)

Figure 10.1. Hydrological cycle. Source: Anishct, Public domain, via Wikimedia Commons

10.2 The SDG Targets

The Sustainable Development Goal is supported by the following Targets:

Target 6.1: By 2030, achieve universal and equitable access to safe and affordable drinking water for all

Target 6.2: By 2030, achieve access to adequate and equitable sanitation and hygiene for all and end open defecation, paying special attention to the needs of women and girls and those in vulnerable situations

Target 6.3: By 2030, improve water quality by reducing pollution, eliminating dumping and minimizing release of hazardous chemicals and materials, halving the proportion of untreated wastewater, and substantially increasing recycling and safe reuse globally

Target 6.4: By 2030, substantially increase water-use efficiency across all sectors and ensure sustainable withdrawals and supply of freshwater to address water scarcity and substantially reduce the number of people suffering from water scarcity

Target 6.5: By 2030, implement integrated water resources management at all levels, including through transboundary cooperation as appropriate

Target 6.6: By 2020, protect and restore water-related ecosystems, including mountains, forests, wetlands, rivers, aquifers, and lakes

Target 6.a: By 2030, expand international cooperation and capacity-building support to developing countries in water- and sanitation-related activities and programmes, including water harvesting, desalination, water efficiency, wastewater treatment, recycling, and reuse technologies

Target 6.b: Support and strengthen the participation of local communities in improving water and sanitation management

10.3 How to Improve Access to Clean Water

Water governance and how to protect, maintain and allocate water resources among all the stakeholders is critical to ensure equitable access to safe and affordable drinking water. Water can be used and affected by many stakeholders by agriculture (irrigation, livestock, food production), industry (natural resource extraction, energy production, water discharge), hydropower, leisure, drinking, washing, and sanitation. Downstream users of water should not suffer from excess water abstractions upstream, or drinking water users should not be affected by agriculture overexploiting or polluting groundwater with pesticides and pollutants or by contamination from industry or human wastes in case of flooding (United Nations, 2022).

The OECD (OECD, 2015) has set up principles for water governance:

- Principle 1. Clearly allocate and distinguish roles and responsibilities for water policymaking, policy implementation, operational management and regulation, and foster coordination across these responsible authorities.

- Principle 2. Manage water at the appropriate scale(s) within integrated basin governance systems to reflect local conditions, and foster coordination between the different scales.

- Principle 3. Encourage policy coherence through effective cross-sectoral coordination, especially between policies for water and the environment, health, energy, agriculture, industry, spatial planning, and land use

- Principle 4. Adapt the level of capacity of responsible authorities to the complexity of water challenges to be met and to the set of competencies required to carry out their duties

- Principle 5. Produce, update, and share timely, consistent, comparable, and policy-relevant water and water-related data and information, and use it to guide, assess and improve water policy

- Principle 6. Ensure that governance arrangements help mobilize water finance and allocate financial resources in an efficient, transparent, and timely manner

- Principle 7. Ensure that sound water management regulatory frameworks are effectively implemented and enforced in pursuit of the public interest

- Principle 8. Promote the adoption and implementation of innovative water governance practices across responsible authorities, levels of government, and relevant stakeholders

- Principle 9. Mainstream integrity and transparency practices across water policies, water institutions, and water governance frameworks for greater accountability and trust in decision-making

- Principle 10. Promote stakeholder engagement for informed and outcome-oriented contributions to water policy design and implementation.

- Principle 11. Encourage water governance frameworks that help manage trade-offs across water users, rural and urban areas, and generations

- Principle 12. Promote regular monitoring and evaluation of water policy and governance where appropriate, share the results with the public and make adjustments when needed

In practice, water governance can be challenging to enforce. It can lead to inequitable outcomes if governments, local authorities, and communities do not manage the trade-offs well because of wrong incentives or are partial stakeholders in the economics of water distribution and usage. Legal frameworks could also be inadequate for good water governance (United Nations, 2022). Water governance might require cooperation between countries when the resources such as rivers are shared.

Access to clean water also requires significant investments in WASH (Water, Sanitation, and Hygiene) services, not only in the treatment and delivery of water but also in the sanitation and disposal of used water and human wastes. These investments are often lacking in poor and remote areas, informal human settlements where there is no tax collection, and minimal public services, such as urban slums, refugee camps, and disaster-affected regions. Decentralized and low-cost WASH solutions would need to be developed (United Nations, 2019).

10.4 What Can AI Do to Improve Access to Clean Water

Prediction

AI can help predict water quality at different stages of the water cycle (source, distribution, consumption). AI can monitor and predict the risk of water contamination and pollution. AI can monitor and predict the water level and supply, consumption, abstraction, and risk of groundwater depletion. AI can help predict the impact on water of climate interaction and weather dynamics such as rainfall, humidity, temperature, ice melting from glaciers, and drought.

Coordination

AI can plan the usage of water by all the stakeholders to maximize the sustainability of its use. AI can help plan and coordinate the efforts to invest and build the water infrastructure to distribute water to all stakeholders. AI can coordinate assistance to human populations, livestock, and crops in case of drought, water pollution, or contamination. AI can help cities and urban people maintain sustainable drinking water access.

Optimization

AI can optimize water supply and usage and possible treatment and recycling of wastewater to minimize shortages and unsustainable uses. AI can set up water pricing to reflect the total cost of supply, distribution, access, scarcity, and sustainability to encourage efficient water use. AI can identify potential polluters and inefficient users and reduce their impacts.

Control

AI can help to limit water contamination and pollution by controlling water and toxic contaminant discharge from agriculture, industry, and urban areas. AI can help manage water abstractions and flows to maximize the collective benefit of all stakeholders, especially in dry seasons. AI can also be used to control the operations of water treatment plants and reduce the risk of water quality degradation.

10.5 The State of the World Seas and Oceans

World Seas and Oceans Trend

Goal 14 is to "conserve and sustainably use the oceans, seas and marine resources for sustainable development." ("Goal 14 | Department of Economic and Social Affairs").

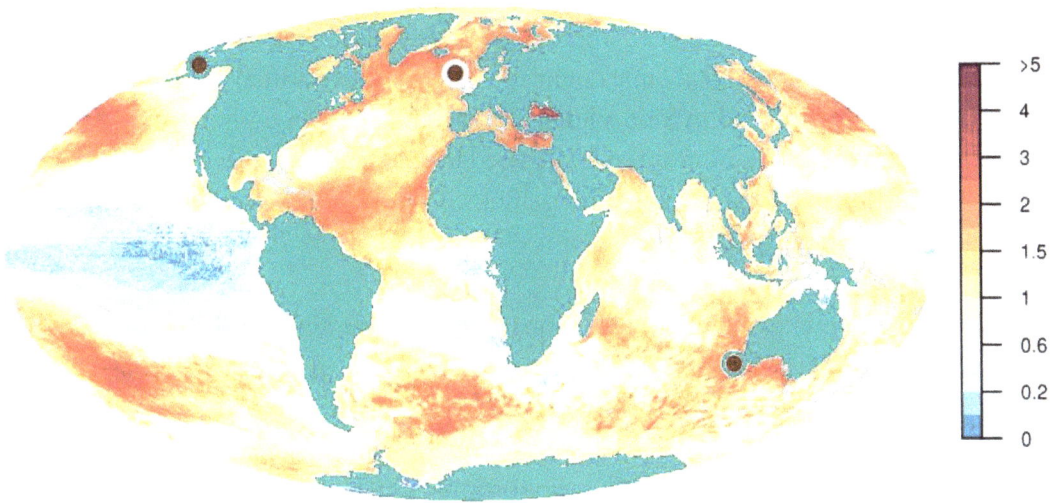

Figure 10.2. Impact of humans on oceans. Source: By Benjamin S. Halpern, Melanie Frazier, Jamie Afflerbach, Julia S. Lowndes, Fiorenza Micheli, Casey O'Hara, Courtney Scarborough & Kimberly A. Selkoe - [1], CC BY 4.0, https://commons.wikimedia.org/w/index.php?curid=84396967

Oceans play an essential role in regulating the climate by producing half of the oxygen, absorbing CO2, and cooling the planet. It brings immense economic benefits to humanity as it is estimated to contribute 1.5 trillion dollars annually to the world economy, including international maritime shipping (Stuchtey et al., 2020). More than 200 million people work in food production from the oceans, and an estimated 3 billion people are consuming it. Coastal areas are homes of many people and provide them with essential ecosystem services such as fisheries, biodiversity, water and climate regulation, and natural protection from sea-level rise (Stuchtey et al., 2020).

Ocean warming

Climate change is affecting the oceans and contributing to their warming and acidification. Coral reefs are very exposed to the rise in temperature, and their disappearance causes loss of biodiversity in the coastal areas with often unknown and unpredictable consequences for life in the oceans.

Marine pollution

Oceans are affected by marine pollution. Despite their size, oceans do not absorb and make all pollutants disappear. In the coastal areas, pollution from nutrients used in agriculture, loose sediments, and loss of biodiversity cause eutrophication (too many nutrients) and dead zones (reduced oxygen), such as in the Chesapeake Bay, the Gulf of Mexico, the Baltic Sea, Japan, and South Korea ("dead zone | National Geographic Society," n.d.).

Plastics, heavy metals, and other chemical pollutants contaminate water and sicken marine life and the food chain in the oceans. Microplastics, tiny plastic particles up to 5mm in size (UNEP, 2017a), are now found in large quantities in ocean water, often close to coastal areas, and are ingested by fishes and marine animals with very uncertain consequences for aquatic health and the environment. Microplastics are used in cosmetics and consumer products and are byproducts of plastic degradation and washing clothes made of synthetic fiber.

Overfishing

Oceans are a food source, with 85 million tons of fish captured in 2018 and an increasingly global food fish consumption of 3.1% from 1961 to 2017 (FAO, 2020). Still, they have suffered from overexploitation due to illegal and unregulated fishing despite international agreements to limit it (FAO, 1995). The FAO monitors and assesses fish stocks and their levels of sustainability and found that the proportion of sustainable fish stocks decreased to 65.8% in 2017 from 90% in 1974. Aquaculture in inland and sea waters has developed a lot since the 1990s to substitute for fisheries, especially in countries like China which has become the dominant producer.

Large Marine Ecosystems (LMEs)

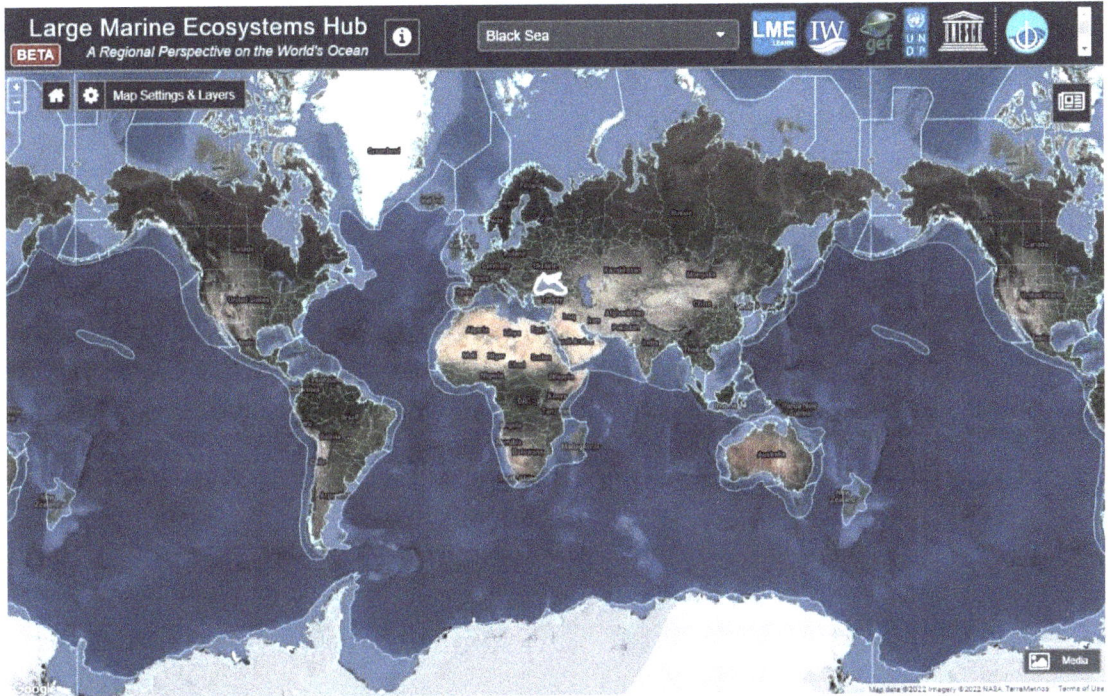

Figure 10.3. Large Marine Ecosystems (LMEs). Source: Large Marine Ecosystems Hub

Large Marine Ecosystems are very productive large maritime coastal areas such as river basins and estuaries throughout the world that provide many nature services such as biodiversity, fish catch, and coastal protection to humans. The UN has identified 66 such LMEs ("Large Marine Ecosystems | IOC UNESCO," n.d.) that produce 3 trillion dollars of economic activity ("Large Marine Ecosystems Hub," n.d.). They are exposed to overfishing, pollution, eutrophication, and acidification.

10.6 The SDG Targets

The Sustainable Development Goal is supported by the following Targets:

Target 14.1: By 2025, prevent and significantly reduce marine pollution of all kinds, in particular from land-based activities, including marine debris and nutrient pollution

Target 14.2: By 2020, sustainably manage and protect marine and coastal ecosystems to avoid significant adverse impacts, including by strengthening their resilience and taking action for their restoration in order to achieve healthy and productive oceans

Target 14.3: Minimize and address the impacts of ocean acidification, including through enhanced scientific cooperation at all levels

Target 14.4: By 2020, effectively regulate harvesting and end overfishing, illegal, unreported, and unregulated fishing, and destructive fishing practices and implement science-based management plans in order to restore fish stocks in the shortest time feasible, at least to levels that can produce maximum sustainable yield as determined by their biological characteristics

Target 14.5: By 2020, conserve at least 10 percent of coastal and marine areas, consistent with national and international law and based on the best available scientific information

Target 14.6: By 2020, prohibit certain forms of fisheries subsidies that contribute to overcapacity and overfishing, eliminate subsidies that contribute to illegal, unreported, and unregulated fishing and refrain from introducing new such subsidies, recognizing that appropriate and effective special and differential treatment for developing and least developed countries should be an integral part of the World Trade Organization fisheries subsidies negotiation

Target 14.7: By 2030, increase the economic benefits to Small Island developing States and least developed countries from the sustainable use of marine resources, including through sustainable management of fisheries, aquaculture, and tourism

Target 14.a: Increase scientific knowledge, develop research capacity and transfer marine technology, taking into account the Intergovernmental Oceanographic Commission Criteria and Guidelines on the Transfer of Marine Technology, in order to improve ocean health and enhance the contribution of marine biodiversity to the development of developing countries, in particular, small island developing States and least developed countries

Target 14.b: Provide access for small-scale artisanal fishers to marine resources and markets

Target 14.c: Enhance the conservation and sustainable use of oceans and their resources by implementing international law as reflected in UNCLOS, which provides the legal framework for the conservation and sustainable use of oceans and their resources, as recalled in paragraph 158 of The Future We Want

10.7 How to Protect the Seas and Oceans

The UNESCO Intergovernmental Oceanographic Commission (UNESCO-IOC, 2022) has a plan to protect the seas and oceans through a set of ten challenges:

- Challenge 1: Understand, document, and address the sources of ocean pollution and contamination

- Challenge 2: Understand, document, and address the stressors on ocean ecosystems and biodiversity

- Challenge 3: Research the role of the ocean in sustainably feeding the world's population

- Challenge 4: Research the equitable and sustainable development of the ocean economy

- Challenge 5: Research the ocean-climate nexus and mitigate, adapt, and build resilience to the effects of climate change

- Challenge 6: Enhance early warning services for all ocean and coastal hazards, community preparedness, and resilience

- Challenge 7: Ensure a sustainable ocean observing system across all ocean basins with accessible, timely, and actionable data and information

- Challenge 8: Develop a comprehensive digital representation of the ocean with free and open access for exploring, discovering, and visualizing ocean conditions

- Challenge 9: Ensure equitable access to data, information, knowledge, and technology across all aspects of ocean science

- Challenge 10: Ensure that people understand the values and services of the ocean for human well-being, culture, and sustainable development

10.8 What Can AI Do to Protect the Seas and Oceans

Prediction

Thanks to remote sensors on satellites and floating devices, AI can help with the prediction of the impact of climate change, such as sea level rise and effects on coastal system erosions, ocean salinity, CO_2 cycle including absorption, and the effect on biodiversity in seas and oceans, fish or specific marine animal population, and coral reefs.

AI could be an early warning system and used for disaster prediction such as underwater earthquakes (Wu et al., 2022), typhoons using satellite imaging and weather data (Su et al., 2020), and tsunamis using ocean sound waves (Gomez and Kadri, 2021).

AI can help predict pollution in the effluents and large marine ecosystems but also from plastic and microplastics in the oceans. AI can help monitor and predict the risk of oil and chemical spills from ship containers and offshore drilling platforms.

AI can help better understand the ocean and the different streams, seabed mapping, the effect of temperature, and the interaction with the atmosphere and ecosystems on seas and oceans. AI can monitor biodiversity and identify marine species and fisheries activities.

Coordination

AI can identify the factors contributing to pollution and contamination of the seas and oceans and prioritize the efforts to protect the marine environment. AI can assist in localizing and identifying ships on the oceans and guide the navigation to ensure the safety of the crew, passengers, shipments, vessels, and the sea.

Optimization

AI can help navigation with computer vision and better geolocation and optimize shipping routes of ships to avoid collisions and minimize travel time with high fuel efficiency. AI can optimize the sustainability of fisheries in some maritime regions, monitor the fish population, and predict its dynamics and replenishment.

Control

AI could control autonomous cargo ships, passenger ships, scientific ships, and even submarines in extreme oceanic areas (at the poles) or provide autopilot assistance to a crew on board for routine navigation or a remote crew on land. A sizeable continuous presence of AI-piloted devices at sea could help understand, monitor, and preserve the oceans. There are, of course, concerns for safety that need to be reviewed (Veitch and Andreas Alsos, 2022).

10.9 Case Studies

Ocean Carbon Storage

Oceans play an essential role in capturing anthropogenic CO_2 emissions (25%, see ("Ocean-Atmosphere CO2 Exchange," 2015)). Zemskova et al. (2022) use a deep learning model to estimate dissolved inorganic carbon (DIC) concentration in the Southern Ocean up to 4km depth. They use satellite surface data as model inputs and DIC estimated by the Biogeochemical Southern Ocean State Estimate (B-SOSE), a data assimilating ocean circulation model, and DIC measured by ships (Lauvset et al., 2021) and Argo floats with biogeochemical sensors ("SOCCOM | Unlocking the Mysteries of the Southern Ocean," n.d.).

They use a U-Net model that combines convolutional neural networks and an LSTM model. They use input features from satellite observations: Horizontal ocean surface velocities, Sea surface height, Zonal and meridional components of 10m wind speed, sea surface temperature (SST), and total heat flux at the ocean surface, Total heat flux, Surface Chlorophyll a concentrations, extrapolated (by neural network) surface CO2 partial pressure.

Some results are shown in Figure 10.4. They obtain time series of DIC concentrations in the Southern pole for different latitudes of the Atlantic, Pacific, and Indian oceans. This helps to follow the trends in DIC and CO2 uptake across time and space and better understand the carbon cycle at the ocean level.

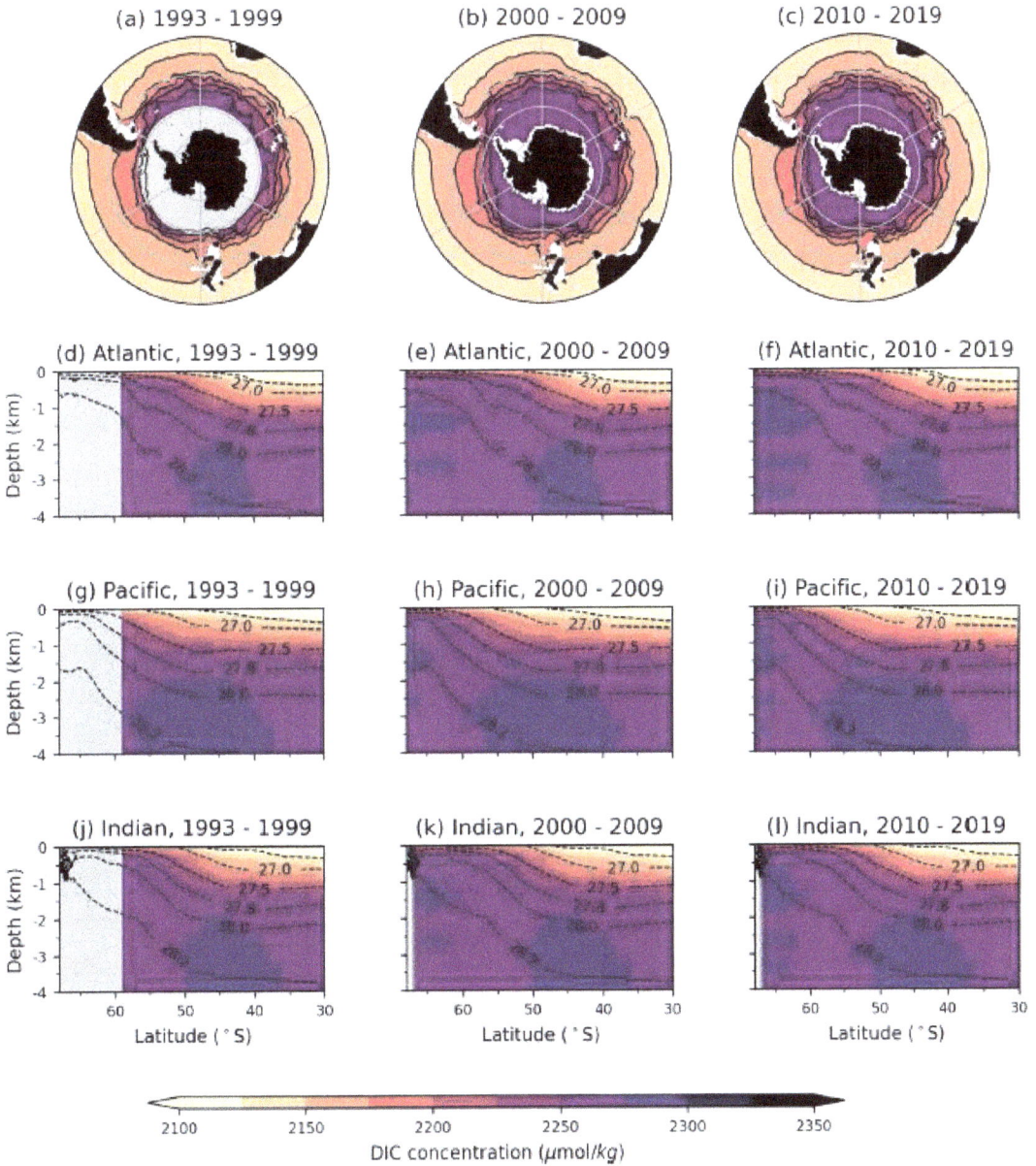

Figure 10.4. Dissolved inorganic carbon (DIC) concentrations computed using our deep learning model. a, d, g, j 1993–1999, (b, e, h, k) 2000–2009, (c, f, i, l) 2010-2019. Source: (Zemskova et al., 2022)

Plastic Pollution

Plastic pollution is a global problem. According to the United Nations, 11 million tons of plastic flow into the ocean annually, possibly tripling by 2040 ("Nations sign up to end global scourge of plastic pollution," 2022).

Garcia-Garin et al. (2021) propose using deep learning to identify floating marine macro-litter (FMML) in aerial images of drones or planes. They focused on the Northwestern Mediterranean sea and used aerial surface water images from drones and aircraft in 2017, 2018, and 2019.

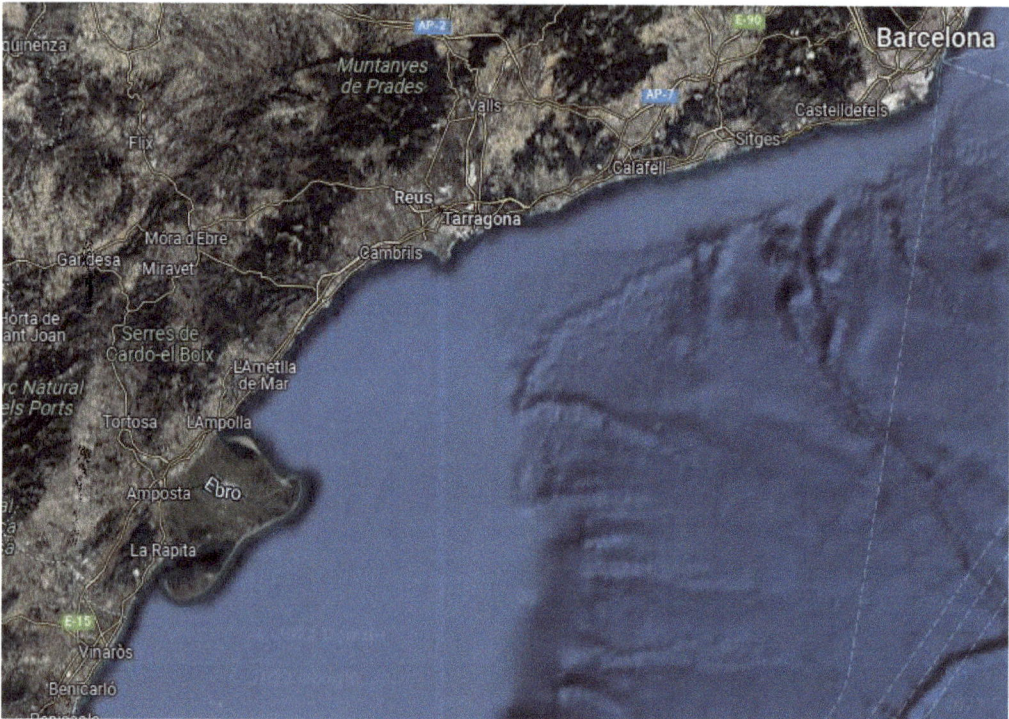

Figure 10.5. Area of the Delta de l'Ebre

Seven hundred ninety-six (796) images were labeled as containing FMML. The images were augmented by shifting, rotating, and zooming to reach 1860 images with litter and 1863 without litter. The authors use a convolutional neural network to classify the images into two categories, FMML or no FMML. The model accuracy is satisfactory at 0.85 for the training sets and 0.79 for the test sets. Errors were made when the sun was reflecting at the same angle as the drones or aircraft (the phenomenon of sunglint).

Fish Tracking

Monitoring and preserving the fish population is vital to maintain a healthy marine ecosystem. Kandimalla et al. (2022) developed a model to detect, classify, and count fish by species using high-resolution visual sonar, underwater video, and deep learning. It is an alternative to more invasive fish tagging or catch-and-release fishing.

High-resolution sonars can help monitor fish behaviors by sending sound pulses and converting the echoes into images. They work well in the dark and murky waters. They include Dual-frequency Identification Sonar (DIDSON) and Adaptive Resolution Imaging Sonar (ARIS). Figure 10.6 shows images produced by a DIDSON system.

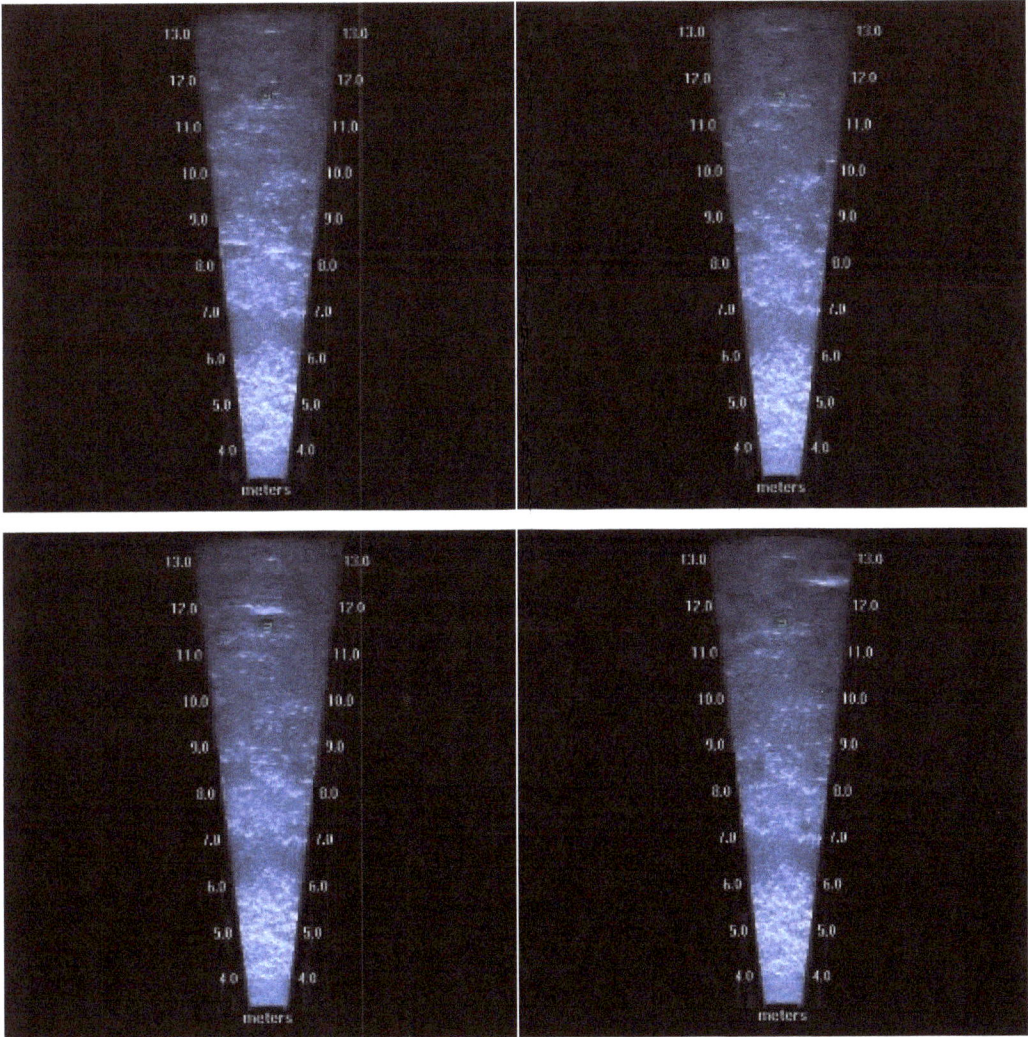

Figure 10.6. Salmon detected by DIDSON. Source: https://www.adfg.alaska.gov/

The authors use 100 hours of high-resolution visual acoustic DIDSON videos captured from the Ocqueoc River in Michigan, USA. These videos are annotated by fish experts who localize and identify the fish species. They also use optical video footage from the Wells Dam fish ladder on the Columbia River in eastern Washington state, USA.

They evaluate three models. Two object detection models, YOLO (you only look once) from Redmon et al. (2016), Mask-RCNN (Mask Region-Based Convolutional Neural Network) from He et al. (2018), and one object tracking library called Norfair from Alori (2020), used in conjunction with an enhanced YOLO model. Object detection assigns a bounding box (for YOLO) or a mask (for Mask-RCNN) and a confidence score to the object detected, such as in Figure 10.7.

Figure 10.7. Detection of a fish with the confidence level

After applying saturation, contrast, hue, and rotation augmentations, they find the models improve their performance, YOLO doing better than Mask-RCNN in terms of mean average precision. They also evaluate the tracking abilities of Norfair with its multiple tracking accuracy (MOTA) and find that it can track fish on videos with high frame rates.

PART IV SUSTAINABLE GROWTH

Chapter 11 | Sustainable Infrastructure, Industrialization, and Innovation

> "Never before in history has innovation offered promise of so much to so many in so short a time."
>
> Bill Gates

11.1 The State of Sustainable Infrastructure, Industrialization, and Innovation

Goal 9 is to "build resilient infrastructure, promote inclusive and sustainable industrialization and foster innovation." ("Goal 9 | Department of Economic and Social Affairs").

Sustainable Infrastructure, Industrialization, and Innovation Trend

Sustainable infrastructure

Infrastructures such as transportation, water and sanitation, irrigation, electricity, and communication are essential for economic growth, health, and prosperity. Without transportation, people might not be able to access job opportunities or trade goods. Without water and sanitation, the health risk is high for the population exposed to communicable diseases and infections. Without irrigation, agriculture is very reliant on rainfalls and can be disrupted by drought. Without electricity, machinery cannot operate, lightning is limited, and people are kept in low-productivity occupations. Without communication, people are isolated and might not have access to information and economic opportunities.

Still, many of the world's population does not have access to these basic infrastructures. According to Rozenberg and Fay (2019), one billion people do not have access to electricity, 663 million do not have access to contaminant-protected drinking water sources, 2.4 billion people lack modern sanitation facilities, and 2.4 billion people are more than 2 km away from a road. They often live in developing countries in Africa and Asia but can be found on all continents.

The capital cost of these infrastructures is often high and has to be paid upfront, while the returns are spread over the long run and are not always privately monetized but can be in the form of social returns. The total annual cost to develop infrastructure in low and middle-income countries is estimated by Rozenberg and Fay (2019) to be between 640 billion dollars (2% of GDP) to 2.7 trillion dollars (8.2% of GDP). Sources of capital might not always be available, especially in the poorest countries and countries that have had financial difficulties in the past or are not well-managed economically. Beyond capital, operation and maintenance costs must be covered directly with user fees or with general taxes. This makes it challenging to build infrastructure in the poorest and most areas in a country.

In addition to the cost, infrastructure needs to be sustainable and resilient to climate change and natural disasters. For instance, electricity production should not rely on fossil fuels such as coal that produce a lot of CO_2 but favor renewable sources such as wind or solar (Chapter 8). According to the OECD ("Strategic Policies for Sustainable Infrastructure - OECD," n.d.), 60% of greenhouse gas emissions are due to infrastructure. Water infrastructure should withstand drought and minimize leakage and waste. Roads and public transportation should be resilient to flooding and other extreme weather events.

A recent trend is investing in green infrastructure in addition to the traditional "gray" infrastructure (Browder et al., 2019). This means using Nature-based solutions such as planting trees and plants to cool cities, preserving Watersheds and Wetlands to improve water quality and filter wastewater, and preserving ecosystems such as coral reefs and Mangrove forests to protect coastal areas from storms and erosion.

Industrialization

Developed countries are the most industrialized ones. Their productivity and high standard of living have benefited from a higher level of capital accumulation and technological progress. This has been the path of Great Britain, Europe, North America, and more recently, East Asia and China, which have become industrial powerhouses. These countries underwent several industrial revolutions led by water and steam power, steel, oil and gas, electricity, mass production, and electronics and information technology.

Lower-income countries tend to be agricultural economies with relatively low productivity, with many small farmers and rural workers. The traditional development path was to use cheap labor to develop labor-intensive light industries such as textiles and then progressively go up the value chain, invest in more infrastructure such as energy and transportation, and produce more sophisticated goods and services. Countries like Turkey, Thailand, and Vietnam have followed this growth path. It is unclear if this traditional path is still open as the old-style industrialization is energy and resource intensive and might not be sustainable.

Innovation

Innovation drives technological progress and contributes to higher productivity. It is usually associated with more R&D investments (public and private), a better-educated workforce, and creative destruction, where new firms innovate and replace older and less innovative firms. The most developed countries tend to be the most innovative, but middle-income countries such as China and India are also very resourceful in manufacturing and services.

11.2 The SDG Targets

Eight targets should contribute to reaching SDG 9:

Target 9.1: Develop quality, reliable, sustainable, and resilient infrastructure, including regional and transborder infrastructure, to support economic development and human well-being, with a focus on affordable and equitable access for all

Target 9.2: Promote inclusive and sustainable industrialization and, by 2030, significantly raise the industry's share of employment and gross domestic product, in line with national circumstances, and double its share in least developed countries

Target 9.3: Increase the access of small-scale industrial and other enterprises, in particular in developing countries, to financial services, including affordable credit, and their integration into value chains and markets

Target 9.4: By 2030, upgrade infrastructure and retrofit industries to make them sustainable, with increased resource-use efficiency and greater adoption of clean and environmentally sound technologies and industrial processes, with all countries taking action in accordance with their respective capabilities

Target 9.5: Enhance scientific research, upgrade the technological capabilities of industrial sectors in all countries, in particular developing countries, including, by 2030, encouraging innovation and substantially increasing the number of research and development workers per 1 million people and public and private research and development spending

Target 9.a: Facilitate sustainable and resilient infrastructure development in developing countries through enhanced financial, technological, and technical support to African countries, least developed countries, landlocked developing countries, and small island developing States

Target 9.b: Support domestic technology development, research, and innovation in developing countries, including by ensuring a conducive policy environment for, inter alia, industrial diversification and value addition to commodities

Target 9.c: Significantly increase access to information and communications technology and strive to provide universal and affordable access to the Internet in least developed countries by 2020

11.3 How to Improve Innovation and Sustainable Infrastructure

Infrastructure projects are expensive, and financing is not always available, especially for the poorest countries. Even in developed countries like the United States, financing infrastructure is challenging as roads, bridges, and airports are aging and need upgrading.

Government fiscal situations have worsened after the pandemic, and even though investments in infrastructure have a positive net economic contribution, there is not much appetite to use massive public funds or debts to pay for them. In low-income countries, borrowing is not an option as domestic savings are insufficient and foreign lenders might be concerned by the higher credit risk.

Smaller-scale projects might be more viable and easier to finance. Public-private partnership projects could be attractive but are unlikely to be sufficient to meet all the investment needs, as PPP will pick the best projects in terms of risk and returns first. Projects that give investors some equity or convertible debt might also be an option.

Infrastructure projects also need to transfer know-how and technology to the local population so that more similar projects can be developed domestically or in partnership. By co-designing the projects and providing co-benefits, they will be more likely to succeed and have a meaningful impact on the country. Lema et al. (2022) give insightful examples of renewable electrification and sustainable industrialization.

Regarding innovation, scientific innovation, and technological capabilities, local institutions such as universities, research labs, and national or regional agencies should be responsible for developing expertise and building partnerships with institutions of more advanced countries to collaborate on research and train local experts, scientists, engineers and technical staff in all fields relevant to economic and human development.

More advanced countries could help finance scholarships, fellowships, research grants, exchange programs to finance domestic and international researchers, and scientific and technical projects in less developed countries with the ultimate goal of building local capacities for research and innovation that would meet the local needs and interests.

11.4 What Can AI Do to Improve Innovation and Sustainable Infrastructure

Prediction

AI can help predict future demand for infrastructure based on population, economic activity, location and geography, urban development, and other variables. AI can predict the cost, schedule, risk, and environmental impacts of such projects, financing costs, and returns on investment. AI can monitor and assess the quality of all the inputs involved in the infrastructure project.

AI can be used with sensors in predictive maintenance and quality control to predict failure and risk of operating infrastructure. The infrastructure could be a power grid, a port, a water treatment plant, and a public transportation network. AI can predict daily usage, required capacity, real-time demand, and revenues.

Coordination

AI can help coordinate infrastructure projects, the resources, and the people they require. AI can help create the documentation, business and technical specifications, and planning for all the components of a project, including its supply chain.

Once the infrastructure is completed, an AI can help in operations to ensure demand is met, quality of service is adequate, and any technical and operational issues are quickly resolved. AI can also coordinate communications with the local authorities, regulators, and end-users.

Optimization

AI can help optimize operations, allocate resources efficiently, and ensure the sustainability and resilience of the infrastructure. For instance, an AI can optimize the volume of water flowing into a power plant to minimize environmental impact in downstream rivers, the amount of fossil fuel to produce electricity in a grid, and the number of vehicles on the road to limit greenhouse gas emissions.

Control

AI can operate autonomous drones and a network of sensors to inspect quality and safety in infrastructure. It can control the collection of user fees through automatic systems such as reading vehicle plate numbers to collect congestion charges or fees for toll bridges.

AI can control an autonomous public transportation system or a network of decentralized power producers and make decisions on maintenance, lengths of operations, safety, and security. AI can operate marketplaces so users and producers can clear and execute contracts in real-time.

AI can operate digital twins of infrastructure to simulate and anticipate issues that could occur on the project. AI could control the infrastructure directly with its digital twin. AI could also exchange information with other market participants and regulators in an emergency.

An AI could oversee the operations of all infrastructures in a particular domain (e.g., energy, health, roads and transportation, communication) to deliver the service efficiently and sustainably. An AI could coordinate the traffic of autonomous vehicles to minimize congestion or a network of charging stations to reduce disruption to car owners.

11.5 Case Studies

Infrastructure Inspection and Monitoring

Spencer et al. (2019) look at AI applications for infrastructure (roads and bridges, tunnels, buildings, dams). These tasks are even more critical today as many infrastructures are aging and have passed their initial lifetimes. They are divided into inspection and monitoring.

Inspection applications

Damage detection can be done on any surface, such as concrete, steel, or asphalt, to look for cracks, spalling, delamination, fatigue, corrosion, and other issues. Convolutional neural networks can be used to classify images as evidence of damage or not and for change detection. Object detection models such as R-CNN (Girshick et al., 2014) can be used to locate cracks in an image. Mask R-CNN (He et al., 2018) can perform semantic segmentation and precisely delineate the damage in an image.

Image classification and semantic segmentation can also be applied to structural component recognition to identify components of a structure and facilitate a more specialized inspection work targeted to the particular segment. Damage detection with structure-level consistency combines the two approaches.

Monitoring applications

Traditional structure health monitoring is done with contact sensors and provides measurements that inform the state of the structure. Computer vision is now a non-contact alternative for static applications and dynamic applications.

Digital image correlation (DIC), which compares pixel changes between images, is a widespread technique for static monitoring. Displacement (an object is moved) and strain (an object is deformed) can be analyzed with DIC.

Figure 11.1. Camera drone

For dynamic applications, video cameras (fixed or on drones) capture images of displacements, mode shapes, and frequencies of a structure and different points of the system. Examples of applications are bridge structures and load estimations.

AI for Predictive Maintenance

Shin et al. (2021) look at the use of AI in the predictive maintenance of wind farms, especially at the benefits of AI assistance to human inspectors. The task is to perform bearing fault diagnostics of wind turbines.

Figure 11.2. Wind turbine

The authors selected 2301 endoscopy images of rolling-element bearing labeled by experts. An AI model using CNNs was developed to classify the images with or without abnormalities of the bearing. The AI model is then used to assist a group of 54 experts (20 specialists and 34 generalists).

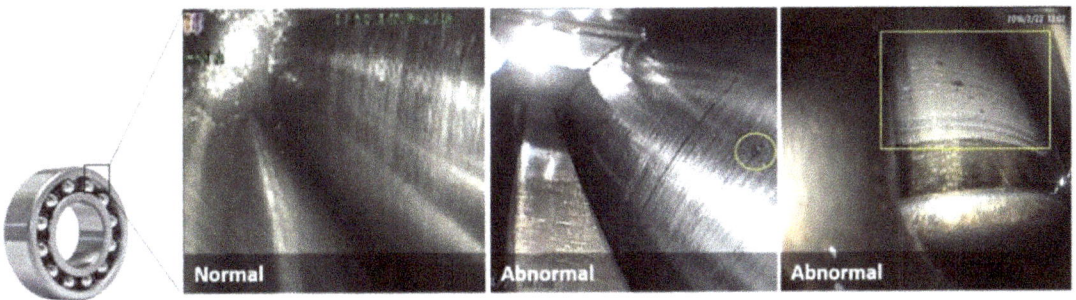

Figure 11.3. Example of endoscope images of bearing. Source: (Shin et al., 2021)

They look at three key metrics to evaluate the tasks: Specificity (True Negative/(True Negative + False Positive)), Sensitivity (True Positive/(True Positive + False Negative)), and Time Efficiency (Number of images in the task/Completion time). Specificity measures out of all normal bearings; what proportion was correctly classified as normal? Sensitivity measures out of all abnormal bearings; what proportion was correctly classified as abnormal?

Experts can give their judgments on a series of images during two tasks with or without knowing the result of the AI system (AI assistance). The authors find that AI assistance improves the specificity of both groups (specialists and generalists), more for the generalist group, and enhances sensitivity only slightly. AI also improves Time Efficiency, especially with generalists.

Scientific Innovation with AI

AI can help innovation by helping the intuition of scientists. Davies et al. (2021) provide examples in mathematics where an AI model (a supervised machine learning model) generates mathematical data $X(z)$ and $Y(z)$, where z are random variables, and finds a pattern $Y(z)=f(X(z))$ between these data that the mathematician can use as conjecture and prove it as a theorem. The AI can also guide the mathematician with attribution techniques such as gradient saliency that calculates the input sensitivity df/dX of the relationships between the input and output variables.

Topology

The authors conjecture a relationship between hyperbolic and algebraic invariants of a knot, simple closed curves in the 3D space of real numbers (Figure 11.4).

Name ⬍	Picture ⬍	Alexander–Briggs–Rolfsen ⬍	Dowker–Thistlethwaite ⬍	Dowker notation ⬍	Conway notation ⬍	crossinglist ⬍
Unknot		0_1	0a1	—	—	0
Trefoil knot		3_1	3a1	4 6 2	[3]	123:123
Figure-eight knot		4_1	4a1	4 6 8 2	[22]	1234:2143 1231\4324
Cinquefoil knot		5_1	5a2	6 8 10 2 4	[5]	12345:12345
Three-twist knot		5_2	5a1	4 8 10 2 6	[32]	12345:12543 1231\452354
Stevedore knot		6_1	6a3	4 8 12 10 2 6	[42]	123456:216543 1231\45632654
6_2 knot		6_2	6a2	4 8 10 12 2 6	[312]	123456:234165 1231\45632456
6_3 knot		6_3	6a1	4 8 10 2 12 6	[2112]	123456:236145 1231\45642356 1231\45236456

Figure 11.4. Example of knots and their representations. Source: Wikipedia

Geometric invariants include the Volume, the Chern–Simons index, and Meridional translation, and Algebraic invariants are the Signature and the Jones polynomial. They define the slope as the real value of the ratio of meridional translation μ and the longitudinal translation λ and find a relationship between the slope(K), signature σ(K), volume vol(K), and the injectivity radius inj(K).

Representation theory

In representation theory, pairs of permutations are represented by directed graphs, the Bruhat intervals (that follow from the Bruhat ordering of permutations), and Kazhdan–Lusztig (KL) polynomials. AI can help find a relationship between these two representations. The authors find that "every Bruhat interval admits a canonical hypercube decomposition along its extremal reflections, from which the KL polynomial is directly computable." and propose the conjecture that "the KL polynomial of an unlabelled Bruhat interval can be calculated using the previous formula with any hypercube decomposition."

Chapter 12 | Sustainable Economy

> "Sustainable development is the development that meets the needs of the present without compromising the ability of future generations to meet their own needs."
>
> Gro Harlem Brundtland

12.1 The State of the Sustainable Economy

Goal 12 is to "ensure sustainable consumption and production patterns." ("Goal 12 | Department of Economic and Social Affairs").

Sustainable Economy Trend

Following One Planet Network and UNEP (2018), we group sustainable consumption and production into three categories: resource efficiency, environment, and human well-being.

Resource efficiency

Economic growth can be unsustainable if the production and consumption of goods and services deplete natural resources and use excess non-renewable materials. They include earth minerals and metal ores, fossil fuels, and groundwater and are used for energy production (Chapter 8), transportation, construction, manufacturing, food, and agriculture (Chapter 2). Some renewable materials, such as timber, can also be exploited in an unsustainable way.

People consume a lot of single-use materials that end up in landfills and beyond. For instance, only a minority of plastics produced are ever recycled, and countries like China now refuse to purchase used plastics for recycling. Plastics are now found in the oceans and the food chain. In general, manufacturers are not responsible for the complete life cycle of their products, so some are trying to make their products fully recyclable. Special products that contain heavy metals, such as car batteries, need special handling and cannot be discarded in landfills.

According to UNEP (2017b), cities produce between 7 to 10 billion tons per year of urban waste, including 2 billion tons of municipal solid waste. So it is more than one ton per person per year. Higher-income countries generate more waste per capita than lower-income countries, but the latter increase their share with a rising population and economic growth. Not all municipal solid waste is collected, and even less is recycled.

Environment

Economic growth can be unsustainable if the production and consumption of goods and services generate too much waste and air pollution with greenhouse gas emissions and microparticles, chemicals, and nitrates in soils, watersheds, lakes, and rivers that have adverse effects on human health and the environment (see Chapters 7, 9, 10).

Private modes of transportation such as automobiles cause congestion and air pollution in cities (see Chapter 8) and are very energy inefficient when only one person commutes in her car. Most cars are idled most of the time, and new car models come out every year though cars can last one to two decades thanks to their improved quality. Public transportation, car sharing, bicycles, and electric vehicles would be more sustainable alternatives.

We have seen that fossil fuels are a source of greenhouse gas emissions, and their consumption needs to be curbed to limit their impact on climate change (Chapter 7). Dependency on fossil fuels can also cause geopolitical risks in consumer countries and distort the economies of producer countries, such as a Dutch disease where other sectors of the economy are not competitive.

Excessive energy use by buildings is also wasteful. Buildings that are not well-isolated and poorly designed can require too much heating in cold seasons and too much air conditioning in warm seasons. Cities that are not well-designed with limited parks, water pounds, and trees for shade can be sweltering in the summer and increase energy consumption and even mortality in poorer countries.

In agriculture, much land and water are used to raise and feed livestock (Chapter 2). Deforestation continues in some regions to expand farming (Chapter 9). 70% of antibiotics are used for livestock and not for humans risking antibiotic resistance. On the consumption side, an estimated 40% of food is not-consumed and is simply wasted. Some foods and diets, such as consuming beef, have a more significant environmental impact than other diets based on other sources of proteins. With a growing world population, agriculture needs to limit its environmental impact on air, water, land, and public health (Chapter 3).

Gross Domestic Product, 2020
Gross domestic product adjusted for price changes over time (inflation) and expressed in US-Dollars

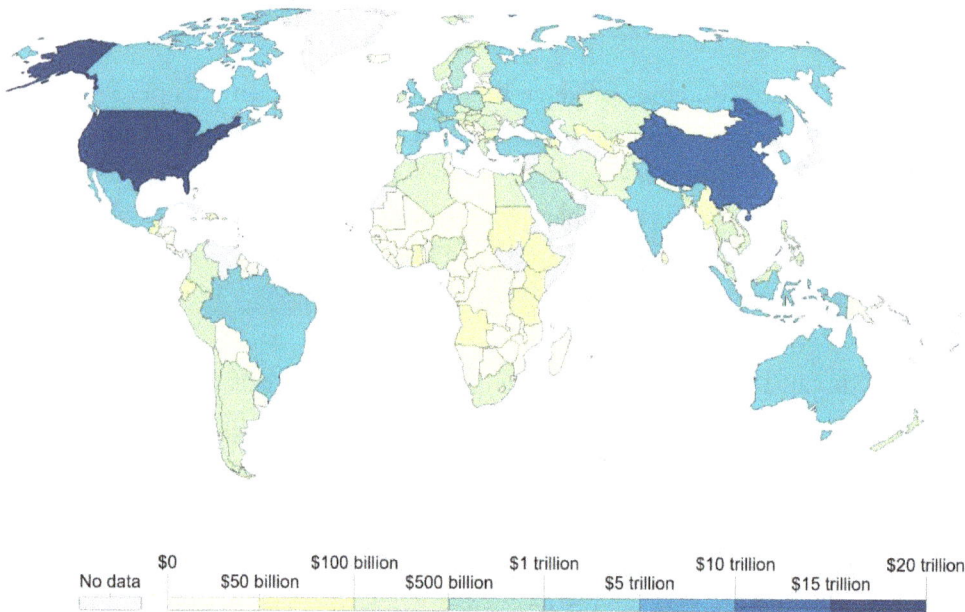

Source: World Bank and OECD

OurWorldInData.org/economic-growth · CC BY

Figure 12.1. Gross Domestic Product, 2020

Human well-being

Human well-being matters because it is the condition for sustainable living, work, and consumption. Humans cannot live and work in unhealthy conditions or consume products that make them sick. Human well-being includes improving health (Chapter 3), providing decent jobs, and reducing poverty, hunger, and inequalities (Chapters 1, 2, and Chapter 5). It is also challenging to convince people to aim for a sustainable economy that has a longer time horizon when the short-term basic human needs are not met.

12.2 The SDG Targets

Eleven targets have been defined to reach the sustainable economy goal (SDG 12):

Target 12.1: Implement the 10-year framework of programmes on sustainable consumption and production, all countries taking action, with developed countries taking the lead, taking into account the development and capabilities of developing countries

Target 12.2: By 2030, achieve the sustainable management and efficient use of natural resources

Target 12.3: By 2030, halve per capita global food waste at the retail and consumer levels and reduce food losses along production and supply chains, including post-harvest losses

Target 12.4: By 2020, achieve the environmentally sound management of chemicals and all wastes throughout their life cycle, in accordance with agreed international frameworks, and significantly reduce their release to air, water, and soil in order to minimize their adverse impacts on human health and the environment

Target 12.5: By 2030, substantially reduce waste generation through prevention, reduction, recycling, and reuse

Target 12.6: Encourage companies, especially large and transnational companies, to adopt sustainable practices and to integrate sustainability information into their reporting cycle

Target 12.7: Promote public procurement practices that are sustainable, in accordance with national policies and priorities

Target 12.8: By 2030, ensure that people everywhere have the relevant information and awareness for sustainable development and lifestyles in harmony with nature

Target 12.a: Support developing countries to strengthen their scientific and technological capacity to move towards more sustainable patterns of consumption and production

Target 12.b: Develop and implement tools to monitor sustainable development impacts for sustainable tourism that creates jobs and promotes local culture and products

Target 12.c: Rationalize inefficient fossil-fuel subsidies that encourage wasteful consumption by removing market distortions, in accordance with national circumstances, to include restructuring taxation and phasing out those harmful subsidies where they exist. This would reflect their environmental impacts, taking fully into account the specific needs and conditions of developing countries and minimizing the possible adverse impacts on their development in a manner that protects the poor and the affected communities.

12.3 How to Make the Economy More Sustainable

Achieving the targets would help make the economy more sustainable, but countries, governments, local authorities, businesses, and consumers need incentives to reach them. Measurement tools such as the Sustainable Consumption and Production Hotspots Analysis Tool (SCP-HAT) ("SCP Hotspots Analysis," n.d.) are valuable and necessary to account for progress towards the targets. They might, however, be insufficient. Partnerships and technical assistance between sustainable cities and cities on the path to sustainability could help share and spread best practices. New laws, regulations, and enforcement tools could also be required to improve resource efficiency, the environment, and human well-being.

Resource Efficiency

Circular Economy

Best practices of a circular economy can be learned. The European Commission has a New Circular Economy Action Plan (European Commission, 2020) to encourage making sustainable products the norm, empowering consumers, and focusing on sectors with high potential for recycling, such as electronics and information and communications technology (ICT), electric vehicle batteries, packaging, plastics, food, and textiles.

This also means that imported products to the EU will likely have to comply with these new norms and spread best practices to exporting countries to the EU. Sustainable circular supply chains can be adopted by companies and trading partners of the EU.

Sharing Economy

Some cities and communities (Chapter 6) are developing a sharing economy in transportation, lodging, and household items. Bicycles, cars, rooms, and power tools can be shared and will reduce the need for multiple people to purchase the same things. Shared ownership in a cooperative could also be a solution, especially when some individuals or households do not have the financial resources to be the sole owner.

Public Goods

Sustainable infrastructures (Chap 11) can provide public (or shared) goods and services such as roads, bridges, water sanitation, and public transportation that can benefit a community without replicating private costs. They do, however, require upfront capital investments that are not always easy to finance.

Environment

We have discussed in Chapters 9 and 10 initiatives that should benefit the environment. We highlight three sets of solutions that could help make the economy more sustainable.

Nature-based Solutions

Nature-based solutions (World Bank, 2022) are viable for coastal area and forest restorations, ecosystem protections, and sustainable agriculture. They are also easier to implement in low-income countries as they require less capital investment and technology than traditional engineering alternatives such as seawalls or offshore breakwaters.

For cities and communities, nature-based solutions have been attractive to address excess urbanization, pollution, disaster, climate change, and low quality of life (United Nations, 2021b). In low-income countries, large rural-urban migrations are causing many problems for the environment and the well-being of vulnerable populations in and around the cities, and nature-based solutions could alleviate some of the urbanization issues such as wastewater, air quality, and urban heat.

Sustainable Business Practices

Businesses must develop more sustainable business practices and account for their environmental footprint. This also means more disclosure to investors and stakeholders. The Financial Stability Board is working on Climate-related Financial Disclosures with the Task Force on Climate-related Financial Disclosures ("Task Force on Climate-Related Financial Disclosures | TCFD)," n.d.). Cities and governments must also adopt greater transparency and be open about their collaborations with businesses and communities.

Natural Capital Accounting

In his biodiversity report (Dasgupta, 2022), the economist Partha Dasgupta recommended to "(i) ensure that our demands on Nature do not exceed its supply, and that we increase Nature's supply relative to its current level; (ii) change our measures of economic success to help to guide us on a more sustainable path; and (iii) transform our institutions and systems – in particular our finance and education systems – to enable these changes and sustain them for future generations."

His work has inspired natural capital accounting to measure economic growth, natural assets, and their returns in the form of biodiversity and ecosystem services more accurately. The UN and the EU are leading the efforts to mainstream natural capital accounting and have so far experimented with this approach in Brazil, China, India, Mexico, and South Africa ("Natural Capital Accounting and Valuation of Ecosystem Services Project," n.d.).

Human Well-being

Human well-being is affected by poverty (Chapter 1), hunger (Chapter 2), health (Chapter 3), education (Chapter 4), work and inequalities (Chapter 5), and their environment (previous section). Any sustainability policy would need to maintain and improve human well-being to be acceptable to the population. Protecting the environment and addressing climate change cannot overlook social justice issues and need, for instance, to look at the impact on local communities, including indigenous populations, and the financial impact on any environmental policy such as carbon taxes, phasing out of fossil fuel subsidies, or more stringent energy-saving standards on the poorest households.

12.4 What Can AI Make the Economy More Sustainable

Prediction

AI can help predict demand more accurately to limit waste and unsold products. AI can help predict resources used and wasted along a supply chain from production to final consumption. With sensors, AI can measure and predict environmental impacts, pollution and contamination risk, and greenhouse gas emissions in a business process (agriculture, manufacturing, distribution, transportation).

AI can help predict waste generation and circularity potentials of materials, energy, and goods produced and sold. AI can help predict the environmental costs of each production step and compare them with the economic costs and benefits. AI can also be used internally within an organization to track the environmental impact of the product cycle accurately.

AI can help measure and predict depletion and unsustainable extraction of natural resources, exploitation of biodiversity, land, soil, and water, and ecosystem services such as a tropical forest, a glacier, or a large marine ecosystem, possibly at a very granular level.

AI could enhance the accuracy of natural capital accounting by measuring natural assets and their services more accurately and on time using, for instance, satellite imaging and sensors. AI would complement the role of markets that do not fully account for nature degradation and natural resource depletion.

Coordination

AI can identify the factors influencing the sustainability of production and consumption and help coordinate the efforts to manage or regulate them. AI can analyze the complete life cycle of a product and identify the parts in the value chain where more sustainability efforts can be made. Zero waste policy for some products can be coordinated by AI so that recycling is done efficiently and is widely adopted and enforced.

Optimization

AI can help optimize production and distribution to minimize the environmental impact and greenhouse gas emissions. AI can help price all resources accurately to reflect their use's unsustainability or negative effect. AI can help optimize and regulate the use of common goods, such as allocating quotas to fisheries or forest exploitation.

Control

AI can control and manage a supply chain to make it more sustainable, switching to more material or energy-efficient suppliers and reducing some inputs and even production if the environmental impact is too high. For instance, if water becomes scarce because of a drought, an AI could decide to limit the size of livestock or pick more drought-resistant types of crops.

On the consumption side, AI can help manage demand more efficiently. For instance, shifting energy demand by production facilities or increasing energy storage when energy is cheap or produced by renewable energy, limiting the use of air conditioning in buildings and offices when energy demand is very high, or adjusting prices to favor more sustainable modes of consumption (higher prices for single-use or non-recyclable items).

12.5 Case Studies

Supply-Chain Management

Toorajipour et al. (2021) survey the literature on AI in supply chain management. It is divided into marketing, logistics, production, and supply chain.

Marketing

In marketing, AI and machine learning are applied to sales forecasting, management and promotion, pricing, market and customer segmentation, consumer behavior, marketing decision support, direct and industrial marketing, design of a new product, and product life-cycle management.

Logistics

AI is applied to container terminal operations and management, inbound logistic processes, logistic system automation, lot-sizing, and logistic workflow in logistics.

Production

In production, AI has helped with assembly line automation, production monitoring and forecasting, scheduling, integrated production management, general manufacturing, quality control, improvement and monitoring, product line optimization, prototyping, and manufacturing of low-volume production.

Supply chain

In the supply chain, AI is applied to demand forecasting, facility location, supplier selection, network design, risk management, inventory management, crisis management, global value chains, supply chain process management, integration and planning, and maintenance.

Battery

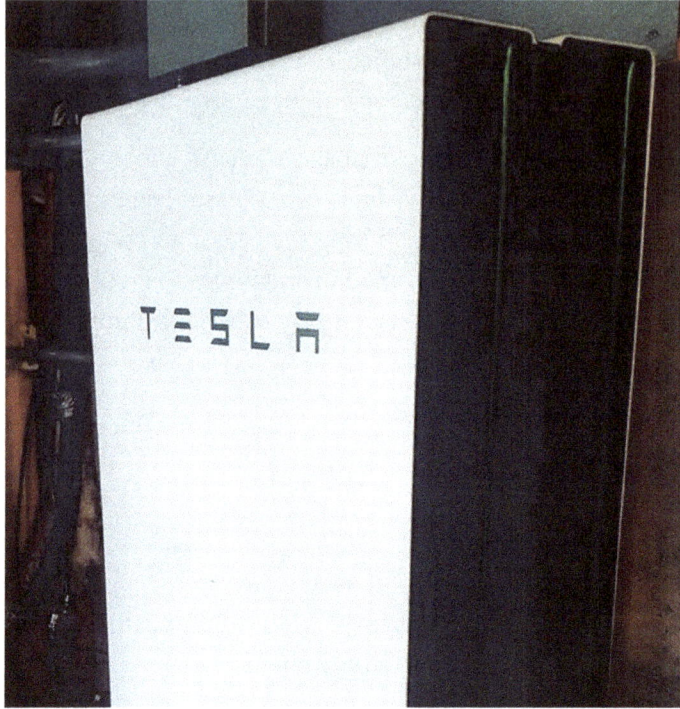

Figure 12.2. Tesla battery. Source: Photo by Greg Johnstone. – U.S. Department of Energy from the United States

Storing clean energy is essential for the energy transition. Lombardo et al. (2022) review AI applied to battery research, in particular to the improvement of Lithium Ion batteries (LIBs) and to look for alternatives to LIBs.

Materials design and synthesis

One way to improve batteries is to research new materials for the electrodes (the terminals of the battery) and the electrolyte (the medium containing ions to conduct electricity). Electrodes can be oxide-based or silicate-based or can contain different active materials. They can have different characteristics: discharge capacity, capacity retention, volume change, Coulombic efficiency, voltage profile, or redox potential. Electrolytes can be of different types and are investigated for their ion conductivity and migration energy.

High throughput experiments or simulated data generate data, and AI maps the material characteristics to specific targets such as migration energy, mechanical property, discharge capacity, and charge efficiency. AI can also help to accelerate molecular and large-scale atomic dynamic simulations and computations.

Application to an electrode and cell manufacturing

The manufacturing of batteries involves complex operations from the electrode production with mixing, coating, drying, cutting, compressing, shaping, assembling, housing, contacting, and finishing, affecting the end-result performance, quality, and cost.

AI is used to map the manufacturing parameters to these results by predicting the properties of electrodes, cells, and the final product. The AI model can then be used to optimize the manufacturing process.

Materials and electrode architecture characterization

Materials and electrode X-ray and electron tomography images, spectroscopic, and diffraction profiles can be analyzed by AI to characterize their structures, crystallography, and properties. This helps improve the understanding of the mechanisms involved in the synthesis reactions and battery operations, particularly the link between the material microstructure and electrochemical performance.

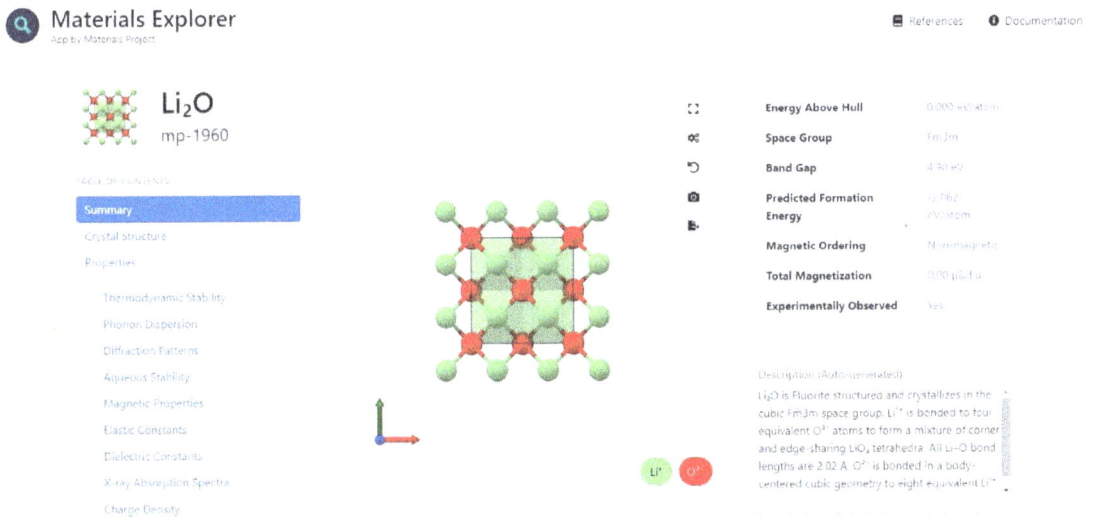

Figure 12.3. Properties of Li2O from the Material Project

Application to battery cell diagnosis and prognosis

AI can be applied for battery cell diagnosis and prognosis. For electric vehicles, this information needs to be very reliable for the safety and security of the driver and passengers. With sufficient data, an AI model can help predict the performance of a battery cell. It is crucial to predict aging, performance degradation, end-of-life, and risk of failure. AI algorithms can be developed based on electrochemical real-time characteristics and sensor input data.

Waste Management

AI can help detect and manage waste with computer vision models. Majchrowska et al. (2022) introduce two new benchmark datasets for waste management: detect-waste and classify-waste and a two-stage detector for litter localization and classification.

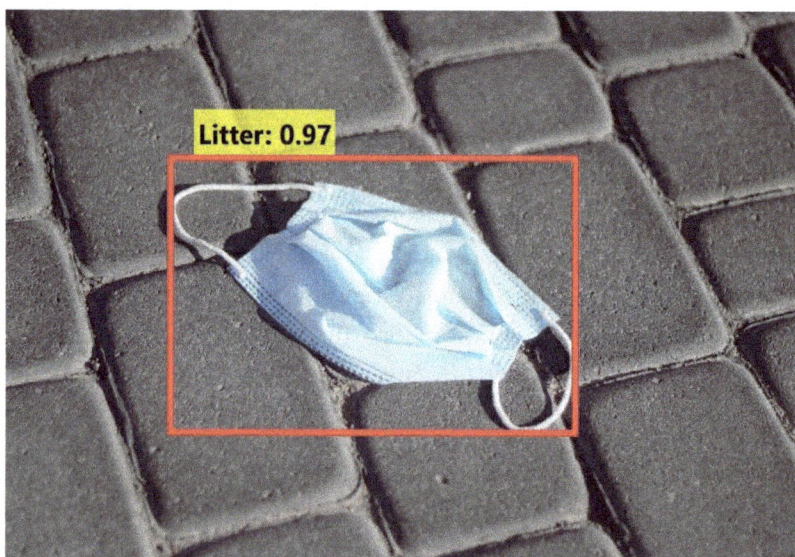

Figure 12.4. Litter detection with a confidence score

The benchmark datasets were built from publicly available waste datasets with proper classifications, labeling, and bounded box annotations for object detection. The detect-waste dataset has 28,000 images, with 40,000 objects appearing indoors, outdoors, or underwater. The classify-waste dataset has eight classes: bio, glass, metals and plastic, non-recyclable, other, paper, unknown, and background.

They ran three models for litter detection and found that EfficientDet (Tan et al., 2020) performs better than R-CNN (Ren et al., 2016) and DETR, a detection model with transformers (Carion et al., 2020). For classification, they use the EfficientNet model (Tan and Le, 2020). They evaluate their detection models with mean Average Precision (mAP), which measures how well the model detects a true litter with a correct label in an image, and the classification model with the F1-score, a combination of precision and recall.

Chapter 13 | Peace, Justice, and Institutions

"Peace does not rest in the charters and covenants alone. It lies in the hearts and minds of all people. So let us not rest all our hopes on parchment and on paper, let us strive to build peace, a desire for peace, a willingness to work for peace in the hearts and minds of all of our people. I believe that we can. I believe the problems of human destiny are not beyond the reach of human beings."

John F. Kennedy

13.1 The State of Peace, Justice, and Institutions

Goal 16 is to "promote peaceful and inclusive societies for sustainable development, provide access to justice for all and build effective, accountable and inclusive institutions at all levels." ("Goal 16 | Department of Economic and Social Affairs").

Peace

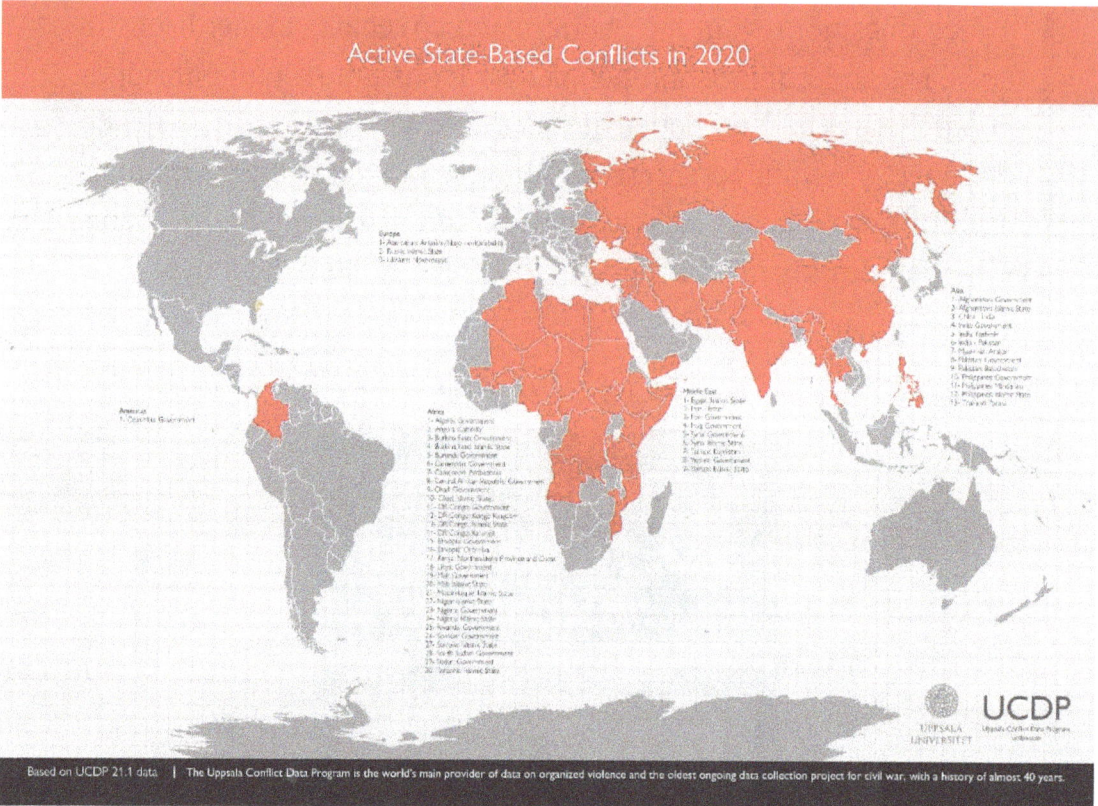

Figure 13.1. Active-based conflicts in 2020. Source: UCDP

Armed Conflicts

Armed conflicts are a widespread source of poverty, hunger, and poor health worldwide, especially in Subsaharan Africa. Armed conflicts can be between States, regions, ethnic groups, religious groups, governments, and rebels. They often force civilian populations to flee their homes to seek safety. Houses, villages, towns, infrastructures, and livestock are destroyed, working in agricultural fields becomes too dangerous, and markets are no longer functioning.

What causes armed conflicts?

The causes of armed conflicts are diverse. We can review the armed conflicts of the 20th and 21st centuries:

We can see several causes of war:

- Civil war:

  Political competition can lead to a civil war if a group wants to seize power with violence and replace the incumbent government. If the group feels it is not fairly represented or has no voice in the political process, that its interests are threatened (expropriation, over taxation, resource allocation away from the group, lack of access to scarce resources), or it perceives the government is illegitimate, biased, or very corrupt.

- Inter-countries war:

  A country can wage war against another nation if it feels it is in its interest. The attacker can search, for instance, to defend its territory, gain more territory, protect or access economic and natural resources, and support or improve its geopolitical position or security. The political or economic advantage will be weighted against some economic, political, and human costs.

  A country can act for prestige, to maintain its reputation as a great power, or to correct some past perceived injustice and regain its reputation. A war can compensate for weaknesses in other areas, such as political stability or economic strength. An armed conflict could also result from some geo-political or economic conflicts.

  A war can be offensive (a country attacks), defensive (a country defends itself), or preemptive (a nation attacks before getting attacked). A war could be waged to defend an ally if it is triggered by a defense treaty or a military alliance such as NATO. Article 4 of the North Atlantic Treaty is called when "the territorial integrity, political independence or security of any of the parties is threatened."

- Proxy war:

  Two countries or groups can wage war on behalf of other countries, usually more powerful but militarily constrained because of ethical, political, or military constraints. For instance, two nuclear powers, the United States and Russia, rarely directly engage in armed conflicts.

Non-armed Conflicts

In times of peace, countries can still compete and attempt to gain advantage through other means: diplomacy and geopolitics, intelligence, and cyberwar.

Diplomacy and geopolitics

Countries can form alliances and partnerships and sign treaties for various reasons: trade, investments, intellectual property, defense, cooperation, or foreign aid. For instance, China is investing a lot in Africa, which should help secure access to natural resources, open markets, and build goodwill. The United States has been a historically strong ally to oil producers in the Middle East to secure energy supply and defense contracts, East Asian countries such as Japan and South Korea to counterbalance China, and NATO countries to defend against Russia.

Intelligence

Intelligence includes traditional human intelligence gathering with spies and informants, communication surveillance (signals intelligence or SIGINT), cyber-hacking, and reconnaissance satellites. The software Pegasus is an example of cyber hacking. Governments have deployed it to spy on foreign dignitaries, including heads of state. The American NSA is well-known for collecting signals intelligence and working with other foreign agencies, especially from the Five Eyes Alliance (Australia, Canada, New Zealand, the United Kingdom, and the United States). The military uses reconnaissance satellites to identify targets and observe enemy troops and military assets at a very high resolution.

Cyber and electronic warfare

According to the Council of Foreign Relations ("Tracking State-Sponsored Cyberattacks Around the World," n.d.), "Since 2005, thirty-four countries have been suspected of sponsoring cyber operations. China, Russia, Iran, and North Korea sponsored 77 percent of all suspected operations. In 2019, there were a total of seventy-six operations, most being acts of espionage."

As infrastructures become more digital and connected, they are exposed to cyber-attacks. The power grid, power plants, water treatment plants, banks, factories, internet and communication networks, computer servers, information technology infrastructures, satellites, electronic and mobile computing devices, social media, and news platforms can be targeted in a cyberwar and put out-of-service by viruses, worms, altered code and data, malicious bots, or ransomware. Chinese, North Korean, and Russian hackers frequently penetrate Western facilities. The United States and Israel have also waged cyber-warfare against Iran. We cannot exclude that terrorists might also attempt to engage in cyber-warfare one day.

Information warfare

Closely related to cyber and electronic warfare is information warfare. Information warfare is relatively inexpensive, given that it happens primarily online. A country that controls its media can fabricate news, false narrative, photos, and videos to spread fake news and lies against another country, censor news, and interfere with or manipulate foreign media. It can use troll factories or bots to propagate fake news on social media at home or abroad. For instance, Russia has conducted an information war against France in Mali and Tchad using social media ("Paris fails to counter Russian propaganda in the Sahel," 2022).

Societies

Promoting peace within societies is also an important goal. Crime and violence against individuals, women, and children, terrorism, and illicit arms flows are happening too often in many countries ("Global Alliance," n.d.). In the same report, the UN reports that "18% of women and girls aged 15 to 49 have experienced physical and/or sexual partner violence in the previous 12 months." and "one billion children globally experience some form of violence every year and one child dies as a result of violence every 5 minutes." Human abuse, exploitation, trafficking, child labor, and child soldiers are also happening and often target the most vulnerable populations. The most disadvantaged people are more exposed to crime because fewer law-enforcement and social service resources are available to deter crime and treat conditions such as mental illness that might lead to crime. This also happens in the richest countries, like the United States.

Justice

Justice and the rule of law are necessary for societies to regulate human behavior. Lawmakers vote laws, but there needs to be an enforcement mechanism to abide by the law. According to *Measuring the Justice Gap* ("Measuring the Justice Gap | World Justice Project," n.d.), 5.1 billion people cannot obtain justice because of malfunctioning justice systems (1.5 billion people), lack of legal documentation or contracts to be protected by the law (4.5 billion people), or are in a situation of extreme injustice because of they are stateless or live in very fragile states (253 million people).

Even in rich countries like the United States, where legal costs can be prohibitive, many people opt to represent themselves in civil or administrative cases, often with worse outcomes ("Everyone Counts," n.d.). In criminal cases, a defendant can get a court-appointed lawyer, but because of low pay and excessive caseload, the outcome can be worse with public defenders (Wihbey et al., 2014).

Financial crimes in illicit money, tax evasion, bribery, and corruption are common in many countries, with a justice system sometimes ill-equipped to catch or prove them. According to the World Bank, "between 2011 and 2018, 19.5% of more than 130,000 firms surveyed across135 countries experienced at least one bribe payment request in the preceding twelve months" ("Global Alliance," n.d.). Briberies are common in developing countries where government jobs sometimes do not cover living expenses. More sophisticated forms of bribery exist in more developed countries, sometimes in the form of illegal political donations. Corruption seems to affect most countries but at different levels of severity ("Global Corruption Barometer," n.d.).

Institutions

Peace and justice require strong institutions such as a legislative assembly, a judiciary, an executive branch with a civil service, a police force, and an armed force that serves the people. Perfect institutions rarely exist, and illegal activities, corruption, and injustice are still present in most countries but to different degrees. Institutions often do not represent or do not let everyone participate equally and are not sufficiently inclusive of women or underrepresented groups. For instance, according to Inter-Parliamentary Union (Inter-Parliamentary Union, n.d.), only 26% of parliamentarians worldwide are women.

13.2 The SDG Targets

The Sustainable Development Goal is supported by the following Targets:

Target 16.1: Significantly reduce all forms of violence and related death rates everywhere

Target 16.2: End abuse, exploitation, trafficking, and all forms of violence against and torture of children

Target 16.3: Promote the rule of law at the national and international levels and ensure equal access to justice for all

Target 16.4: By 2030, significantly reduce illicit financial and arms flows, strengthen the recovery and return of stolen assets, and combat all forms of organized crime

Target 16.5: Substantially reduce corruption and bribery in all their forms

Target 16.6: Develop effective, accountable, and transparent institutions at all levels

Target 16.7: Ensure responsive, inclusive, participatory, and representative decision-making at all levels

Target 16.8: Broaden and strengthen the participation of developing countries in the institutions of global governance

Target 16.9: By 2030, provide legal identity for all, including birth registration

Target 16.10: Ensure public access to information and protect fundamental freedoms in accordance with national legislation and international agreements

Target 16.a: Strengthen relevant national institutions, including through international cooperation, for building capacity at all levels, in particular in developing countries, to prevent violence and combat terrorism and crime

Target 16.b: Promote and enforce non-discriminatory laws and policies for sustainable development

13.3 How to Improve Peace, Justice, and Institutions

Peace

Wars between large developed countries are sporadic but cannot be ruled out as China and Russia are more confident in challenging the US superpower position. Conflicts between middle-income and low-income countries are more common in South Asia or Africa.

Economic Integration

Economic integration will help if we believe that the decision to wage war is rational. The benefit of war has to be weighed against its cost. Loss of trade of goods and services and economic and business opportunities can be very costly. This was the fundamental idea behind the European Union (formerly the EEC) and the World Trade Organization, G8, and United Nations (established in 1945 after World War II and before the League of Nations, founded in 1920 after World War I).

War can seem irrational if the cost is the private cost of the political leader or a political elite instead of the social cost for the country. Therefore a nation and its population might lose out economically and wage a senseless war while its leaders have assets hidden in safe havens. This is also true when the private benefit differs from the social benefit. Remaining in power might bring many personal benefits to a government leader, such as access to state financial resources, even though a country might benefit from having a more competent or less corrupt leader.

Shared Goal and New Narrative

Having a shared goal can foster cooperation and limit the chance of conflicts. Addressing the narrative of past international relations between countries can decrease the risk of conflicts. For instance, a weakened nation can blame another one for its decline. Past armed conflicts can be used to foster nationalism for political gains.

As an example, France and Germany (formerly Prussia) had three major conflicts in the past: the Franco–Prussian War (1870 – 1871), World War I (1914 – 1918), and World War II (1939 – 1945). Today war between France and Germany or any member of the European Union would be implausible thanks to new shared goals. Its first goal within its border is to "promote peace, its values, and the well-being of its citizens" ("Aims and values," n.d.)—the economic integration between these European countries.

Deconcentration of Power

When one country is dominant, like the United States after the fall of the Berlin Wall, but faces the challenge of a rising power such as China, the risk of conflict can occur. This didn't happen with Japan in the 80s, but a reason could be that Japan had vowed not to wage war any longer after its defeat in World War II.

Justice

People must have access to a fair and effective justice system and face a reduced justice gap. This task looks unlikely to be completed anytime soon as these problems exist even in the most developed countries ("Measuring the Justice Gap | World Justice Project," n.d.).

At the international level, the mission of the United Nations Office on Drugs and Crime ("UNODC Strategy 2021-2025," n.d.) is to contribute to global peace, human rights, security, and development and help nations fight against drugs, crime, corruption, and terrorism. Its strategy focuses on five domains: drugs, organized crime, corruption, economic crime, terrorism, crime prevention, and criminal justice.

Drugs

To address the world drug problems, UNODC proposes several measures, including identifying and monitoring emerging substances of abuse and drug trafficking, the link with transnational criminality, the treatment and prevention of substance abuse, and exploring alternatives to cultivating drugs in poor communities.

Organized crime, corruption, economic crime, and terrorism

Cooperation between countries is necessary to prevent and fight organized crime, corruption and economic crime, and terrorism. Crimes include human trafficking, drug and arms trafficking, money laundering, environmental crimes such as illicit mining, maritime crime, and cybercrime. Law enforcement and justice officials need the means to uncover these crimes and access all the relevant information and people to prosecute them.

For transnational crimes overlapping different national jurisdictions, sharing information such as illicit financial flows and joint investigations between regional and international law enforcement teams is necessary. Under-resourced national crime-fighting capacities, inconsistent national legal systems, extradition limits, and bank secrecy laws could limit such efforts.

Crime prevention and criminal justice

Crime prevention and criminal justice are important issues for all countries and governments. Better policing and surveillance, bail reforms, better prison management, alternatives to incarceration, treatment of mental illness, youth crime prevention and rehabilitation, access to affordable legal counsel, fairness of the legal system, coordination between different jurisdictions (precinct, municipal, regional, national, federal, international), and coordination with health and social policies are all tools that can help.

Institutions

People need to have better access to political institutions. These institutions must be more effective, representative, open, transparent, and accountable. This requires giving access to information used in public decision making, such as in the freedom of information act, transparency on how the decisions are made and who has access to lawmakers and the executive branch, sharing and publicity of budgetary, financial, and asset information and relevant performance indicators, a stable and non-political civil service, and effective independent monitors and judicial systems to investigate and prosecute wrongdoings including political corruptions and illegal campaign financing.

13.4 What Can AI Do to Improve Peace, Justice, and Institutions

Prediction

AI can help predict peace and conflicts using socio-economic and political factors. History of conflicts, miscalculation, overconfidence, and ideology, could be factors in such AI models. An AI could provide conflict risk assessment per country and region. If a conflict has already started, AI can help predict the outcome of a conflict and the human and economic losses to all parties due to the conflict. AI could also help predict adversary positions, movements, and offensive, defensive, and logistical capabilities during a conflict.

In the field of justice, AI can help predict and classify crimes and provide risk assessment before crimes are committed. AI will use historical crime data and determine features to predict future crime occurrences. Because crime is sometimes correlated with poverty and racial diversity, there is a risk of biases (Sankin et al., 2021).

Where surveillance is allowed, AI can identify offenders, victims, and crime scenes and provide assistance in investigation and forensics to find and prosecute criminals. AI can also monitor and predict trial outcomes and evaluate their fairness and accuracy.

AI can help predict the quality of state or local institutions and evaluate the risk of breakdown, corruption, or political instability. AI can track performance indicators and use an early warning system for institutional degradation and decline.

Coordination

AI can identify the features leading to conflicts, crimes, or injustice and coordinate the efforts to correct or address them. If gun violence is due to the ease of access to weapons, AI can help design or implement a policy of gun control regulation such as red flag laws or gun repurchases. If injustice is caused by bad preventable policing such as racial profiling, AI could help train and inform police officers to reduce their biases.

Optimization

AI can help optimize resources to solve conflicts and reduce crime and injustice. Before a conflict, factors conducive to war can be addressed and replaced by other factors that lead to economic integration and a shared destiny and reduce the risk of miscommunication, overconfidence, and inaccurate information. During a conflict, resources must be constantly optimized to reach a resolution that will yield the best outcomes for both parties and the international community.

In crime, AI can optimize resources dedicated to crime prevention, deterrence, investigation, arrest, and detention. In particular, AI can optimize the social cost of the crime-fighting value chain, focusing on where the cost yields the maximum benefit. AI can also coordinate with other domains, such as social services, health departments, or judicial authorities from other regions or countries.

Control

AI can operate remote sensors and unmanned aerial vehicles to monitor and prevent conflicts. AI can control drones and autonomous vehicles to bring humanitarian or military supplies to conflict zones. AI can provide resources to investigate war crimes and illegal activities.

AI can assist criminal prevention and investigation in dangerous urban areas with increased intelligence surveillance and community tools to connect neighborhoods and communities with city services and police forces.

AI can be used to limit fraud and corruption in institutions by monitoring and triggering investigations when suspicious transactions are detected, such as illegal campaign financing or there is suspicion of conflict of interests among public servants or political appointees.

13.5 Case Studies

Satellite Imaging

Mueller et al. (2021) use satellite imaging to measure destruction in conflict zones, such as in cities in a country at war. They study the destruction in the city of Aleppo in Syria from 2013 to 2017. They use high-resolution images with damage label data from the United Nations

Operational Satellite Applications Programme (UNOSAT) of the United Nations Institute for Training and Research (UNITAR).

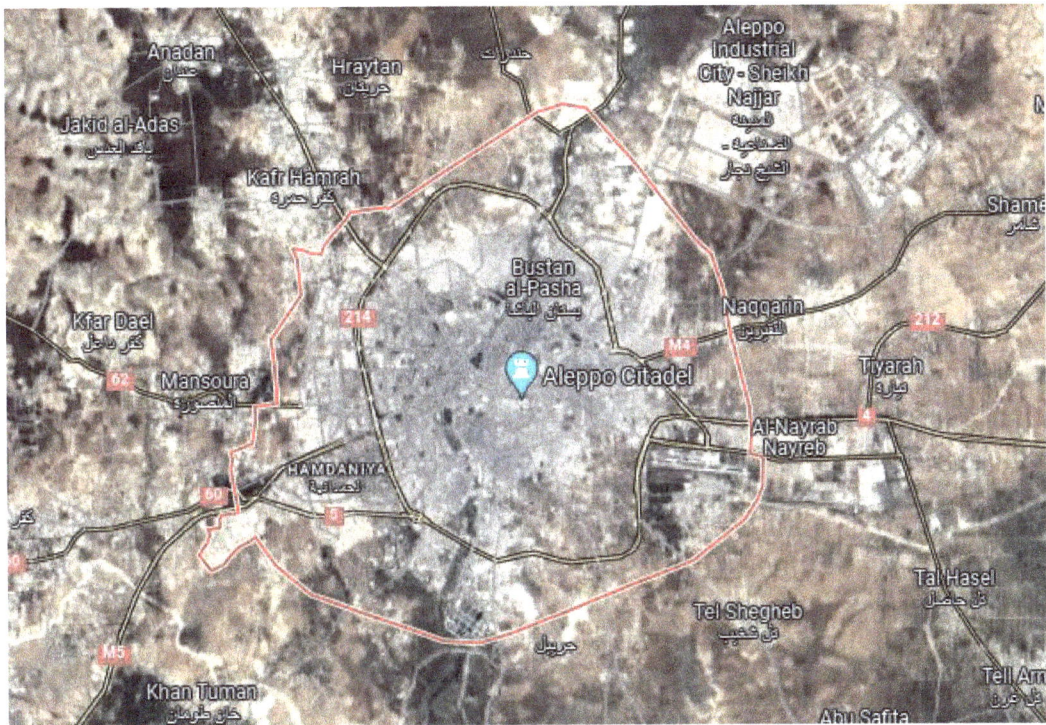

Figure 13.2. Aleppo, Syria. Source Google Earth

UNOSAT does the annotation. Images are divided into patches labeled using the annotation. The labels are carried forward assuming no reconstruction during wartime. They end up with 2.2 million labeled images, with 45,000 images (2%) containing destructions.

They run a two-step model composed of a CNN classifier and a random forest model that leverages the classifications of the CNN. The AUC is 0.84 in the first stage and rises to 0.90 in the second stage, thanks to increased precision.

Institutions: Anti-corruption Tools

Köbis et al. (2022) look at AI as an anti-corruption tool. More government data is available to the public but needs to be screened and analyzed to bring insights and more transparency. AI has the potential to detect, predict, and report risks.

Input data for such AI models can be open government data, leaked data, crowdsourced data, and social media. These data offer opportunities to uncover corruption, such as when the public shares when it has to pay bribes and ethical questions if the data is inaccurate, biased, or illegally acquired.

Regarding algorithm design, the model accuracy, the false positives, and the false negatives are essential. Falsely accusing someone of corruption (false positive) can damage her reputation, and missing corruption cases (false negative) might be costly for society. There is often a trade-off between these two types of errors.

As for the institutional implementation, humans might still be required to remain in the loop as a pure AI-driven system to monitor and catch corruption cases might not be acceptable or make people less trusting of technology and cause them to be wary of surveillance altogether.

Warfare

AI can be used in warfare, lead to an armed race, and escalating violence. The attractiveness of AI for military applications is evident ("Pros and Cons of Autonomous Weapons Systems," n.d.). It can reduce the number of human warfighter casualties, as we see with unmanned aerial vehicles (UAV) today, lower the cost of maintaining troops on a battlefield, make the human warfighters more effective with support and intelligence, and be potentially more lethal by moving to enemy territories unreachable to human soldiers.

With drones, pilots are safe in places like Nevada and can destroy targets remotely without putting their lives at risk. Without pilots, combat aircraft can be lighter, faster, and potentially cheaper to produce. Suppose a drone is a fully autonomous aerial weapons system without a human-on-the-loop. In that case, it will reduce the psychological damage that some drone pilots, intelligence officers, and support staff still suffer. Studies show that they can suffer from "emotional disengagement, Post Traumatic Stress Syndrome (PTSD), emotional exhaustion, and burnout" (Saini et al., 2021).

The US Navy has tested Unmanned Surface Vessels (USVs) with its Ghost Fleet Overlord program (Eckstein, 2021). Removing a human crew allows for new forms of naval warfare as unmanned ships can also be equipped with weapons and sensors for reconnaissance, protecting traditional warships, or maritime surveillance and coastal protection.

With fewer human lives at stake and cheaper AI-based weapons, the political cost of going to war could be lower and war more acceptable. A war that involves no human casualties would also be less likely to escalate (a drone shooting down another drone). A drawback is that an AI-based conflict will likely have civil losses and might even be more deadly as AI weapons can be deployed at scale but fail to distinguish between civilians and armed combatants.

Suppose a country chooses to equip its military force with combat robots and autonomous weapons. In that case, its adversaries will likely follow, leading to an armed race with unpredictable consequences. Autonomous anti-missile systems would be attractive to protect a country against missile attacks, especially if these missiles are hypersonic and might be too fast for humans to react in time. But it then makes it "safer" for a country to attack another because it is confident it will be protected from counter-attacks.

Many scientists oppose using autonomous weapons ("Autonomous Weapons Open Letter: AI & Robotics Researchers - Future of Life Institute," n.d.). Most autonomous weapon systems have humans in the loop. The debate today is whether to forbid human out-of-the-loop systems, especially if the risk that they become unsafe and unreliable is high.

Chapter 14 | Partnerships for Sustainable Development

> "It is time for all of us to remember the values of our common humanity, the values that are fundamental to all religions and that form the basis of the U.N. Charter: peace, justice, respect, human rights, tolerance and solidarity. All those with power and influence have a particular responsibility to recommit to these ideals. We face enormous global challenges. They can be solved only if we work together."
>
> António Guterres

14.1 The State of World Partnerships

Goal 17 is to "strengthen the means of implementation and revitalize the global partnership for sustainable development." ("Goal 17 | Department of Economic and Social Affairs").

Lack of SDG Progress

A recent report from the Sustainable Development Solutions Network (Sachs et al., 2022) shows that the world has not made progress on SDGs since 2019. The Covid-19 pandemic, the war in Ukraine, and the uncertain economic situation have distracted countries from achieving more steps toward these goals. The report identifies six investment priorities:

- Education and social protection

- Health systems

- Zero-carbon energy and circular economy

- Sustainable food, land use, biodiversity, and ecosystems

- Sustainable infrastructure

- Universal digital services

- Financing Constraints

Developing countries are facing a fiscal and investment gap to meet their SDGs. Sachs et al. (2022) recommend financing this gap with increased tax revenues, increased borrowing from development banks, sovereign borrowing in capital markets, increased Official Development Aid (ODA), and debt restructuring for the poorest countries. In particular, donor countries in the OECD have pledged to give 0.7% of their GDP to ODA but have delivered only 0.33% in 2021. For climate change, developed countries have promised 100 billion dollars of aid per year till 2020 but have fallen short (Bhandari et al., 2022).

Technology

Many developing countries lack the technology and human capital to reach the SDGs. For instance, electric car battery technology comes from Japan, South Korea, and China. Large infrastructure projects require engineering, design, and construction expertise. Pharmaceutical companies are based in the United States, Western Europe, India, and China and are well ahead in research and development.

Capacity Building

Many SDGs require not only financing but also capacity building. Health requires healthcare professionals and healthcare equipment and facilities. Education requires qualified teachers, schools, books, and ICTs. Farmers need farming equipment, storage, and transportation networks. Energy requires generating plants, solar panels, wind farms, and modernized electric grids. SDGs also require data and statistics to monitor progress.

14.2 The SDG Targets

The following Targets support the Sustainable Development Goal:

Finance

Target 17.1: Strengthen domestic resource mobilization, including through international support to developing countries, to improve domestic capacity for tax and other revenue collection

Target 17.2: Developed countries to implement fully their official development assistance commitments, including the commitment by many developed countries to achieve the target of 0.7 percent of ODA/GNI to developing countries and 0.15 to 0.20 percent of ODA/GNI to least developed countries ODA providers are encouraged to consider setting a target to provide at least 0.20 percent of ODA/GNI to least developed countries

Target 17.3: Mobilize additional financial resources for developing countries from multiple sources

Target 17.4: Assist developing countries in attaining long-term debt sustainability through coordinated policies aimed at fostering debt financing, debt relief, and debt restructuring, as appropriate, and address the external debt of highly indebted poor countries to reduce debt distress

Target 17.5: Adopt and implement investment promotion regimes for least developed countries

Technology

Target 17.6: Enhance North-South, South-South, and triangular regional and international cooperation on and access to science, technology, and innovation and enhance knowledge sharing on mutually agreed terms, including through improved coordination among existing mechanisms, in particular at the United Nations level, and through a global technology facilitation mechanism

Target 17.7: Promote the development, transfer, dissemination, and diffusion of environmentally sound technologies to developing countries on favorable terms, including on concessional and preferential terms, as mutually agreed

Target 17.8: Fully operationalize the technology bank and science, technology, and innovation capacity-building mechanism for least developed countries by 2017 and enhance the use of enabling technology, in particular information and communications technology

Capacity building

Target 17.9: Enhance international support for implementing effective and targeted capacity-building in developing countries to support national plans to implement all the sustainable development goals, including through North-South, South-South, and triangular cooperation

Trade

Target 17.10: Promote a universal, rules-based, open, non-discriminatory, and equitable multilateral trading system under the World Trade Organization, including through the conclusion of negotiations under its Doha Development Agenda

Target 17.11: Significantly increase the exports of developing countries, in particular with a view to doubling the least developed countries' share of global exports by 2020

Target 17.12: Realize timely implementation of duty-free and quota-free market access on a lasting basis for all least developed countries, consistent with World Trade Organization decisions, including by ensuring that preferential rules of origin applicable to imports from least developed countries are transparent and simple, and contribute to facilitating market access

Systemic issues

Policy and institutional coherence

Target 17.13: Enhance global macroeconomic stability, including through policy coordination and policy coherence

Target 17.14: Enhance policy coherence for sustainable development

Target 17.15: Respect each country's policy space and leadership to establish and implement policies for poverty eradication and sustainable development

Multi-stakeholder partnerships

Target 17.16: Enhance the global partnership for sustainable development, complemented by multi-stakeholder partnerships that mobilize and share knowledge, expertise, technology, and financial resources, to support the achievement of the sustainable development goals in all countries, in particular developing countries

Target 17.17: Encourage and promote effective public, public-private, and civil society partnerships, building on the experience and resourcing strategies of partnerships

Data, monitoring, and accountability

Target 17.18: By 2020, enhance capacity-building support to developing countries, including least developed countries and small island developing States, to increase significantly the availability of high-quality, timely, and reliable data disaggregated by income, gender, age, race, ethnicity, migratory status, disability, geographic location and other characteristics relevant in national contexts

Target 17.19: By 2030, build on existing initiatives to develop measurements of progress on sustainable development that complement gross domestic product and support statistical capacity-building in developing countries

14.3 How to Improve Partnerships

Financing

Financial flows to developing countries are insufficient. The same report recommends a global finance plan to help low-income and middle-income countries achieve their SDGs. It asks the G20 to increase its financing to these countries, the lending capacity of the multilateral development banks, the flow of official development aid (to the level they have already committed), philanthropy, and debt refinancing to review credit ratings to account for future growth. Further, it asks developing countries to strengthen their debt management to prevent future liquidity crises, restructure their debts if needed, and increase domestic tax revenues.

Technology and Capacity Building

Developing countries need technology transfer, training, and assistance to manage their SDGs. Foreign direct investments and development aids should help with capacity and local knowledge building. Local companies and communities should organize to lead the SDG projects with international partners from the private and public sectors and NGOs. This could lead to better solutions using local knowledge and resources.

Accountability, Data, and Statistics

The scale of the SDGs makes the risk of failure and mismanagement non-negligible. If billions and trillions of dollars of investments go to finance such projects, accountability, data, and statistics would be necessary to monitor progress, manage the projects efficiently and avoid waste. Best practices for project management should be adopted with the involvement of all local stakeholders.

14.4 What Can AI Do to Improve Partnerships

Prediction

AI can help predict the financing, capabilities, and factors required to reach the SDGs for each country. Financing will come from better tax collections, public debt, foreign debt, and development assistance. Capabilities will include people, technology, infrastructure, and working institutions. Factors will be economic, social, political, institutional, and environmental.

AI can evaluate the probability of reaching the SDGs and calculate SDG indexes to inform policymakers, citizens, and other stakeholders. AI can predict the areas most at risk of falling short and the policies more likely to succeed.

AI can also predict the factors influencing development aid flows from developed countries to assist lower-income countries in managing their transition and finance their mitigation and adaptation strategies.

Coordination

AI can guide policymakers by identifying the necessary factors that drive the path to the SDGs and coordinating the efforts of national and local governments, international development organizations, NGOs, and developed nations to elicit these factors. The previous chapters have listed many of these factors already.

Optimization

AI can help optimize the factors, the appropriate policy mix to reach the SDG, and the timing of these policies. New circumstances will always occur, and AI will need to re-optimize the policies to account for them. For instance, the 2022 Ukraine invasion by Russia requires a reexamination of energy and food policies across Europe, Asia, and Africa.

Control

The large financial flows to help pay for the SDGs risk being misused or not accounted for. Proper control by AI could help all the stakeholders that the money is used efficiently for the benefit of the recipient countries. AI can authorize and monitor transactions, flag suspicious transactions for further auditing or reporting, and recommend the best use of funds to reach the SDG.

14.5 Case Studies

Monitoring the SDGs

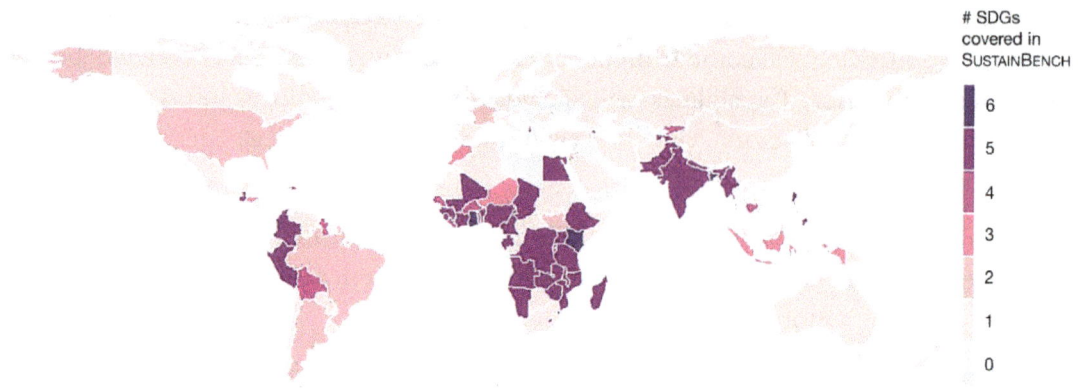

Figure 14.1. SDGs covered in SustainBench. Source: (Yeh et al., 2020)

Yeh et al. (2020) propose SustainBench ("SustainBench," n.d.), a set of 15 benchmarks related to 7 SDGs: No Poverty (SDG 1), Zero Hunger (SDG 2), Good Health and Well-being (SDG 3), Quality Education (SDG 4), Clean Water and Sanitation (SDG 6), Climate Action (SDG 13), and Life on Land (SDG 15). These SDGs are covered in Chapter 1 (Poverty), Chapter 2 (Hunger), Chapter 3 (Health), Chapter 4 (Education), Chapter 10 (Clean Water), Chapter 7 (Climate Action), and Chapter 9 (Life on Land) of this book.

The benchmarks take the form of datasets and tasks. The datasets are usually publicly available datasets. The tasks include regression, classification, semantic segmentation, and prediction. For each task, the authors define some metrics that new models need to outperform.

For poverty, health, education, and clean water and sanitation, they rely on the Demographic and Health Surveys from USAID ("The DHS Program - Quality information to plan, monitor and improve population, health, and nutrition programs," n.d.) and the Living Standards Measurement Study from the World Bank ("Living Standards Measurement Study," n.d.). The task is to predict outcomes such as cluster-level asset wealth index, changes in asset ownership, women's BMI and child mortality rates, average years of educational attainment by women of reproductive age, water quality index, and sanitation index.

For zero hunger, the tasks are performed on satellite images and consist of mapping croplands and crop types, predicting crop yields, and delineating fields.

The task is to identify brick kilns from Sentinel-2 satellite imagery for climate action. The idea is that brick kilns are emitters of CO_2 and other pollutants though they are probably not the largest ones.

For life on land, the task is to perform land cover classification of satellite images. They use a global dataset with MODIS satellite inputs and land classification of 17 types.

Development Aid

Interactive monitoring of global development aid

By Malte Toetzke, last updated: 30.11.2021

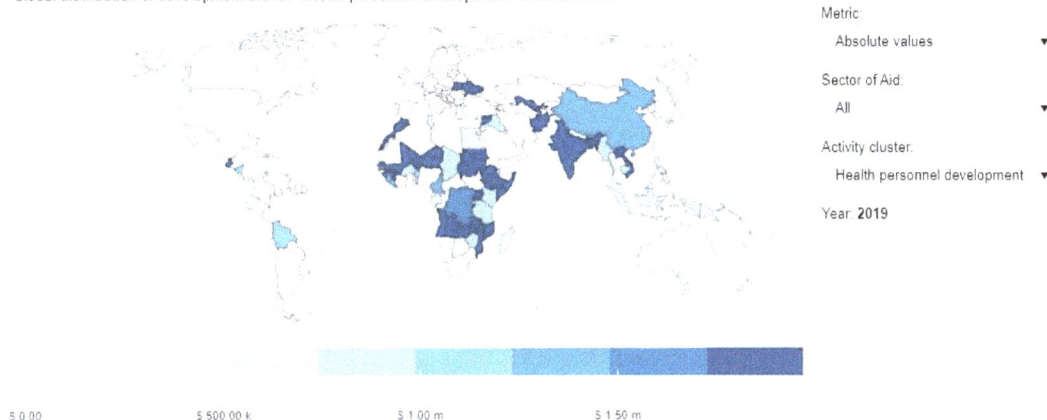

Global distribution of development aid for "Health personnel development" in million USD

Metric:
Absolute values ▼

Sector of Aid:
All ▼

Activity cluster:
Health personnel development ▼

Year: 2019

$ 0.00 $ 500.00 k $ 1.00 m $ 1.50 m

Figure 14.2. Interactive monitoring of global development aid. Source: https://maltetoetzke.github.io/Monitoring-Global-Development-Aid/

Toetzke et al. (2022) developed a classification system to monitor global development aid. They use reports covering around 3.2 million aid activities from 747 donors from 2000 to 2019 found in the creditor reporting system (CRS) of the Organization of Economic Cooperation and Development (OECD). These aid activities sum up to 3.2 trillion dollars.

The authors translate and preprocess all the texts, use word embeddings to represent them in vector forms, use clustering algorithms (k-means) on the document vectors to group them, and find names for 173 activity clusters. Names of clusters include PRIMARY EDUCATION, BASIC NUTRITION, and BIODIVERSITY.

This allows them to look at the distribution of activities by donors, recipient countries, and across time. They see, for instance, new emerging activities such as YOUTH EMPOWERMENT and MICROFINANCE that were not initially officially categorized.

ESG Investing

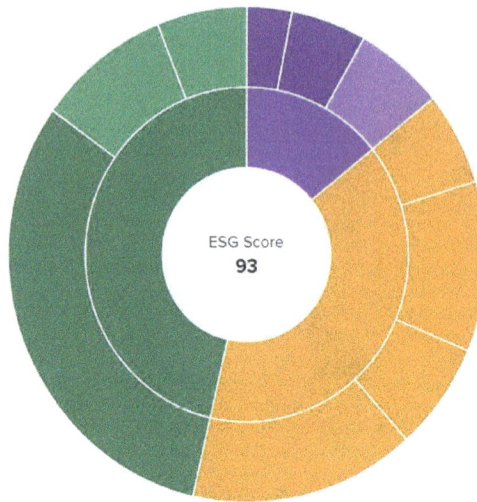

Microsoft Corp ESG score (out of 100): **93**	
■ **Environment** ⓘ	78
Emissions	96
Resource Use	100
Innovation	53
■ **Social** ⓘ	97
Human Rights	96
Product Responsibility	98
Workforce	99
Community	96
■ **Governance** ⓘ	93
Management	98
Shareholders	80
CSR Strategy	87

COMPARISON AND RANK

Microsoft Corp is a Software & IT Services company. Below is the rank of this company out of all the companies in its industry. Get the most comprehensive, detailed, and up to date sector and industry classification available with the Refinitiv Business Classification here

2/895

Out of Software & IT Services Companies.

USEFUL LINKS

ESG brochure →

Contribute ESG data →

ESG scores methodology →

Figure 14.3. ESG Score of Microsoft. Source: Refinitiv
https://www.refinitiv.com/en/sustainable-finance/esg-scores

ESG ratings ("Environmental, social, and corporate governance," 2022) are new ratings that measure environmental (climate change, greenhouse gas emissions, biodiversity loss, deforestation, pollution, energy efficiency, and water management), social (gender and diversity, equity, and inclusion), and governance (board composition, cybersecurity practices, management structure, executive compensation, preventing bribery and corruption) risks on companies.

Krappel et al. (2021) developed an ensemble model to predict ESG ratings based on fundamental data. The authors use fundamental data and ESG scores data from Refinitiv. The data are general information (industry, location) and financial reporting data. The ESG score data are commercial data from Refinitiv (Figure 14.3) constructed from 186 ESG metrics, aggregated into Environmental, Social, and Governance categories and pillars, and then combined into a final ESG Score.

Several machine learning models are trained to map the fundamental data to the ESG Score. An ensemble of CatBoost, XGBoost, and Feedforward Neural Network models is used to give the final ESG Score prediction. R2 measures performance. They find an R2 of 54%, which is not a bad result given that the fundamental data do not explicitly include any ESG information. This approach could be helpful in rapidly calculating ESG Scores using only relatively easily accessible fundamental data.

Conclusion

> "The world will not be destroyed by those who do evil, but by those who watch them without doing anything."
>
> Albert Einstein

The Sustainable Development Goals must be achieved by 2030 in less than a decade. A lot of problems raised by the SDGs are man-made. Poverty, hunger, climate change, wars, and conflicts often find their roots in poorly aligned private incentives and inadequate public policy.

The Sustainable Development Report (Sachs et al., 2022) indicates that significant and major challenges remain to achieve these Goals (Figure 15.1 for no poverty, Figure 15.2 for zero hunger, Figure 15.3 for health and well-being, Figure 15.4 for education, and Figure 15.5 for climate action). It seems, therefore, that humanity will fall short of these Goals unless there are some breakthroughs in how it addresses them.

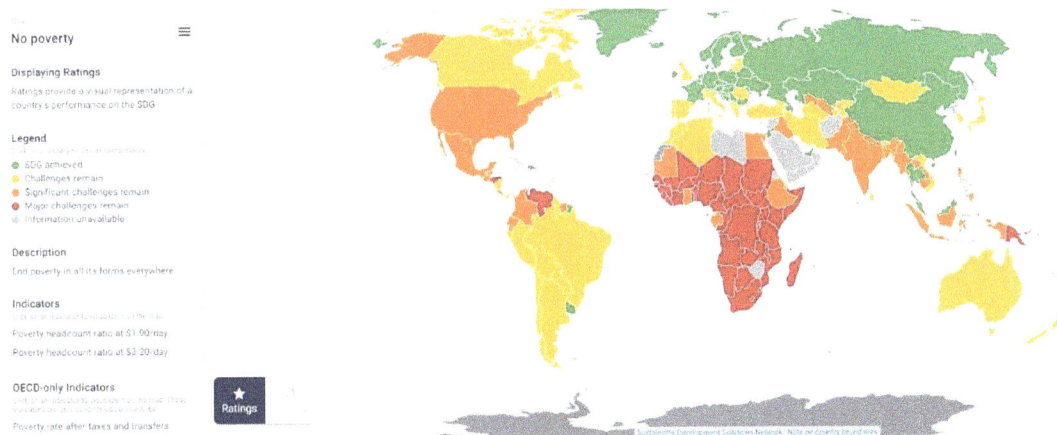

Figure 15.1. No poverty progress. Ratings range from major challenges remain (red) to SDG achieved (green). Source: https://dashboards.sdgindex.org/

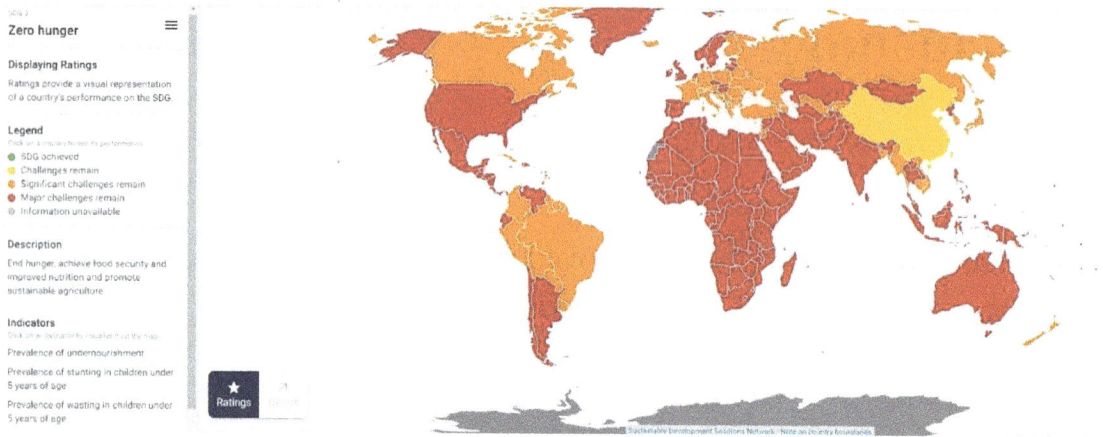

Figure 15.2. Zero hunger progress. Ratings range from major challenges remain (red) to SDG achieved (green). Source: https://dashboards.sdgindex.org/

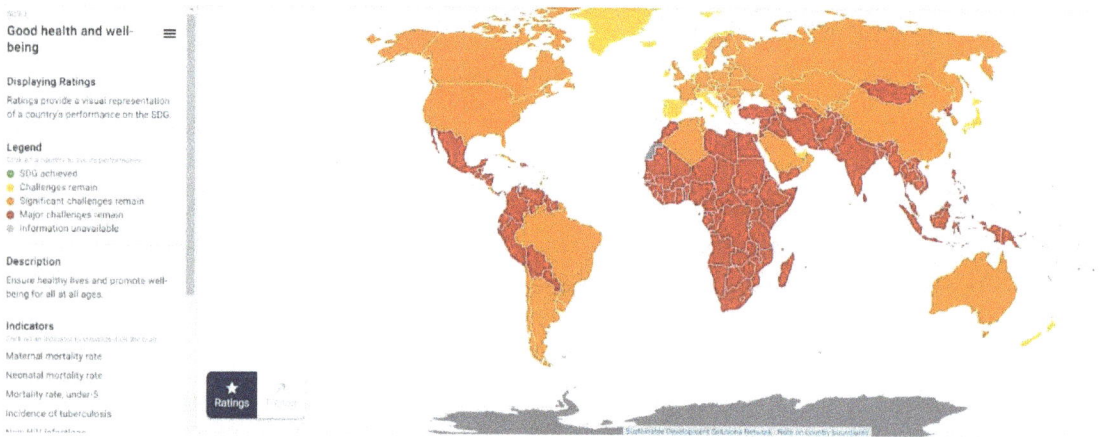

Figure 15.3. Health and well-being progress. Ratings range from major challenges remain (red) to SDG achieved (green). Source: https://dashboards.sdgindex.org/

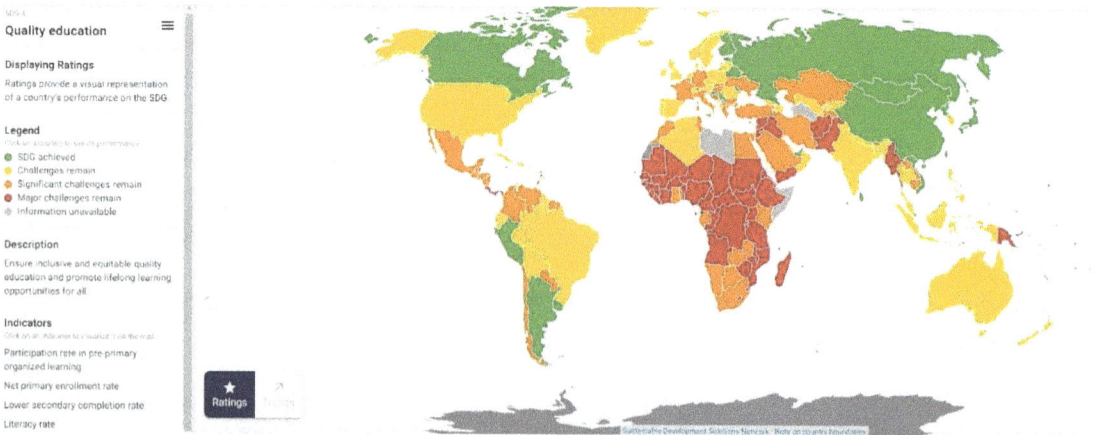

Figure 15.4. Education progress. Ratings range from major challenges remain (red) to SDG achieved (green). Source: https://dashboards.sdgindex.org/

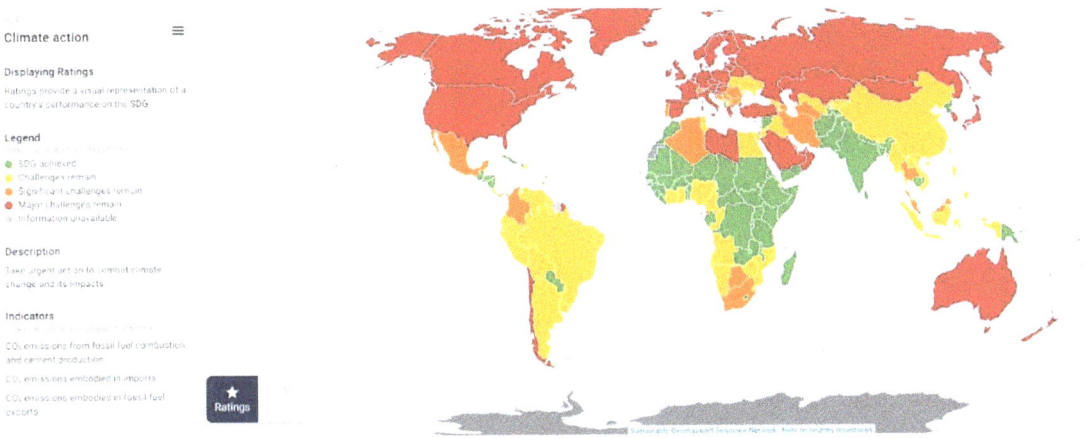

Figure 15.5. Climate action progress. Ratings range from major challenges remain (red) to SDG achieved (green). Source: https://dashboards.sdgindex.org/

We might already see some of these breakthroughs with this new era of big data and AI. From a top-down perspective, satellite imaging has the potential to give us precious near real-time data and insights on many SDGs, such as poverty, hunger, climate change, and land and water ecosystems. From the bottom-up, AI is becoming a powerful tool to progress at the atomic and molecular level in biology, medicine, or energy to find new drugs or materials. As the world becomes more digital, more data becomes accessible to researchers, practitioners, and citizens. AI is on the path to offering the keys to making sense of them.

Depending on the Goals, different regions will be closer or farther to achieving them. Nations such as the United States or China are better positioned to use AI to reach the SDGs if they have the political will. Other countries, especially in Sub-Saharan Africa and some parts of Asia, will need assistance to adopt and deploy AI that meets their needs.

We have mentioned the PCOC framework (Prediction, Coordination, Optimization, and Control) in several case studies that showcase the power of AI to address issues raised by the SDGs. Many applications are still in the Prediction phase, but there is no doubt that AI will make a lot of progress in coordinating, optimizing, and controlling resources and efforts to deal with the SDGs.

It is likely that powerful AI will be adopted first in the more developed countries as they already have the technological and institutional resources to do so. It is crucial, however, not to leave the other countries behind. AI could be very effective where human expertise is lacking or scarce, such as in the medical field for health screening, nature conservation, or climate action. More advanced countries will need to share expertise and models and collaborate to help collect regional data and develop new AI models that meet the needs of less advanced nations.

All AI users have concerns about privacy, human rights, ethics, safety and trust, and responsibility. They should be addressed so that society supports the use of AI. Europe is leading the way with its project of regulating Artificial Intelligence (European Commission, 2021). The United Nations (UNESCO, 2021) and the OECD (Council on Artificial Intelligence, 2019) have their proposals too. Other countries are following and adopting their own regulations.

If used responsibly, we will undoubtedly see more AI for Good applications as domain experts, AI and machine learning experts, data scientists, engineers, technicians, environmentalists, regional, national, and local government officials, NGOs, and regulators work together to meet the 2030 Agenda for Sustainable Development and beyond.

Please contact me at contact@rodeopress.com to share your ideas, experience, and lessons learned during your journey to AI.

Appendix: The AI Agile Manifesto

1) YOU NEED TO KNOW WHAT YOU WANT TO ACHIEVE WITH AI. THERE IS A TRADE-OFF BETWEEN FEASIBILITY AND BUSINESS IMPACT.

2) THE ORGANIZATION HAS TO BE COMMITTED TO THE AI PROJECT.

3) THE AI TEAM LEADER NEEDS TO BE AN EFFECTIVE MANAGER AND A LEADER WITH A SHARED VISION OF AI.

4) DESIGN THINKING AND AGILE ARE VALUABLE TOOLS. BE LASER-FOCUSED ON THE TO-DO LIST TO CONTROL THE SCOPE, COST, AND SCHEDULE OF THE AI PROJECT.

5) YOU NEED TO KNOW ALL THE FACTORS THAT CAN INFLUENCE THE AI PROJECT.

6) THE AI PROJECT NEEDS TO LEVERAGE AND BE CONSISTENT WITH ALL THE ORGANIZATIONAL PROCESS ASSETS.

7) AN AI PROJECT NEEDS GREAT PEOPLE, MODELS, AND DATA.

8) AI QUALITY IS NOT ONLY ABOUT MODEL AND SOFTWARE QUALITY BUT ALSO ABOUT PEOPLE AND DATA.

9) AI RISK MANAGEMENT REQUIRES A CONSTANT RISK ASSESSMENT, A RISK STRATEGY, AND HUMAN-IN-THE-LOOP.

10) YOU NEED TO INVOLVE ALL THE STAKEHOLDERS AND HAVE A CLEAR COMMUNICATION PLAN, ESPECIALLY WHEN THINGS GO WRONG.

11) YOU NEED TO IDENTIFY, UNDERSTAND AND ADDRESS THE ETHICAL CONCERNS CAUSED BY AI.

12) AGILE FOR AI REQUIRES A SPECIFIC APPROACH WITH LONGER CYCLES AND MORE EXPLORATION.

Source:

Trinh, M. 2021. The AI Project Handbook: How to manage a successful artificial intelligence project. Rodeo Press.

The AI Agile Manifesto. http://aiagile.org/

References

A hunger catastrophe | World Food Programme [WWW Document], n.d. URL https://www.wfp.org/hunger-catastrophe (accessed 3.9.22).

Acemoglu, D., Robinson, J.A., 2012. Why Nations Fail: The Origins of Power, Prosperity and Poverty, Main edition. ed. Profile Books.

Aghion, P., Antonin, C., Bunel, S., 2021. The Power of Creative Destruction: Economic Upheaval and the Wealth of Nations. Belknap Press.

Aiken, E., Bellue, S., Blumenstock, J.E., Karlan, D.S., Udry, C., 2021. Machine Learning and Mobile Phone Data Can Improve the Targeting of Humanitarian Assistance.

Aims and values [WWW Document], n.d. URL https://european-union.europa.eu/principles-countries-history/principles-and-values/aims-and-values_en (accessed 5.27.22).

Alori, J., 2020. Releasing Norfair: an open source library for object tracking | Tryolabs. Tryo Labs Blog. URL https://tryolabs.com/blog/2020/09/10/releasing-norfair-an-open-source-library-for-object-tracking (accessed 8.30.22).

Antonopoulos, I., Robu, V., Couraud, B., Kirli, D., Norbu, S., Kiprakis, A., Flynn, D., Elizondo-Gonzalez, S., Wattam, S., 2020. Artificial intelligence and machine learning approaches to energy demand-side response: A systematic review. Renew. Sustain. Energy Rev. 130, 109899. https://doi.org/10.1016/j.rser.2020.109899

Autonomous Weapons Open Letter: AI & Robotics Researchers - Future of Life Institute [WWW Document], n.d. URL https://futureoflife.org/2016/02/09/open-letter-autonomous-weapons-ai-robotics/ (accessed 6.11.22).

Azizi, S., Culp, L., Freyberg, J., Mustafa, B., Baur, S., Kornblith, S., Chen, T., MacWilliams, P., Mahdavi, S.S., Wulczyn, E., Babenko, B., Wilson, M., Loh, A., Chen, P.-H.C., Liu, Yuan, Bavishi, P., McKinney, S.M., Winkens, J., Roy, A.G., Beaver, Z., Ryan, F., Krogue, J., Etemadi, M., Telang, U., Liu, Yun, Peng, L., Corrado, G.S., Webster, D.R., Fleet, D., Hinton, G., Houlsby, N., Karthikesalingam, A., Norouzi, M., Natarajan, V., 2022. Robust and Efficient Medical Imaging with Self-Supervision. https://doi.org/10.48550/arXiv.2205.09723

Balboni, C.A., Bandiera, O., Burgess, R., Ghatak, M., Heil, A., 2021. Why do people stay poor? (Working Paper No. 29340), Working Paper Series. National Bureau of Economic Research. https://doi.org/10.3386/w29340

Baldocchi, D., 2014. Measuring fluxes of trace gases and energy between ecosystems and the atmosphere – the state and future of the eddy covariance method. Glob. Change Biol. 20, 3600–3609. https://doi.org/10.1111/gcb.12649

Barnes, M.L., Farella, M.M., Scott, R.L., Moore, D.J.P., Ponce-Campos, G.E., Biederman, J.A., MacBean, N., Litvak, M.E., Breshears, D.D., 2021. Improved dryland carbon flux predictions with explicit consideration of water-carbon coupling. Commun. Earth Environ. 2, 1–9. https://doi.org/10.1038/s43247-021-00308-2

Basu, S., Biswas, G., Kinnebrew, J.S., 2017. Learner modeling for adaptive scaffolding in a Computational Thinking-based science learning environment. User Model. User-Adapt. Interact. 27, 5–53. https://doi.org/10.1007/s11257-017-9187-0

Bergman, P., Chetty, R., deLuca, S., Hendren, N., Katz, L., Palmer, C., 2019. Creating Moves to Opportunity. Oppor. Insights.

Bhandari, P., Warszawski, N., Thangata, C., 2022. 5 Things COP27 Must Achieve for Vulnerable Countries.

BiodiverCities by 2030: Fostering nature-positive urban development | IUCN Urban Alliance [WWW Document], n.d. URL https://iucnurbanalliance.org/biodivercities-by-2030-fostering-nature-positive-urban-development/ (accessed 6.2.22).

Blanchard, O., Tirole, J., 2021. Major Future Economic Challenges.

Browder, G., Ozment, S., Rehberger Bescos, I., Gartner, T., Lange, G.-M., 2019. Integrating Green and Gray: Creating Next Generation Infrastructure. World Bank, Washington, DC. https://doi.org/10.1596/978-1-56973-955-6

Brown, C.F., Brumby, S.P., Guzder-Williams, B., Birch, T., Hyde, S.B., Mazzariello, J., Czerwinski, W., Pasquarella, V.J., Haertel, R., Ilyushchenko, S., Schwehr, K., Weisse, M., Stolle, F., Hanson, C., Guinan, O., Moore, R., Tait, A.M., 2022. Dynamic World, Near real-time global 10 m land use land cover mapping. Sci. Data 9, 251. https://doi.org/10.1038/s41597-022-01307-4

Carion, N., Massa, F., Synnaeve, G., Usunier, N., Kirillov, A., Zagoruyko, S., 2020. End-to-End Object Detection with Transformers. https://doi.org/10.48550/arXiv.2005.12872

Case, A., Deaton, A., 2021. Deaths of Despair and the Future of Capitalism. Princeton University Press.

Cedric, L.S., Adoni, W.Y.H., Aworka, R., Zoueu, J.T., Mutombo, F.K., Krichen, M., Kimpolo, C.L.M., 2022. Crops yield prediction based on machine learning models: Case of West African countries. Smart Agric. Technol. 2, 100049. https://doi.org/10.1016/j.atech.2022.100049

Chen, M., Tworek, J., Jun, H., Yuan, Q., Pinto, H.P. de O., Kaplan, J., Edwards, H., Burda, Y., Joseph, N., Brockman, G., Ray, A., Puri, R., Krueger, G., Petrov, M., Khlaaf, H., Sastry, G., Mishkin, P., Chan, B., Gray, S., Ryder, N., Pavlov, M., Power, A., Kaiser,

L., Bavarian, M., Winter, C., Tillet, P., Such, F.P., Cummings, D., Plappert, M., Chantzis, F., Barnes, E., Herbert-Voss, A., Guss, W.H., Nichol, A., Paino, A., Tezak, N., Tang, J., Babuschkin, I., Balaji, S., Jain, S., Saunders, W., Hesse, C., Carr, A.N., Leike, J., Achiam, J., Misra, V., Morikawa, E., Radford, A., Knight, M., Brundage, M., Murati, M., Mayer, K., Welinder, P., McGrew, B., Amodei, D., McCandlish, S., Sutskever, I., Zaremba, W., 2021. Evaluating Large Language Models Trained on Code. https://doi.org/10.48550/arXiv.2107.03374

Chen, T., Guestrin, C., 2016. XGBoost: A Scalable Tree Boosting System, in: Proceedings of the 22nd ACM SIGKDD International Conference on Knowledge Discovery and Data Mining, KDD '16. Association for Computing Machinery, New York, NY, USA, pp. 785–794. https://doi.org/10.1145/2939672.2939785

Chi, G., Fang, H., Chatterjee, S., Blumenstock, J.E., 2022a. Microestimates of wealth for all low- and middle-income countries. Proc. Natl. Acad. Sci. 119, e2113658119. https://doi.org/10.1073/pnas.2113658119

Chi, G., Fang, H., Chatterjee, S., Blumenstock, J.E., 2022b. Micro-Estimates of Wealth for all Low- and Middle-Income Countries. Proc. Natl. Acad. Sci. 119, e2113658119. https://doi.org/10.1073/pnas.2113658119

Chowdhery, A., Narang, S., Devlin, J., Bosma, M., Mishra, G., Roberts, A., Barham, P., Chung, H.W., Sutton, C., Gehrmann, S., Schuh, P., Shi, K., Tsvyashchenko, S., Maynez, J., Rao, A., Barnes, P., Tay, Y., Shazeer, N., Prabhakaran, V., Reif, E., Du, N., Hutchinson, B., Pope, R., Bradbury, J., Austin, J., Isard, M., Gur-Ari, G., Yin, P., Duke, T., Levskaya, A., Ghemawat, S., Dev, S., Michalewski, H., Garcia, X., Misra, V., Robinson, K., Fedus, L., Zhou, D., Ippolito, D., Luan, D., Lim, H., Zoph, B., Spiridonov, A., Sepassi, R., Dohan, D., Agrawal, S., Omernick, M., Dai, A.M., Pillai, T.S., Pellat, M., Lewkowycz, A., Moreira, E., Child, R., Polozov, O., Lee, K., Zhou, Z., Wang, X., Saeta, B., Diaz, M., Firat, O., Catasta, M., Wei, J., Meier-Hellstern, K., Eck, D., Dean, J., Petrov, S., Fiedel, N., 2022. PaLM: Scaling Language Modeling with Pathways. https://doi.org/10.48550/arXiv.2204.02311

Climate Change 2022: Mitigation of Climate Change [WWW Document], n.d. URL https://www.ipcc.ch/report/ar6/wg3/ (accessed 4.4.22).

Collins, G.S., Reitsma, J.B., Altman, D.G., Moons, K.G., 2015. Transparent reporting of a multivariable prediction model for individual prognosis or diagnosis (TRIPOD): the TRIPOD Statement. BMC Med. 13, 1. https://doi.org/10.1186/s12916-014-0241-z

Conati, C., Porayska-Pomsta, K., Mavrikis, M., 2018. AI in Education needs interpretable machine learning: Lessons from Open Learner Modelling. https://doi.org/10.48550/arXiv.1807.00154

Council on Artificial Intelligence, 2019. The OECD Artificial Intelligence (AI) Principles.

Dasgupta, P., 2021. The economics of biodiversity: the Dasgupta review: full report, Updated: 18 February 2021. ed. HM Treasury, London.

Davies, A., Veličković, P., Buesing, L., Blackwell, S., Zheng, D., Tomašev, N., Tanburn, R., Battaglia, P., Blundell, C., Juhász, A., Lackenby, M., Williamson, G., Hassabis, D., Kohli, P., 2021. Advancing mathematics by guiding human intuition with AI. Nature 600, 70–74. https://doi.org/10.1038/s41586-021-04086-x

dead zone | National Geographic Society [WWW Document], n.d. URL https://education.nationalgeographic.org/resource/dead-zone (accessed 6.3.22).

Deaton, A., 2013. The Great Escape: Health, Wealth, and the Origins of Inequality. Princeton University Press.

Declaration of Alma-Ata International Conference on Primary Health Care, Alma-Ata, USSR, 6–12 September 1978, 2004. Development 47, 159–161. https://doi.org/10.1057/palgrave.development.1100047

Degrave, J., Felici, F., Buchli, J., Neunert, M., Tracey, B., Carpanese, F., Ewalds, T., Hafner, R., Abdolmaleki, A., de las Casas, D., Donner, C., Fritz, L., Galperti, C., Huber, A., Keeling, J., Tsimpoukelli, M., Kay, J., Merle, A., Moret, J.-M., Noury, S., Pesamosca, F., Pfau, D., Sauter, O., Sommariva, C., Coda, S., Duval, B., Fasoli, A., Kohli, P., Kavukcuoglu, K., Hassabis, D., Riedmiller, M., 2022. Magnetic control of tokamak plasmas through deep reinforcement learning. Nature 602, 414–419. https://doi.org/10.1038/s41586-021-04301-9

Dieppe, A., 2021. Global Productivity: Trends, Drivers, and Policies. World Bank, Washington, DC. https://doi.org/10.1016/978-1-4648-1608-6

Easterly, W., 2007. The White Man's Burden: Why the West's Efforts to Aid the Rest Have Done So Much Ill and So Little Good. Penguin Books.

Eckstein, M., 2021. US Navy, Pentagon to test large unmanned ships as program winds down [WWW Document]. Def. News. URL https://www.defensenews.com/naval/2021/07/13/us-navy-pentagon-to-test-large-unmanned-ships-in-operationally-relevant-scenarios-as-program-winds-down/ (accessed 6.11.22).

Economics of Innovation in the Energy Sector, 2022.

Elite Capture of Foreign Aid : Evidence from Offshore Bank Accounts [WWW Document], n.d. URL https://openknowledge.worldbank.org/handle/10986/33355 (accessed 6.10.22).

Environmental, social, and corporate governance, 2022. Wikipedia.

European Commission, 2021. Proposal for a Regulation laying down harmonised rules on artificial intelligence (Artificial Intelligence Act) | Shaping Europe's digital future

[WWW Document]. URL https://digital-strategy.ec.europa.eu/en/library/proposal-regulation-laying-down-harmonised-rules-artificial-intelligence-artificial-intelligence (accessed 4.27.21).

European Commission, 2020. New Circular Economy Action Plan.

Everyone Counts: Taking a Snapshot of Self-Represented Litigants in Miami-Dade [WWW Document], n.d. URL https://www.americanbar.org/groups/legal_services/publications/dialogue/volume/20/fall-2017/pro-bono-everyone-counts/ (accessed 6.9.22).

FAO, 2022a. The State of the World's Forests 2022 | FAO | Food and Agriculture Organization of the United Nations.

FAO, 2022b. The State of the World's Land and Water Resources for Food and Agriculture 2021 – Systems at breaking point: Main Report. FAO, Rome, Italy. https://doi.org/10.4060/cb9910en

FAO, 2021. The State of Food and Agriculture 2021: Making agrifood systems more resilient to shocks and stresses, The State of Food and Agriculture (SOFA). FAO, Rome, Italy. https://doi.org/10.4060/cb4476en

FAO, 2020. The State of World Fisheries and Aquaculture -2020 | FAO | Food and Agriculture Organization of the United Nations. Rome, Italy. https://doi.org/10.4060/ca9229en

FAO, 1995. Fisheries and Aquaculture - Fisheries and Aquaculture - Code of Conduct for Responsible Fisheries.

Farr, E., Finnegan, L., Grace, J., Truscott, M., 2022. Dangerous delay 2: The cost of inaction (Technical Report). Jameel Observatory, Oxfam, Save the Children. https://doi.org/10.7488/era/2231

Feldman, T., Peake, A., 2021. End-To-End Bias Mitigation: Removing Gender Bias in Deep Learning. https://doi.org/10.48550/arXiv.2104.02532

Fields, G.S., 2019. Self-employment and poverty in developing countries. IZA World Labor. https://doi.org/10.15185/izawol.60

Garcia-Garin, O., Monleón-Getino, T., López-Brosa, P., Borrell, A., Aguilar, A., Borja-Robalino, R., Cardona, L., Vighi, M., 2021. Automatic detection and quantification of floating marine macro-litter in aerial images: Introducing a novel deep learning approach connected to a web application in R. Environ. Pollut. 273, 116490. https://doi.org/10.1016/j.envpol.2021.116490

Girshick, R., Donahue, J., Darrell, T., Malik, J., 2014. Rich feature hierarchies for accurate object detection and semantic segmentation. ArXiv13112524 Cs.

GLEAM | Global Land Evaporation Amsterdam Model [WWW Document], n.d. GLEAM Glob. Land Evaporation Amst. Model. URL https://www.gleam.eu/ (accessed 8.28.22).

Global Alliance: Enabling the Implementation of the 2030 Agenda Through SDG 16+: Anchoring Peace, Justice and Inclusion [WWW Document], n.d. URL https://www.sdg16hub.org/topic/global-alliance-enabling-implementation-2030-agenda-through-sdg-16-anchoring-peace-justice (accessed 6.3.22).

Global Alliance for Literacy – Member countries | UIL [WWW Document], 2021. URL https://uil.unesco.org/literacy/global-alliance/global-alliance-literacy-member-countries-0 (accessed 5.16.22).

Global Corruption Barometer [WWW Document], n.d. Transparency.org. URL https://www.transparency.org/en/gcb (accessed 6.9.22).

Global Platform for Sustainable Cities, 2021. GPSC's Webinar Series: Bringing Nature to Cities [WWW Document]. GPSC. URL https://www.thegpsc.org/blogs/gpsc%E2%80%99s-webinar-series-bringing-nature-cities (accessed 7.1.22).

Global Poverty Map [WWW Document], n.d. URL http://beta.povertymaps.net/#4.09/-12.84/27.34/-15.2/60 (accessed 6.11.22).

Goal 1 | Department of Economic and Social Affairs [WWW Document], n.d. URL https://sdgs.un.org/goals/goal1 (accessed 4.12.22).

Goal 2 | Department of Economic and Social Affairs [WWW Document], n.d. URL https://sdgs.un.org/goals/goal2 (accessed 4.12.22).

Goal 3 | Department of Economic and Social Affairs [WWW Document], n.d. URL https://sdgs.un.org/goals/goal3 (accessed 4.12.22).

Goal 4 | Department of Economic and Social Affairs [WWW Document], n.d. URL https://sdgs.un.org/goals/goal4 (accessed 4.12.22).

Goal 5 | Department of Economic and Social Affairs [WWW Document], n.d. URL https://sdgs.un.org/goals/goal5 (accessed 4.12.22).

Goal 6 | Department of Economic and Social Affairs [WWW Document], n.d. URL https://sdgs.un.org/goals/goal6 (accessed 4.12.22).

Goal 7 | Department of Economic and Social Affairs [WWW Document], n.d. URL https://sdgs.un.org/goals/goal7 (accessed 4.12.22).

Goal 8 | Department of Economic and Social Affairs [WWW Document], n.d. URL https://sdgs.un.org/goals/goal8 (accessed 4.12.22).

Goal 9 | Department of Economic and Social Affairs [WWW Document], n.d. URL https://sdgs.un.org/goals/goal9 (accessed 4.12.22).

Goal 10 | Department of Economic and Social Affairs [WWW Document], n.d. URL https://sdgs.un.org/goals/goal10 (accessed 4.12.22).

Goal 11 | Department of Economic and Social Affairs [WWW Document], n.d. URL https://sdgs.un.org/goals/goal11 (accessed 4.12.22).

Goal 12 | Department of Economic and Social Affairs [WWW Document], n.d. URL https://sdgs.un.org/goals/goal12 (accessed 4.12.22).

Goal 13 | Department of Economic and Social Affairs [WWW Document], n.d. URL https://sdgs.un.org/goals/goal13 (accessed 4.12.22).

Goal 14 | Department of Economic and Social Affairs [WWW Document], n.d. URL https://sdgs.un.org/goals/goal14 (accessed 4.12.22).

Goal 15 | Department of Economic and Social Affairs [WWW Document], n.d. URL https://sdgs.un.org/goals/goal15 (accessed 4.12.22).

Goal 16 | Department of Economic and Social Affairs [WWW Document], n.d. URL https://sdgs.un.org/goals/goal16 (accessed 4.12.22).

Goal 17 | Department of Economic and Social Affairs [WWW Document], n.d. URL https://sdgs.un.org/goals/goal17 (accessed 4.12.22).

Gomez, B., Kadri, U., 2021. Earthquake source characterization by machine learning algorithms applied to acoustic signals | Scientific Reports. Sci. Rep.

Gorelick, N., Hancher, M., Dixon, M., Ilyushchenko, S., Thau, D., Moore, R., 2017. Google Earth Engine: Planetary-scale geospatial analysis for everyone. Remote Sens. Environ., Big Remotely Sensed Data: tools, applications and experiences 202, 18–27. https://doi.org/10.1016/j.rse.2017.06.031

He, K., Gkioxari, G., Dollár, P., Girshick, R., 2018. Mask R-CNN. https://doi.org/10.48550/arXiv.1703.06870

Hoffmann, F., Lee, D.S., Lemieux, T., 2020. Growing Income Inequality in the United States and Other Advanced Economies. J. Econ. Perspect. 34, 52–78. https://doi.org/10.1257/jep.34.4.52

Human Development Report 2020, 2020.

Huot, F., Hu, R.L., Goyal, N., Sankar, T., Ihme, M., Chen, Y.-F., 2022. Next Day Wildfire Spread: A Machine Learning Data Set to Predict Wildfire Spreading from Remote-Sensing Data. https://doi.org/10.48550/arXiv.2112.02447

IEA, 2021a. About CCUS – Analysis.

IEA, 2021b. World Energy Outlook 2021. Paris.

IEA, 2021c. Net Zero Emissions by 2050 Scenario (NZE) – World Energy Model – Analysis. Paris.

ILO, 2020. Global Employment Trends for Youth 2020: Technology and the future of jobs (Report).

ILO, 2019. These are the countries with the most teachers. ILOSTAT. URL https://ilostat.ilo.org/these-are-the-countries-with-the-most-teachers/ (accessed 6.22.22).

Inter-Parliamentary Union, n.d. Gender equality [WWW Document]. Inter-Parliam. Union. URL https://www.ipu.org/our-impact/gender-equality (accessed 6.9.22).

IPBES, 2019. Global assessment report on biodiversity and ecosystem services of the Intergovernmental Science-Policy Platform on Biodiversity and Ecosystem Services. Zenodo. https://doi.org/10.5281/zenodo.6417333

IPC Global Partners, 2021. IPC Manual 3.1 | IPC Global Platform. Rome.

Iyer, L.S., 2021. AI enabled applications towards intelligent transportation. Transp. Eng. 5, 100083. https://doi.org/10.1016/j.treng.2021.100083

Jumper, J., Evans, R., Pritzel, A., Green, T., Figurnov, M., Ronneberger, O., Tunyasuvunakool, K., Bates, R., Žídek, A., Potapenko, A., Bridgland, A., Meyer, C., Kohl, S.A.A., Ballard, A.J., Cowie, A., Romera-Paredes, B., Nikolov, S., Jain, R., Adler, J., Back, T., Petersen, S., Reiman, D., Clancy, E., Zielinski, M., Steinegger, M., Pacholska, M., Berghammer, T., Bodenstein, S., Silver, D., Vinyals, O., Senior, A.W., Kavukcuoglu, K., Kohli, P., Hassabis, D., 2021. Highly accurate protein structure prediction with AlphaFold. Nature 596, 583–589. https://doi.org/10.1038/s41586-021-03819-2

Kandimalla, V., Richard, M., Smith, F., Quirion, J., Torgo, L., Whidden, C., 2022. Automated Detection, Classification and Counting of Fish in Fish Passages With Deep Learning. Front. Mar. Sci. 8.

Köbis, N., Starke, C., Rahwan, I., 2022. The promise and perils of using artificial intelligence to fight corruption. Nat. Mach. Intell. 4, 418–424. https://doi.org/10.1038/s42256-022-00489-1

Koppa, A., Rains, D., Hulsman, P., Poyatos, R., Miralles, D.G., 2022. A deep learning-based hybrid model of global terrestrial evaporation. Nat. Commun. 13, 1912. https://doi.org/10.1038/s41467-022-29543-7

Korinek, A., Stiglitz, J.E., 2017. Artificial Intelligence and Its Implications for Income Distribution and Unemployment (Working Paper No. 24174), Working Paper Series. National Bureau of Economic Research. https://doi.org/10.3386/w24174

Krappel, T., Bogun, A., Borth, D., 2021. Heterogeneous Ensemble for ESG Ratings Prediction. https://doi.org/10.48550/arXiv.2109.10085

Kruse, J., Schäfer, B., Witthaut, D., 2021. Revealing drivers and risks for power grid frequency stability with explainable AI. Patterns 2, 100365. https://doi.org/10.1016/j.patter.2021.100365

Landsat 8, 2022. Wikipedia.

Large Marine Ecosystems | IOC UNESCO [WWW Document], n.d. URL https://ioc.unesco.org/topics/large-marine-ecosystems (accessed 6.28.22).

Large Marine Ecosystems Hub [WWW Document], n.d. URL https://www.lmehub.net/ (accessed 6.28.22).

Lauvset, S.K., Lange, N., Tanhua, T., Bittig, H.C., Olsen, A., Kozyr, A., Álvarez, M., Becker, S., Brown, P.J., Carter, B.R., Cotrim da Cunha, L., Feely, R.A., van Heuven, S., Hoppema, M., Ishii, M., Jeansson, E., Jutterström, S., Jones, S.D., Karlsen, M.K., Lo Monaco, C., Michaelis, P., Murata, A., Pérez, F.F., Pfeil, B., Schirnick, C., Steinfeldt, R., Suzuki, T., Tilbrook, B., Velo, A., Wanninkhof, R., Woosley, R.J., Key, R.M., 2021. An updated version of the global interior ocean biogeochemical data product, GLODAPv2.2021. Earth Syst. Sci. Data 13, 5565–5589. https://doi.org/10.5194/essd-13-5565-2021

Lema, R., Andersen, M.H., Hanlin, R., Nzila, C., 2022. Building Innovation Capabilities for Sustainable Industrialisation: Renewable Electrification in Developing Economies (Pathways to Sustainability). Routledge.

Lewkowycz, A., Andreassen, A., Dohan, D., Dyer, E., Michalewski, H., Ramasesh, V., Slone, A., Anil, C., Schlag, I., Gutman-Solo, T., Wu, Y., Neyshabur, B., Gur-Ari, G., Misra, V., 2022. Solving Quantitative Reasoning Problems with Language Models. https://doi.org/10.48550/arXiv.2206.14858

List of famines, 2022. Wikipedia.

Living Standards Measurement Study [WWW Document], n.d. URL https://www.worldbank.org/en/programs/lsms (accessed 9.2.22).

Lombardo, T., Duquesnoy, M., El-Bouysidy, H., Årén, F., Gallo-Bueno, A., Jørgensen, P.B., Bhowmik, A., Demortière, A., Ayerbe, E., Alcaide, F., Reynaud, M., Carrasco, J., Grimaud, A., Zhang, C., Vegge, T., Johansson, P., Franco, A.A., 2022. Artificial Intelligence Applied to Battery Research: Hype or Reality? Chem. Rev. 122, 10899–10969. https://doi.org/10.1021/acs.chemrev.1c00108

Long, Y., Aleven, V., 2017. Enhancing learning outcomes through self-regulated learning support with an Open Learner Model. User Model. User-Adapt. Interact. 27, 55–88. https://doi.org/10.1007/s11257-016-9186-6

Lundberg, S., Lee, S.-I., 2017. A Unified Approach to Interpreting Model Predictions. https://doi.org/10.48550/arXiv.1705.07874

Mahendra, A., King, R., Du, J., Dasgupta, A., Beard, V.A., Kallergis, A., Schalch, K., 2022. Seven Transformations for More Equitable and Sustainable Cities.

Majchrowska, S., Mikołajczyk, A., Ferlin, M., Klawikowska, Z., Plantykow, M.A., Kwasigroch, A., Majek, K., 2022. Deep learning-based waste detection in natural and urban environments. Waste Manag. 138, 274–284. https://doi.org/10.1016/j.wasman.2021.12.001

Martini, M., Cerrato, S., Salvetti, F., Angarano, S., Chiaberge, M., 2022. Position-Agnostic Autonomous Navigation in Vineyards with Deep Reinforcement Learning. https://doi.org/10.48550/arXiv.2206.14155

McKinney, S.M., Sieniek, M., Godbole, V., 2020. International evaluation of an AI system for breast cancer screening. Nature 89–94. https://doi.org/10.1038/s41586-019-1799-6

Measuring the Justice Gap | World Justice Project [WWW Document], n.d. URL https://worldjusticeproject.org/our-work/research-and-data/access-justice/measuring-justice-gap (accessed 6.9.22).

MODIS Web [WWW Document], n.d. URL https://modis.gsfc.nasa.gov/ (accessed 8.28.22).

Mueller, H., Groeger, A., Hersh, J., Matranga, A., Serrat, J., 2021. Monitoring war destruction from space using machine learning. Proc. Natl. Acad. Sci. 118, e2025400118. https://doi.org/10.1073/pnas.2025400118

Myers, A., 2022. Methane leaks much worse than estimates; fix available. Stanf. News. URL https://news.stanford.edu/2022/03/24/methane-leaks-much-worse-estimates-fix-available/ (accessed 6.24.22).

Nations sign up to end global scourge of plastic pollution, 2022. UN News. URL https://news.un.org/en/story/2022/03/1113142 (accessed 8.30.22).

Natural Capital Accounting and Valuation of Ecosystem Services Project | System of Environmental Economic Accounting [WWW Document], n.d. URL https://seea.un.org/home/Natural-Capital-Accounting-Project (accessed 9.26.22).

Ocean-Atmosphere CO2 Exchange [WWW Document], 2015. Sci. Sphere. URL https://sos.noaa.gov/catalog/datasets/ocean-atmosphere-co2-exchange/ (accessed 8.30.22).

OECD, 2015. The OECD Principles on Water Governance.

One Planet Network, UNEP, 2018. One Planet network Indicators of Success.

ORNL DAAC MODIS SUBSETS [WWW Document], n.d. URL https://daac.ornl.gov/cgi-bin/dataset_lister.pl?p=12 (accessed 8.28.22).

Paris fails to counter Russian propaganda in the Sahel, 2022. Le Monde.fr.

Peng, A., Nushi, B., Kiciman, E., Inkpen, K., Kamar, E., 2022. Investigations of Performance and Bias in Human-AI Teamwork in Hiring. https://doi.org/10.48550/arXiv.2202.11812

PISA - PISA [WWW Document], n.d. URL https://www.oecd.org/pisa/ (accessed 5.16.22).

Plasma shaping, 2022. Wikipedia.

Porayska-Pomsta, K., Rizzo, P., Damian, I., Baur, T., André, E., Sabouret, N., Jones, H., Anderson, K., Chryssafidou, E., 2014. Who's Afraid of Job Interviews? Definitely a Question for User Modelling, in: Dimitrova, V., Kuflik, T., Chin, D., Ricci, F., Dolog, P., Houben, G.-J. (Eds.), User Modeling, Adaptation, and Personalization, Lecture Notes in Computer Science. Springer International Publishing, Cham, pp. 411–422. https://doi.org/10.1007/978-3-319-08786-3_37

Pörtner, H.-O., Roberts, D.C., Tignor, M.M.B., Poloczanska, E.S., Mintenbeck, K., Alegría, A., Craig, M., Langsdorf, S., Löschke, S., Möller, V., Okem, A., Rama, B. (Eds.), 2022. Climate Change 2022: Impacts, Adaptation and Vulnerability. Contribution of Working Group II to the Sixth Assessment Report of the Intergovernmental Panel on Climate Change.

Programme (UNDP), U.N.D., Initiative (OPHI), O.P. and H.D., 2021. Global MPI 2020 – Charting pathways out of multidimensional poverty: Achieving the SDGs.

Pros and Cons of Autonomous Weapons Systems [WWW Document], n.d. Army Univ. Press. URL https://www.armyupress.army.mil/Journals/Military-Review/English-Edition-Archives/May-June-2017/Pros-and-Cons-of-Autonomous-Weapons-Systems/ (accessed 6.11.22).

Qian, I., Xiao, M., Mozur, P., Cardia, A., 2022. Four Takeaways From a Times Investigation Into China's Expanding Surveillance State. N. Y. Times.

Ralaidovy, A.H., Adam, T., Boucher, P., 2020. Resource allocation for biomedical research: analysis of investments by major funders. Health Res. Policy Syst. 18, 20. https://doi.org/10.1186/s12961-020-0532-0

Ravilious, K., 2020. Biomass energy: green or dirty? [WWW Document]. Phys. World. URL https://physicsworld.com/a/biomass-energy-green-or-dirty/ (accessed 6.24.22).

Realtime Inequality [WWW Document], n.d. URL https://realtimeinequality.org/ (accessed 6.21.22).

Redmon, J., Divvala, S., Girshick, R., Farhadi, A., 2016. You Only Look Once: Unified, Real-Time Object Detection. https://doi.org/10.48550/arXiv.1506.02640

Ren, S., He, K., Girshick, R., Sun, J., 2016. Faster R-CNN: Towards Real-Time Object Detection with Region Proposal Networks. https://doi.org/10.48550/arXiv.1506.01497

Renewable Energy Statistics 2021, n.d. 460.

Rolnick, D., Donti, P.L., Kaack, L.H., Kochanski, K., Lacoste, A., Sankaran, K., Ross, A.S., Milojevic-Dupont, N., Jaques, N., Waldman-Brown, A., Luccioni, A., Maharaj, T., Sherwin, E.D., Mukkavilli, S.K., Kording, K.P., Gomes, C., Ng, A.Y., Hassabis, D., Platt, J.C., Creutzig, F., Chayes, J., Bengio, Y., 2019. Tackling Climate Change with Machine Learning. ArXiv190605433 Cs Stat.

Rozenberg, J., Fay, M., 2019. Beyond the Gap: How Countries Can Afford the Infrastructure They Need while Protecting the Planet. World Bank, Washington, DC. https://doi.org/10.1596/978-1-4648-1363-4

Sachs, J., 2006. The End of Poverty: Economic Possibilities for Our Time. Penguin Books.

Sachs, J., Lafortune, G., Kroll, C., Fuller, G., Woelm, F., 2022. Sustainable Development Report 2022. Cambridge University Press.

Saini, R.K., V. K. Raju, M.S., Chail, A., 2021. Cry in the sky: Psychological impact on drone operators. Ind. Psychiatry J. 30, S15–S19. https://doi.org/10.4103/0972-6748.328782

Sankin, A., Gizmodo, D.M. for, Mattu, S., Gilbertson, A., 2021. Crime Prediction Software Promised to Be Free of Biases. New Data Shows It Perpetuates Them – The Markup [WWW Document]. URL https://themarkup.org/prediction-bias/2021/12/02/crime-prediction-software-promised-to-be-free-of-biases-new-data-shows-it-perpetuates-them (accessed 7.6.22).

SCP Hotspots Analysis, n.d. URL http://scp-hat.lifecycleinitiative.org/ (accessed 6.29.22).

SEI CEEW, 2022. Stockholm+50: Unlocking a Better Future.

Shin, W., Han, J., Rhee, W., 2021. AI-assistance for predictive maintenance of renewable energy systems. Energy 221, 119775. https://doi.org/10.1016/j.energy.2021.119775

SOCCOM | Unlocking the Mysteries of the Southern Ocean [WWW Document], n.d. URL https://soccom.princeton.edu/ (accessed 8.30.22).

Spencer, B.F., Hoskere, V., Narazaki, Y., 2019. Advances in Computer Vision-Based Civil Infrastructure Inspection and Monitoring. Engineering 5, 199–222. https://doi.org/10.1016/j.eng.2018.11.030

Stern, N., 2006. The Economics of Climate Change: The Stern Review.

Stouhi, D., 2022. Toronto Plans on Stopping the Construction of Smart Cities Following Concerns of Privacy [WWW Document]. ArchDaily. URL https://www.archdaily.com/984561/toronto-plans-on-stopping-the-construction-of-smart-cities-following-concerns-of-privacy (accessed 8.24.22).

Strategic Policies for Sustainable Infrastructure - OECD [WWW Document], n.d. URL https://www.oecd.org/finance/sustainable-infrastructure.htm (accessed 4.16.22).

Stuchtey, M., Vincent, A., Merkl, A., Bucher, M., 2020. Ocean Solutions that Benefit People, Nature, and the Economy. World Resources Institute, Washington, DC.

Su, H., Wu, L., Jiang, J.H., Pai, R., Liu, A., Zhai, A.J., Tavallali, P., DeMaria, M., 2020. Applying Satellite Observations of Tropical Cyclone Internal Structures to Rapid Intensification Forecast With Machine Learning. Geophys. Res. Lett. 47, e2020GL089102. https://doi.org/10.1029/2020GL089102

SustainBench [WWW Document], n.d. SustainBench. URL https://sustainlab-group.github.io/sustainbench/ (accessed 9.2.22).

Tan, M., Le, Q.V., 2020. EfficientNet: Rethinking Model Scaling for Convolutional Neural Networks. https://doi.org/10.48550/arXiv.1905.11946

Tan, M., Pang, R., Le, Q.V., 2020. EfficientDet: Scalable and Efficient Object Detection. https://doi.org/10.48550/arXiv.1911.09070

Task Force on Climate-Related Financial Disclosures | TCFD) [WWW Document], n.d. Task Force Clim.-Relat. Financ. Discl. URL https://www.fsb-tcfd.org/ (accessed 7.1.22).

The DHS Program - Quality information to plan, monitor and improve population, health, and nutrition programs [WWW Document], n.d. URL https://dhsprogram.com/ (accessed 9.2.22).

The Economist, 2017. The Worldwide Educating for the Future Index 2017.

The IUCN Red List of Threatened Species [WWW Document], n.d. IUCN Red List Threat. Species. URL https://www.iucnredlist.org/en (accessed 3.18.22).

The Paris Agreement | UNFCCC [WWW Document], n.d. URL https://unfccc.int/process-and-meetings/the-paris-agreement/the-paris-agreement (accessed 3.11.22).

The State of Cities Climate Finance [WWW Document], n.d. CPI. URL https://www.climatepolicyinitiative.org/publication/the-state-of-cities-climate-finance/ (accessed 6.2.22).

The State of Food Security and Nutrition in the World 2021, 2021. FAO, IFAD, UNICEF, WFP and WHO. https://doi.org/10.4060/cb4474en

The World #InequalityReport 2022 presents the most up-to-date & complete data on inequality worldwide [WWW Document], n.d. World Inequal. Rep. 2022. URL //wir2022.wid.world/ (accessed 6.10.22).

The World's Largest Slums: Dharavi, Kibera, Khayelitsha & Neza [WWW Document], 2017. Habitat Humanity GB. URL https://www.habitatforhumanity.org.uk/blog/2017/12/the-worlds-largest-slums-dharavi-kibera-khayelitsha-neza/ (accessed 4.12.22).

Toetzke, M., Banholzer, N., Feuerriegel, S., 2022. Monitoring global development aid with machine learning. Nat. Sustain. 1–9. https://doi.org/10.1038/s41893-022-00874-z

Toorajipour, R., Sohrabpour, V., Nazarpour, A., Oghazi, P., Fischl, M., 2021. Artificial intelligence in supply chain management: A systematic literature review. J. Bus. Res. 122, 502–517. https://doi.org/10.1016/j.jbusres.2020.09.009

Towards the vision 2050 on biodiversity: living in harmony with nature [WWW Document], 2019. UNEP. URL http://www.unep.org/news-and-stories/story/towards-vision-2050-biodiversity-living-harmony-nature (accessed 5.8.22).

Tracking State-Sponsored Cyberattacks Around the World [WWW Document], n.d. Counc. Foreign Relat. URL https://www.cfr.org/cyber-operations (accessed 5.25.22).

Tramontana, G., Jung, M., Schwalm, C.R., Ichii, K., Camps-Valls, G., Ráduly, B., Reichstein, M., Arain, M.A., Cescatti, A., Kiely, G., Merbold, L., Serrano-Ortiz, P., Sickert, S., Wolf, S., Papale, D., 2016. Predicting carbon dioxide and energy fluxes across global FLUXNET sites with regression algorithms. Biogeosciences 13, 4291–4313. https://doi.org/10.5194/bg-13-4291-2016

Trinh, M., 2021a. The AI Model Handbook: A guide to the world of artificial intelligence modeling, 1st ed, The Artificial Intelligence Handbook Series. Rodeo Press, New York.

Trinh, M., 2021b. The AI Project Handbook: How to manage a successful artificial intelligence project, 1st ed, The Artificial Intelligence Handbook Series. Rodeo Press, New York.

Tseng, G., Zvonkov, I., Nakalembe, C.L., Kerner, H., 2021. CropHarvest: A global dataset for crop-type classification. Presented at the Thirty-fifth Conference on Neural Information Processing Systems Datasets and Benchmarks Track (Round 2).

UNEP, 2017a. Microplastics [WWW Document]. UNEP - UN Environ. Programme. URL http://www.unep.org/resources/report/microplastics (accessed 6.4.22).

UNEP, 2017b. Global Waste Management Outlook.

UNESCO, 2021. Draft text of the Recommendation on the Ethics of Artificial Intelligence. UNESCO, Paris.

UNESCO, I.C.O.T.F.O.E., 2021. Reimagining our futures together: a new social contract for education.

UNESCO-IOC, 2022. Ocean Decade progress report, 2021-2022. UNESCO, Paris.

UNICEF, 2020. Gender and education [WWW Document]. UNICEF DATA. URL https://data.unicef.org/topic/gender/gender-disparities-in-education/ (accessed 6.22.22).

United Nations, 2022. UN World Water Development Report 2022. UNESCO, Paris.

United Nations, 2021a. UN World Water Development Report 2021. UNESCO, Paris.

United Nations, 2021b. Smart, Sustainable and Resilient cities: the Power of Nature-based Solutions.

United Nations, 2019. UN World Water Development Report 2019. Paris.

United Nations Convention to Combat Desertification, 2022. Global Land Outlook (No. 2nd edition). UNCCD, Bonn.

UNODC Strategy 2021-2025 [WWW Document], n.d. URL https://www.unodc.org/unodc/en/strategy/index.html (accessed 6.9.22).

U.S. Energy Information Administration, 2022. Biomass explained - U.S. Energy Information Administration (EIA) [WWW Document]. URL https://www.eia.gov/energyexplained/biomass/ (accessed 6.24.22).

Varadi, M., Anyango, S., Deshpande, M., Nair, S., Natassia, C., Hassabis, D., Velankar, S., 2022. AlphaFold Protein Structure Database: massively expanding the structural coverage of protein-sequence space with high-accuracy models. Nucleic Acids Res. 50, D439–D444. https://doi.org/10.1093/nar/gkab1061

Veitch, E., Andreas Alsos, O., 2022. A systematic review of human-AI interaction in autonomous ship systems. Saf. Sci. 152, 105778. https://doi.org/10.1016/j.ssci.2022.105778

Wagner, M., de Vries, W.T., 2019. Comparative Review of Methods Supporting Decision-Making in Urban Development and Land Management. Land 8, 123. https://doi.org/10.3390/land8080123

Wang, K., Zhao, Y., Gangadhari, R.K., Li, Z., 2021. Analyzing the Adoption Challenges of the Internet of Things (IoT) and Artificial Intelligence (AI) for Smart Cities in China. Sustainability 13, 10983. https://doi.org/10.3390/su131910983

What are the origins of gender inequality? | For Researchers | Springer Nature [WWW Document], n.d. URL https://www.springernature.com/gp/researchers/the-source/blog/blogposts-communicating-research/what-are-the-origins-of-gender-inequality/18901980 (accessed 6.12.22).

Wihbey, J., May 14, T.J.R., 2014, 2014. Public defenders, attorney quality and trial outcomes: Research on legal representation. Journal. Resour. URL https://journalistsresource.org/criminal-justice/indigent-defense-counsel-attorney-quality-defendant-outcomes-research-legal-respresentation/ (accessed 6.9.22).

Wolff, R.F., Moons, K.G.M., Riley, R.D., Whiting, P.F., Westwood, M., Collins, G.S., Reitsma, J.B., Kleijnen, J., Mallett, S., PROBAST Group†, 2019. PROBAST: A Tool to Assess the Risk of Bias and Applicability of Prediction Model Studies. Ann. Intern. Med. 170, 51–58. https://doi.org/10.7326/M18-1376

World Bank, 2022. Climate Explainer: Nature-Based Solutions [WWW Document]. World Bank. URL https://www.worldbank.org/en/news/feature/2022/05/19/what-you-need-to-know-about-nature-based-solutions-to-climate-change (accessed 7.1.22).

World Bank, 2020. Poverty and Shared Prosperity 2020 : Reversals of Fortune. Washington, DC: World Bank. https://doi.org/10.1596/978-1-4648-1602-4

World Bank, 2019. World Development Report 2019: The Changing Nature of Work (Text/HTML).

World Bank, 2017. Monitoring Global Poverty: Report of the Commission on Global Poverty. World Bank, Washington, DC. https://doi.org/10.1596/978-1-4648-0961-3

World Employment and Social Outlook: Trends 2022 (Report), 2022.

World Health Organization, 2022. World health statistics 2022: monitoring health for the SDGs, sustainable development goals. Geneva.

World Health Organization, 2021a. HIV/AIDS [WWW Document]. WHO Reg. Off. Afr. URL https://www.afro.who.int/health-topics/hivaids (accessed 6.18.22).

World Health Organization, 2021b. WHO guidance on preparing for national response to health emergencies and disasters. Geneva.

World Health Organization, 2020. The top 10 causes of death. URL https://www.who.int/news-room/fact-sheets/detail/the-top-10-causes-of-death (accessed 6.18.22).

World Health Organization, 2019. Maternal mortality [WWW Document]. URL https://www.who.int/news-room/fact-sheets/detail/maternal-mortality (accessed 6.20.22).

World urbanization prospects: the 2018 revision, 2019. United Nations, New York.

Wu, X., Huang, S., Xiao, Z., Wang, Y., 2022. Building Precise Local Submarine Earthquake Catalogs via a Deep-Learning-Empowered Workflow and its Application to the Challenger Deep. Front. Earth Sci. 10.

WWF, 2019. Below the Canopy.

Wynants, L., Calster, B.V., Collins, G.S., Riley, R.D., Heinze, G., Schuit, E., Bonten, M.M.J., Dahly, D.L., Damen, J.A., Debray, T.P.A., Jong, V.M.T. de, Vos, M.D., Dhiman, P., Haller, M.C., Harhay, M.O., Henckaerts, L., Heus, P., Kammer, M., Kreuzberger, N., Lohmann, A., Luijken, K., Ma, J., Martin, G.P., McLernon, D.J., Navarro, C.L.A., Reitsma, J.B., Sergeant, J.C., Shi, C., Skoetz, N., Smits, L.J.M., Snell, K.I.E., Sperrin, M., Spijker, R., Steyerberg, E.W., Takada, T., Tzoulaki, I., Kuijk, S.M.J. van, Bussel, B.C.T. van, Horst, I.C.C. van der, Royen, F.S. van, Verbakel, J.Y., Wallisch, C., Wilkinson, J., Wolff, R., Hooft, L., Moons, K.G.M., Smeden, M. van, 2020. Prediction models for diagnosis and prognosis of covid-19: systematic review and critical appraisal. BMJ 369, m1328. https://doi.org/10.1136/bmj.m1328

Yan, Yongliang, N. Borhani, T., Gokul Subraveti, S., Nagesh Pai, K., Prasad, V., Rajendran, A., Nkulikiyinka, P., Odianosen Asibor, J., Zhang, Z., Shao, D., Wang, L., Zhang, W., Yan, Yong, Ampomah, W., You, J., Wang, M., J. Anthony, E., Manovic, V., T. Clough, P., 2021. Harnessing the power of machine learning for carbon capture, utilisation, and storage (CCUS) – a state-of-the-art review. Energy Environ. Sci. 14, 6122–6157. https://doi.org/10.1039/D1EE02395K

Yeh, C., Perez, A., Driscoll, A., Azzari, G., Tang, Z., Lobell, D., Ermon, S., Burke, M., 2020. Using publicly available satellite imagery and deep learning to understand economic well-being in Africa. Nat. Commun. 11, 2583. https://doi.org/10.1038/s41467-020-16185-w

Zemskova, V.E., He, T.-L., Wan, Z., Grisouard, N., 2022. A deep-learning estimate of the decadal trends in the Southern Ocean carbon storage. Nat. Commun. 13, 4056. https://doi.org/10.1038/s41467-022-31560-5

Zizka, A., Andermann, T., Silvestro, D., 2022. IUCNN – Deep learning approaches to approximate species' extinction risk. Divers. Distrib. 28, 227–241. https://doi.org/10.1111/ddi.13450

www.ingramcontent.com/pod-product-compliance
Lightning Source LLC
Chambersburg PA
CBHW080420270326
41929CB00018B/3101